B
THE
SOLUTION

HOW TO TRANSFORM the QUALITY of YOUR LIFE

Darel Rutherford

Warning Disclaimer

This book is designed to provide information in regard to the subject matter covered. It is sold with the understanding that the publisher and author are not engaged in rendering legal, accounting or other professional services. If legal or other expert assistance is required, the services of a competent professional should be sought.

The purpose of this book is to educate and entertain. The Author and DAR Publishing shall have neither liability nor responsibility to any person or entity with respect to any loss or damage, caused or alleged to be caused, directly or indirectly by the information contained in this book.

If you do not wish to be bound by the above, you may return this book to the publisher for a full refund.

BEING THE SOLUTION
By Darel Rutherford

Published by DAR Publishing
7116 Arroyo Del Oso NE
Albuquerque, NM 87109

All rights reserved. No part of this book may be reproduced, transmitted in any form or by any means, electronic or mechanical, including photocopying, recording, or by any information storage and retrieval system without permission in writing from the author, except for inclusion of brief quotations in a review.

Copyright 2002 by Darel A. Rutherford
Printed in the United States of America
First Edition Feb 2001
ISBN # 0-9670540-2-8

CONTENTS

1	POVERTY IS A STATE OF BEING ...not the state of your finances	5
2	NINE STEPS TO PERSONAL FREEDOM ...your way out of the box	19
3	IN THE IMAGE AND LIKENESS OF GOD ...what that really means	31
4	THE GAME BOARD ...for The Game of Life	41
5	YOUR SELF IMAGE ...the mental blue print running your life	49
6	HOW TO KNOW WHAT YOU WANT ...by thinking out of the box	61
7	CREATING A BURNING DESIRE ...the prime ingredient to your success	71
8	CHOOSING TO BE RICH ...your fifth step out of the box	89
9	BEING TRANSFORMED ...means having what you want from life	101
10	UNDERSTANDING EGO'S RESISTANCE ...puts you back in charge of your life	115
11	YOUR WAY PAST THE RESISTANCE ...the three minute Power Pause	123

12	CREATING YOUR SUPPORT TEAM ...empowering your success	135
13	WHAT YOU'VE LEARNED SO FAR ...has no value until you put it to work	151
14	SOLVING SELF-IMAGE PROBLEMS ...with the Power Pause	165
15	SOLVING RELATIONSHIP PROBLEMS ...with the Power Pause	185
16	IMPROVING YOUR HEALTH ...with the Power Pause	199
17	HOW YOU ATTRACT MONEY ...with a Prosperity Consciousness	213
18	FIND THE UNWRITTEN AGREEMENT ...and the solution to your problem	233
19	FIND YOURSELF ON THE CYCLE ...a roadmap for the rest of your life	249
20	YOUR RELATIONSHIP TO MONEY ...will make you rich or keep you poor	265

1
POVERTY IS A STATE OF BEING
...not the state of your finances

What you have or don't have in your life is there as the result of your BEING choice

Power Pause success stories

Living on the edge for two years, almost evicted, electricity turned off more than once, three months behind on car payments and bills, bills, bills, Delores Jackson asked for help. I sent her the Power Pause.

After one week of using the Power Pause, Delores had a songwriter's contract with a record label and an offer to write the music for a radio show. She also had a well-paying job, scoring a movie script for a major player in the music industry.

Delores reports,

> *These are just a few of the miracles happening in my life since I began using the Power Pause. Thank you for bringing the Power Pause to my life.*

Want more Power Pause success stories?

- Hattie Pembrook, used the Power Pause to change who she was BEING in the relationship with her husband and transformed that unhappy alliance into a loving relationship.
- Sherry Jaramillo, after years of suffering frequent migraine headaches, used the Power Pause to cancel out the emotional stress that had caused those headaches. Sherry says, "Wow! No more

headaches! You couldn't possibly imagine how powerful I feel, being back in charge of my life!"
- Maria Mays said, "Last month was my greatest month ever in my massage business! I used the Power Pause to visualize what my business would be like if clients who scheduled massages on a regular basis filled my schedule. I had been trying for five years to increase my volume. "In just one month of using the Power Pause, my business increased by one-third, for my best month ever. I'm truly grateful for the Power Pause!"

Miracles? No, these seeming miracles are the natural result of what happens when we take charge of our thinking patterns to move past our barriers to Success. What powerful spiritual principle makes the Power Pause such a great transformational tool? This truth: We become what we think about with passion.

The Power Pause, by design, changes who you are being relative to whatever you perceive to be a problem and the problem simply dissolves and disappears.

The intent of *BEING* is to show you how to transform yourself into being the person who can have whatever you want in life. The Power Pause is a great tool for transformation; however, it is only one of the nine transformation steps necessary to having the life you've always wanted.

One cannot alter a condition
with the same mind set that created it in the first place.
--Albert Einstein

The truth about having what you've always wanted is that you won't have it as long as you insist on being who you are now. You're being deprived of that want by another spiritual law, the Law of Correspondence, which says that You can only have from life that which belongs to you by right of consciousness.

But if you can change who you're BEING, this same law will provide you with everything that belongs with your new BEING choice. So, if you're ready to consider a change in who you are BEING so you can have the life you want, I'm ready to show you the way. Are you ready for a quality of life change?

POVERTY IS A STATE OF BEING

Your concept of reality

If you have a concept of reality (everybody does), you live in a box. Everyone lives in a box! Everything belonging in that box is already there. Everything you want from life that you don't have is outside the box. The odds are that you will never get to have what you want from life, simply because your wants are not powerful enough to overcome the insecurity of being outside the box.

Armed with what you learn from this book, you WILL overcome your insecurities. I will give you a sure-fire way out of your box so that you WILL have what you want from life. But before I do that, let me show you what a box looks like.

An erroneous conclusion

As a prosperity coach, I often smile and play an imaginary violin when someone tells me his or her sad victim story. When he or she gets over being offended by my lack of sympathy, we laugh together and then get serious about solving the problem. The following was once my own victim story (my box).

When I was four years old, I idolized my oldest brother; in fact, you might say I worshiped him. One morning when he left for school, I followed him. Four blocks from home, he noticed that I was following him and he chased me all the way home, angry that I was making him late for school.

Feeling hurt and sorry for myself, I pouted for a while and then decided I would never be hurt again! As a result of that obviously insignificant and meaningless incident in my life, I came to the absurd conclusion that nobody loved me. And then, to make matters worse, I compounded my error in judgment by deciding that I didn't need anyone. (Talk about dumb conclusions!)

Although no real basis existed for my erroneous conclusion, that decision controlled much of my life for many years to come. So, while growing up, whenever anyone tried to hug me, I pushed him or her away. A loving hug did not fit the victim role I had chosen to play. If you are feeling sorry for me, you've missed the point. By now, you should be playing your own imaginary victim-story violin.

But that was my box, my story, and at first glance, you may not relate my victim story to your own. I suggest you look again. I'm saying that you could have anything you want from life if you were not rejecting it the same way I was rejecting love. If you are lacking

BEING THE SOLUTION

anything—anything at all—you live in a self-limiting box that prevents you from having your wants fulfilled.

When it's their victim story

The best thing about a victim story is that you can easily see how the other person caused his or her problem. And in most cases you could offer an easy solution (a way out of the box) if only that person were willing to give up being a victim. The light bulb goes on (ah ha!) when you suddenly realize that they're telling your story! I want you to get that this IS your story! A different tune, different characters, different circumstances, but the same plot!

I've shared my victim's story so that you can see the lack of love in my life for what it was—ridiculous, self-inflicted poverty. My situation could be likened to someone dying of thirst while swimming in a lake of drinkable water. Love was there for me, but I would not or could not allow myself to partake of it as long as I maintained my nobody-loves-me attitude. Does this ring any bells for you?

During all those early years of feeling unloved and sorry for myself, I could have solved my problem at any moment, with a simple change of attitude and/or perspective. Can you see how that would have worked for me? Then you must see that a change of perspective could solve your problem or fulfill your need as well. I'll be showing you how you can make that viewpoint change.

How does this story relate to you?

If there is anything you lack that you feel would make your life whole and complete if you had it, then you are poor—not as poverty's victim, but because you reject riches in that form, just as I once rejected love. If you are not rich in ALL aspects of your life—if you feel that you lack love, self-confidence, money, or anything else—it's because being rich in that aspect of your life does not fit your concept of reality. It's outside the box for you.

Poverty or abundance in any form is a state of mind (a state of BEING), not the state of your love life, your relationships or your finances. With the message in this book, I intend to take away your victim story and change your mind about the reason for your poverty. In fact, you probably have a dozen reasons you could give me, right now, for why you are poor in some way. None of your reasons are any more valid than my silly excuse for lacking love!

POVERTY IS A STATE OF BEING
If rich is a four-letter word

If you've always thought of "rich" as a four-letter word, you were right. But if you are somehow turned off by the word, your prejudice against it may prevent you from hearing me. That would be a shame, because when I use the term, "rich" I'm not just talking about the money you have or don't have.

I can name a great number of ways that you can be rich, and most of them are a great deal more important than having lots of money. As you read this book, I want you to think about being rich in terms of what ever you most need in your life. Think of what your life would be like if you were rich in self-worth, self-esteem, love, friends, good health, a good job, or even money.

Try to think of yourself as "rich" in consciousness, in a way that attracts an abundance of whatever you thought you were lacking.

Rich is not about what you have

If you think wanting the good life makes you greedy, if you think poverty is next to Godliness, if you think becoming rich is a non-spiritual journey, I have news for you: being rich is not about what you have; it's about who you are. This doesn't mean that having money or any other kind of wealth makes you spiritually enlightened; what it does mean is that you can't go from poverty to riches without a change in consciousness.

Your spiritual journey through life is about discovering who you are. Allowing yourself to have that better life you've always wanted is part of the self-discovery process. BEING financially independent will be one of the side benefits in your spiritual journey toward self-discovery.

The most common error you can make when thinking about becoming rich is to assume that having money, or whatever else you lack, would make you rich. The exact opposite is the truth. You must be rich in consciousness before you can have the riches you want—before you can have love, money or anything else in abundance.

If you already had all the money you could possibly spend, your wealth would only be the consequence, not the root cause, of your becoming rich. That's because BEING rich is not about what you have; it's about who you are. Well, who are you, really? You are a spiritual BEING experiencing reality in a material world. And it is because you are a spiritual BEING that you have the power to choose the reality of your dreams. I intend to prove that, but not just yet.

BEING THE SOLUTION

Poverty is not about what you DON'T have

Another common notion concerning money is that a lack of it makes one poor. Nothing could be farther from the truth. When you are poor in any aspect of your life, it is not your lack of wealth that keeps you from having more of what you want, it's your way of thinking about what you lack that perpetuates your poverty.

For instance, if you made up your mind to increase your income, right now, how would you plan to earn it? Take on another job? Work more hours? Are these solutions acceptable? No? They are not acceptable, because your trading-hours-for-dollars earning strategy has you trapped in a set of assumptions about how money is earned—a reality concept that won't let you be financially rich. Your way out of the box will require a paradigm shift away from those presumptions toward an earning strategy that would allow you to receive income from sources other than hourly pay.

Your lack of wealth is just the natural end result of a mind-set that cancels out any possibility of wealth accumulation. The poor have a negative polarity when it comes to attracting money; it just naturally flows away from them. Have you not wondered why?

Quite the opposite is true of the wealthy. Like a magnet attracts metal filings, wealthy people attract money. Being poor was never about the money you didn't have; it has always been about who you are.

What would your life be like if you changed your polarity to one that attracted abundance? Take time to imagine who you would be BEING if money were no longer a problem.... Feel free to substitute whatever fills your need in place of the word, "money" in any sentence.

If I Could Show You

So, what if I could show you a way to change your mind-set from one that repels money to one that would attract money and make you rich; would you be interested? Sure you would!

Or, then again, maybe you wouldn't. Maybe you've decided against becoming wealthy. (In fact, if this were not true—think about it—wouldn't you already be rich?) The reasons you give yourself for why you are not rich is the stand you've taken against becoming rich! If you are not wealthy, you will be defending your decision to remain poor AS YOU READ THIS. If you don't believe me, stop and listen to your mind chatter!

POVERTY IS A STATE OF BEING

But before you take (re-take) your stand against becoming rich, let's agree on what we mean by the terms "rich" and "poor." Once we're on the same page, you can take your position, one way or the other. The important thing, now, is that you "get" that you had a choice in the matter of being rich or poor. And when you rethink the term "rich" as meaning "rich in consciousness," you will see how becoming rich through a change in consciousness is, in fact, a spiritual journey.

Defining *Rich* or *Poor*

Although rich is about who you are, not about what you have, what you have is truly a measure of who you are.

"Ye shall know them by their fruits."
--Mathew 7.16

So, let's use what you have (or don't have) in your life as our gauge for defining "rich" and "poor."

I say you are rich when you have everything you think you need to make your life whole and complete and that you are poor when something you want from life is missing. Think about it! When using this broad a measure for defining rich and poor, most of us could not back up our claim to be "already rich."

If you thought money was the only possible measure for riches, you have been mistaken. A great many things in life are more important than having money, including spiritual growth, health, self-love and self-confidence, just to name a few. If you lack any of these, or anything else, having money won't make you rich or happy.

Only a few would qualify

For example, even if you had Bill Gates' money, you would not qualify as "rich" if you didn't love yourself; and if your life was filled with loving relationships, but you were struggling to pay your bills, you could not honestly claim to be rich.

If you've been telling yourself that you are "already rich," you may change your mind after doing the following Rich/Poor Exercise. Your "I'm-already-rich" story may have kept you from seeing that you were not as rich as you thought in some other areas in your life. You might even find that you are better off than you thought.

Almost without exception, we each lack something we think we need to make our lives whole and complete. It doesn't matter whether that lack is of love, health, or financial independence, lack in any form

BEING THE SOLUTION

points to a need for further spiritual growth. More than anything else, most of us lack the spiritual awareness that would allow us to know who we really are.

Anyway, if you want to know where you most need to grow, complete the following exercise. On a scale of 10 to 1, rate yourself in each of the following areas of your life, with "10" being the best, and "1" being the worst.

RICH OR POOR EXERCISE

Rate Yourself From 10 to 1	RICH 10 9 8 7 6	POOR 5 4 3 2 1	Rating Scale	Rate
Healthy			Couldn't be better	10
Self-esteem			Pretty Good	9
Self-worth			Just Fair	8
Self-love			Just Okay	7
Self-confidence			Not Good/Not Bad	6
Loving Relationships			Not Okay	5
Good paying job			Unsatisfactory	4
Like what I'm doing			Pretty Bad	3
Time to enjoy life			Very Bad	2
Financial Independence			Couldn't be worse	1
Spiritually nurtured				

What Did You Learn About Yourself?

So, in doing this exercise, have you learned something about yourself you didn't know before? Are you richer or poorer than you thought?

If you lack anything in life that would make your life whole and complete, if you had it, you are poor—not as a victim of that lack, but because you haven't found yourself worthy of having it. You are poor only because being rich in that way does not fit your current concept of reality.

Poverty in any form is a state of mind,
not the state of your circumstances.
--Darel Rutherford

If you scored poorly in any of the categories in this exercise, you will need to admit to yourself that you are poor. What you want

POVERTY IS A STATE OF BEING

from life is outside your box, and so is the growth in consciousness that would allow you to know who you are and have what you want. So, if there's anything missing from your life, now is the time to acknowledge that lack and to make up your mind to deal with it.

If you are ready for this change, right now would be a good time to commit to it with the following affirmation:

I am now ready to give up my victim story and choose out of poverty! As of this moment, I choose to be rich in ....
(whatever you scored lowest)

Poor again!

Even those who seem to have it all will become dissatisfied with their lot in life from time to time. In that moment of discontent, they become poor again.

Russell Conwell, in his great little book, <u>Acres of Diamonds</u>, tells the true story of a very prosperous farmer who was rich because he had everything a man could possibly want in life. He had a loving wife, two beautiful, loving daughters, and servants to tend the livestock and care for his needs. This farmer led a very happy and contented life (he was rich) until someone suggested that he could buy a kingdom and put his daughters on the throne if he owned a diamond mine.

In that moment, the farmer became so obsessed with the desire to own a diamond mine that he could think of nothing else. In that split second, his contentment flew out the window, and he became a poor man.

In this sad tale, the farmer sold his farm and went off in search of the diamond mine he would never find. The irony in this true story is that the Anaconda Diamond Mine, the richest in the whole world, was discovered on the property this farmer sold so he could afford to go searching for a diamond mine.

Diamonds by the handful were picked from the stream bed that flowed through this man's farm, first noticed because they lay there in plain sight, sparkling in the sun light.

This farmer made two serious mistakes:
1. He thought owning a diamond mine would make him rich; he didn't know that rich is about who you are, not about what you have.
2. He gave up everything a man could possibly want in life to go looking for what he could have found in his own back yard!

BEING THE SOLUTION

The moral to this story

The lesson to be learned from this story is that, you too, will find acres of diamonds in your own backyard if you know what you're looking for. Want a clue? You're looking for your inner power. The joke is that what you are looking for, you are looking with!

The diamond mine you seek, the real riches you search for in life, won't be found, in the material wealth you accumulate, but in your spiritual growth—in who you will become in the process of making up your mind that you're worthy of being materially rich. Your diamond mine (becoming rich in all aspects of your life) only seems to be about having what you want; the real riches will be found in knowing who you really are.

Once you can see your lack of wealth as a reflection of what you are, it must become apparent to you that you could be rich by changing who you're BEING relative to whatever it is that you lack. If it's sufficient income you lack, you can be rich by changing the way you relate to money. So, how do you do that? How does one go about changing who they are BEING?

First, you'll need to realize that you're boxed in by a reality concept (a Belief System) that's keeping you poor. Then you'll need powerful motivation for coming out of that box. The first step toward changing who you are (coming out of your box) is to acknowledge what's missing in your life. The second most important step out of your box is in choosing to BE the one who HAS what you've been missing.

The gap between wanting and choosing

Unless you're above average in grit and personal power, you probably won't have the determination it takes to choose out of your box. I'm saying this to challenge to you, because I've noticed that most of those who say they want out of their box never actually choose out. I suspect they got stuck in wanting because they didn't know the difference between wanting and choosing.

Wanting is what you do from inside the box—the box that keeps you from NOT HAVING what you want. Choosing out of your box is a brave new step that most won't take, because it's outside their comfort zone.

*Crossing the gap between wanting and choosing
requires a giant leap of faith in yourself.* --Darel Rutherford

POVERTY IS A STATE OF BEING

If you want something that's outside the box, you need to ask yourself a couple of questions:
1. If I am shown the way out my box, will my desire for what I want be great enough to move me to choose?
2. Will I actually have the courage to take that step?

In the Rich/Poor exercise, you probably discovered that you are not rich in some area of your life. In some ways, that's not good, because before you knew you were poor, you could blissfully say, "I'm already rich," conning yourself into believing that you were. But now you KNOW otherwise. Knowing you're poor wouldn't be sad if it weren't for the fact that you'll likely do nothing about it. Why do I say that?

In a recent survey, the Internal Revenue Service reported that 85% of all U.S. citizens will retire without sufficient income to live comfortably for the rest of their lives. In my book, that's poor! Think about it! You could end up being one of the 85% who retire poor, unless you make up your mind (right now) that you won't be one of THEM.

You can start by understanding why these people never bridged the gap between wanting and choosing.

What happened to their dream?

The world is filled with people who want things they'll never have simply because they never got around to choosing to BE the one who would have it.

Did they want to retire poor? I doubt it! I'm sure these people didn't want their lives to end in poverty. Each and every one of them, at some point in their lives, had a dream that some day they would be living that better life. But their someday never came. So, what went wrong? Their problem: they never got past the wanting to the choosing.

In fact, everyone of these people had a good reason why they couldn't choose. They each had a natural resistance to choosing a new reality. And because they were totally unaware of that powerful, built-in resistance to change, none of them were equipped to deal with it.

Before you can choose that better life and succeed in having it, you will need to know how to overcome that resistance. You'll learn more about overcoming resistance in the next chapter.

BEING THE SOLUTION

A lottery mentality

The popular TV game show, <u>Who Wants To Be A Millionaire?</u>, has helped a great many people acquire what I call a "lottery mentality."

Hoping to win the lottery, as Earl Nightingale once said, is like *"waiting for your ship to come in when you didn't send one out."* And if you were like most lottery winners, even if you won, you wouldn't have the consciousness that would allow you to keep the million dollars for long. Why do I say this? Those who make a business of tracking winners say that a large percentage of lottery winners end up broke in two years or less. Why? They didn't have a millionaire's consciousness to match their good fortune.

If you have a sincere desire to become a millionaire, you can be, and I will show you the path you must take to get there. But becoming wealthy is not about hoping to win a lot of money; it's about CHOOSING to BE a millionaire.

It worked for me

There was a time in my life when I believed that knowing what you want was the only key to having it.

After reading Napoleon Hill's <u>Think and Grow Rich</u> and by putting his thinking-your-way-to-riches philosophy to work in my life, I had this amazing experience; whenever I decided I wanted something, it became almost automatically mine. And because wanting always turned into having for me, I came to the conclusion that knowing what you want from life was the key to having it. But I was wrong! I was unconsciously taking a step that most people leave out. What do you suppose that step was?

The world is full of people who don't know what they want. They haven't given themselves permission to want, because they don't know who they really are. And since they don't know what they want, they don't choose.

And then there are also those who know what they want, but can't choose!

The missing step

Knowing that you want to be rich won't make you rich, because unless you take the most important step in the becoming-rich process—that of CHOOSING to BE rich—it will never happen.

POVERTY IS A STATE OF BEING

*When you don't know what you want from life,
you'll end up getting what you want... nothing!*
--Darel Rutherford

In researching my first book, So, Why Aren't You Rich?, I soon came to realize that the only real difference between the rich and the poor was that the rich had chosen to be rich and the poor had chosen not to be. Life really is that simple—it's about choice! Whatever you want from life will be yours, but only IF you can want it with a passion and then come up with the self-worth that will allow you to choose it.

Just a matter of choice

About three months after reading Hill's book, I came to the conclusion that becoming a millionaire was just a matter of choice, and I chose! To get the significance of this choice, you need to be able to see the difference between having a million dollars and BEING a millionaire. When you choose to BE a millionaire, you become the magnet that attracts millions. The BEING must always come before the HAVING. I didn't just decide that I wanted to have a million dollars, I chose to BE A MILLIONAIRE. I set no time limit on reaching that goal and never became obsessed with the idea. In fact, I actually forgot about it.

I committed to the image of myself BEING a millionaire, totally believed in it, accepted that as my reality, and promptly forgot to keep thinking consciously about it. In fact, I became so engrossed in the managing of my growing business, I didn't really think much about my millionaire goal until almost two years later.

When I finally remembered that I had chosen to be a millionaire, I decided it was time to check the score. I was already half way toward my second million!

Are you impressed that I'm a millionaire? Don't be! Be impressed with the idea that becoming a millionaire is just a matter of choice! You see, I'm not a millionaire because I'm smarter than you. I had no special education; I had no special advantages to start with, no money to invest. The only difference between you and me is that I chose to be a millionaire and you didn't. It really is that simple.

What can you learn from this?

Conclusion: Becoming a millionaire is just a matter of choice! Believe me. If I could choose and have it happen, so can you! If I've convinced you, now would be a good time for your affirmation:
I don't need to know HOW it will happen;
All I need do is choose, so I choose. I will BE a millionaire!

If the idea of becoming a millionaire is too rich for your blood, make the affirmation, but substitute whatever BEING statement suits you at the moment. You could choose to BE, rich, abundant, happy, healthy, self-confident, or whatever, just as long as your new BEING choice takes you outside your comfort zone.

In the following chapters you'll learn;
- Why you are not already rich in all ways.
- How to come to know what you really want from life.
- Why becoming rich is a BEING choice.
- Why a BEING change will be the solution to all your problems.
- How to create the burning desire that will motivate your new BEING choice.
- How to become a magnet that attracts money.
- Why most people never make it past the mind set that keeps them poor.
- How to use the Power Pause as the way past your resistance to becoming rich.

2
NINE STEPS TO PERSONAL FREEDOM
...your way out of the box

*Improving the quality of your life
will require a change in who you are BEING.*
--Darel Rutherford

You can avoid their mistakes

About 40% of my prosperity workshop participants doubled their incomes in the year of their participation. Sounds good, until you begin to wonder—what happened to the 60% who failed to accomplish that mission?

According to the IRS report I referred to in the last chapter, about 15% of us will retire rich enough to live comfortably in retirement. Maybe that's good news, but I don't think so. The negative side of those statistics tells a very sad story. While living in the richest nation in the world 85% of us will retire poor. Why?

BEING THE SOLUTION

If you're wise, you'll want to learn the reason for their failure so that you can avoid their mistakes and perhaps, retire rich instead of poor.

So here are their four biggest mistakes:
1. They failed because they thought wanting was the same as choosing. They just never got around to the point of choosing to BE the one who could have what they wanted from life.
2. They failed because they were not aware that having what they wanted would require a change in who they were being.
3. They failed because they were not aware of, and therefore, unable to deal with their own built-in resistance to that attempted being change.
4. They failed because their desire for that change was not powerful enough to overcome ego's resistance to change.

What you want from life that you don't already have can only be found outside your box.
--Darel Rutherford

Wanting without choosing is a trap

I want you to see how easy it is to get stuck in the trap of wanting something you will never have. Once you've identified with the condition of lack, (unless you choose out of it) you almost automatically become one who will not have what you wanted. This is because almost every decision we make in life is actually a BEING choice. By wanting and not choosing, you've actually chosen to BE the one who will NOT have what you want.

This is the trap into which many fall. We knew what we wanted, but when it came time to choose it, we chose not to choose. It never dawned on us that choosing not to choose is choosing not to have. If you are not rich, it's because, when the time came for choosing, you didn't choose to be.

The power to choose whom you will BE is a far greater power than you ever imagined. What you may not know is that, once you've chosen, everything that belongs with that choice will become available to you. You must still choose it, but now it's there for you, when it seemed not to be before. By failing to realize that you used your power of choice even when you choose not to choose, you become the victim of your unconscious choices.

NINE STEPS TO PERSONAL FREEDOM
*Wanting it and not choosing it
is choosing not to have it.*
--Darel Rutherford

When you don't know what you want

Some workshop participants fizzle out in the goal-setting process because they don't really know what they want. This "not knowing" is their ego not wanting them to know, because it sees goal setting as a threat to its survival. Your ego (your concept of self) knows that having what you want means changing who you are. You need to know that your ego is dead set against that change.

In the prosperity workshops that I have taught, close to half of the room would doze off during goal-setting sessions. This was because their ego took them out of harms way by putting them to sleep. Goal setting, a brave new step out of your box, is contrary to your ego's wishes.

To have it, you must BE it

You have been given the power, the power to make a new BEING choice. Your job in life is to learn to use that power wisely. Once you've chosen abundance over poverty, a spiritual law, the Law of Correspondence, takes over to bring within your reach everything that belongs to you by right of your new BEING choice.

It's not magic; it's that law. But don't say "I'm a millionaire," snap your fingers, and expect to be spending your million the next day. Choosing to be a millionaire, metaphorically speaking, is like choosing to go to New York from Los Angeles. Having made the decision to go, you won't magically appear in New York. You'll be figuring out the best way to get yourself there. If you're driving, you'll find your destination on a map, and plot the best course for getting yourself there. On the way, you'll find that there are some detours and direction choices you must make—decisions you will make with your destination always in mind.

Once you've chosen to be a millionaire, you must work at being and becoming one who feels worthy of having what just naturally comes with BEING a millionaire.

You've taken the first step out of your box by choosing to be more than you were, but choosing out is only the beginning. Now you must work at playing out the role; that's the becoming part of being. Most people fizzle out during the becoming process. Let me explain why they fail.

BEING THE SOLUTION

Why they fail after they've chosen
When you understand why most people fail, your chances for success will improve exponentially. They fail for two reasons:
1. Their desire for the change was not powerful enough to overcome their ego's very powerful, built-in resistance to change.
2. And, since they were not aware of that resistance, they were not prepared to deal with it.

That resistance comes from what I call ego. I would define ego as:

our self-concept, functioning in and as
our individualized adaptation to our perception of reality.

In other words, your ego is your concept of self acting out the role in life that seems to best fit your current concept of reality.

The fact that you and I have an ego will come as no surprise to you, but you may not have noticed just how determined your ego is to resist any change you try to make in status quo. Your ego feels that it must keep everything the way it is if it is to survive. It sees a change in your point of view about life as a serious threat to its survival; it will resist any attempted change with all of its considerable might.

Your ego is quite aware of the fact that changing the way you relate to money, or anything else, will change who you are, and that self-image change is what it must avoid if your old image of self is to survive. Your ego's mission in life is:

the survival of its being whoever it perceives itself to be.
--Werner Erhard

A grand and glorious experience
Your ego fears change, because changing who you are BEING, for the ego, is like dying in order to be reborn into a new reality. It is only natural that the ego would do everything within its power to avoid dying.

Of course, being reborn into a new way of life, like a caterpillar being reborn as a butterfly, is a grand and glorious experience. But your ego doesn't see it that way. Your ego sees change as the death of who you are being. Your ego hopes you never discover that your lack of

NINE STEPS TO PERSONAL FREEDOM

abundance is simply a consequence of your BEING choice. Your ego hides this truth, because it does not want you making a new choice. It doesn't want you changing who you are.

If, after reading this far, you are considering the possibility of becoming rich, you must accept the fact that your ego will do everything within its power to block your attempt! And if that IRS report is correct, about 85% of the egos in the U.S. will succeed in blocking the attempted change in consciousness.

Unless you're determined

Changing what you have in life is as simple as changing your mind about which you will be, rich or poor. But because of your ego's resistance; your change of mind will be a little more complicated than it appears on the surface. Changing your self-concept is a little like planting a seed.

You can't plant a tomato seed today and pluck ripe tomatoes from the vine tomorrow. You must water that seed and nurture it for a few months before you can reap the harvest. And if you decide to become a millionaire today, you won't be spending the money tomorrow. Becoming rich is a being and becoming process that can only begin in earnest AFTER your ego has bought into the new program.

An example of wanting without choosing

When I was a kid, I learned to play the harmonica. I played by ear, couldn't read a note of music, but I loved making music and thought that, one day, I would learn to play the piano. So a few years ago, I bought one of those electronic keyboards with the intention of teaching myself to read music and play the piano. But I never became the piano player I said I wanted to be.

I learned to pick out a few tunes and enjoyed the playing for a while, but I didn't follow through with learning to read music. There are several reasons for my failure to learn. First of all, my heart wasn't in the practice. The desire was there, but not the commitment. I wanted the enjoyment of playing, but I hadn't actually chosen to BE a piano player. I had made a DOING choice, not a BEING choice, and because I lacked the necessary commitment, my want was never fulfilled. My desire to be a piano player was simply not great enough to overcome my resistance to a BEING change.

BEING THE SOLUTION

Why we make and break resolutions

I'm sure you've had the same experience. How many New Year's resolutions have you broken in your lifetime? Unless you're way above average in determination and will power, probably quite a few. We make and break resolutions, because changing what we do would require a change in who we are—a transformation in consciousness. We fail because our ego does not want us being transformed!

What you want from life is the bait that will, hopefully, motivate your choosing out of your box, but having it won't be your real gain. Your growth in consciousness will be the most important benefit of your coming out. Each trip out of the box empowers you, bringing you a little closer to knowing who you really are. The real purpose of your life is self-discovery, and that can only happen if we can get you outside the box. Every trip out of your box becomes a transformation in consciousness—if you can make it out to stay.

Transformation, a 21 day process

In Chapter Eight of this book, you will find the formula for a transformation. With this process, you will easily transform yourself into BEING the one who will have what you want from life. The change in your thinking habits, a transformation in consciousness, should take about 21 days to complete—that's according to Maxwell Maltz in his book, Psycho-cybernetics.

But I've learned, from conducting prosperity workshops for over 35 years, that about 60% of those who begin the transformation process never finish. They fail, because they don't make it past their ego's resistance. In Chapter Ten, you will find the Power Pause solution to that resistance.

When the ego takes on the new reality

Your powerful ego is "in charge" of your life most of the time (it maintains the box you call reality). But during the self-discovery process, you will come to realize that you are much more than an ego—much more than you know. Even so, if you are to transform the quality of your life, your ego—the one in charge of maintaining status quo—must finally come to accept your new vision as the new reality, or you will surely fail in the attempt.

The tool for enlisting your ego in your new vision is called the Power Pause, a transformational tool that will get you past your ego's

NINE STEPS TO PERSONAL FREEDOM

first line of defense and set you free of your box. You'll learn how to use the Power Pause in Chapter Ten.

When the transformation is successful, your ego will take over the job of defending the new reality as it has the old one. In short, before you can have what you want from life, you must BE the one to whom it belongs. Once ego is recruited into the new reality, you're practically home free. The purpose of this book is to show you how you can put your ego to work on making your dream BE your reality.

TRANSFORMATION: THE KEY

You've learned that most hopefuls who want a better life will end up retiring poor. They live in a box, a concept of reality, that has them believing that there's no way out. There is a way out, but they haven't found it! If you want your life to change for the better, you must make up your mind that you WILL NOT retire poor; you must choose out of your box.

The key to having what you want from life is a transformation in consciousness. I've offered this solution to workshop participants for years. And for all of those years, I've been frustrated by the high percentage of participants who did not follow through to complete the transformation process. They wanted riches, but never quite made it out of the box to stay and be rich.

REVIEWING THE REASONS FOR THEIR FAILURE

You live in a box, and I'm offering you the way out, right here, right now. But first, let's review the reasons why most people fail in their attempt to improve the quality of their lives.

- With the power to choose who they will be, most people become a victim of their own poor choices; they've staked their claim on poverty, instead of riches. They don't know who they are and haven't discovered their power of choice.
- They fail, because they're locked into their own victim story, without a clue that they're poor because they've chosen not to be rich.
- They've left out the number-one step in the becoming-rich process, that of choosing to be rich. They never chose to BE the one who would have the life they wanted.
- Because they don't know who they are, they don't know what they want. And since they don't know what they want, they can't choose anything different from what they have now. It's a "catch 22."

BEING THE SOLUTION

- They've made the mistake of believing that wanting and choosing was one and the same. They've never gotten past wanting that better life to choosing it.
- No one told them they'd need a transformation in consciousness in order to have what they wanted.
- No one told them their ego would resist that transformation. Totally unaware of this powerful resistance to change, some chose that better life and had their dreams shot down with ego's "yeah buts," and "what ifs."
- Most of all, they failed for lack of a burning desire for the change they wanted.
- They failed because no one told them they'd need a support group to reinforce their courage for making it past their weaker moments. You'll learn more about setting up your support group in Chapter Eleven.

Those are the reasons for most people's failure to become rich. Now, let's talk about the nine steps you MUST take if you are to overcome those reasons for your failing to become rich.

The Nine Steps

1. **Rediscover your personal power, the power of choice**
   In the next chapter, you will see why the true purpose of life is self-discovery. In the process of discovering your power to choose, you will learn who you really are. You will come to see that you have the power of the Universe behind your ability to make a new BEING choice. You will understand why I can promise you that the Universe will provide whatever belongs with your new BEING choice.

2. **Accepting that you chose what you have**
   In order to have that better life you've always wanted, you must change your mind about who you are. But you can't get from where you are now to where want to be, until you know from where you're starting. Knowing how you came to be where you are now is the first step in the process. To exit your box you must, first, admit that you chose the victim role you now play. You will be stuck in that box for as long as you continue to defend your reasons for being stuck!

3. **Knowing what you really want**
   Knowing what you want from life is the third step in the transformation process, and it's, obviously, the most essential ingredient to making a new choice in life. A greater sense of personal power comes from finally knowing who you really are, and that level of awareness gives you back something you've temporarily lost--the power to choose. Once you reconnect with your power of choice, you will know what you want. Just be aware that knowing what you want won't get it for you. Another step must be taken first.

4. **Develop a burning desire**.
   Workshop participants, who succeeded in doubling their incomes, had a burning desire to become financially independent. Those who failed to accomplish their income-doubling mission lacked the necessary burning desire. In Chapter Seven, you will learn how to develop a simple want into a burning desire and then to fan the flame until it's white-hot.

5. **Choosing to BE the one**
   The next and most important step in the direction of having what you want from life, the one most wannabes leave out, is in choosing to BE the one who will have it. When your burning desire has you wanting it so bad you can taste it, you will cancel out your poverty by CHOOSING to be rich. It is in your commitment to BE that you find the real power behind the power of choice! Some are transformed in the instant of making this commitment. Others may need the next step to complete the process.

6. **Transforming yourself**
   The key to having what you want in life is a transformation in consciousness. Quite simply, this means: *a change of mind about who you are and how you will relate to the circumstances in your perceived reality.* This sounds like a big deal, but it's really not. Transformation is a simple process that takes thirty minutes a day for about 21 days. In Chapter Nine, you will be given the formula for transforming yourself into BEING the

BEING THE SOLUTION

one who will have what you want. The process is guaranteed to work if you complete the exercise as directed.

7. **Understanding the resistance**
   Chapter Ten will show you how failing to understand ego's resistance to change can put you back in your box. Most people fail in the attempt to change the quality of their lives because they didn't really understand just how determined their egos would be to resist that change. But once you understand and learn how to deal with the resistance, you will easily find your way past it.

8. **Overcoming the resistance**
   Most of the ego's resistance comes in the form of mind chatter—it's that little voice in the back of your head that keeps telling you why a change in your life style couldn't, shouldn't or wouldn't happen. It's probably talking to you right now, telling you to drop this book and run for the nearest exit! In Chapter Eleven, I will introduce to you, the Power Pause, a perfect tool for replacing ego's mind chatter with the vision of your new and prosperous reality.

9. **Forming a support group**
   To transform yourself into "being" the one who can have what you want from life, your ego must die and be reborn into your new identity. During the dying process, the ego goes through the emotional crisis of detaching itself from the old reality. During this period of emotional upset, when the ego is trying its best to survive, about 60% of those who start the transformation process will give up on their dream and fail to follow through for the full 21 days.
   To get you through this stressful period, I will show you how to form the support group that will take you past those moments when fear has you wanting to crawl back into your box. My name for a support group is, "Powerpact." You'll learn about support groups in Chapter Twelve.

THE CREATIVE PROCESS

If there's anything you lack, that would make your life whole and complete, a BEING change will solve that problem. The nine steps

NINE STEPS TO PERSONAL FREEDOM

necessary to that transformation will be explained in detail in the balance of this book.

Most self-help books are based on the premise that what you have makes you who you are. They offer DO HAVE BE as the correct order of the creative process. They have the order backwards. The truth is; you won't DO what they suggest, unless you can, first, BE whomever you would need to be to do those successful things naturally. DO is not the first step in the becoming rich process. In fact, DO HAVE BE just doesn't work. The correct order of creation for mankind is BE DO HAVE.

Who you are determines what you can have; that means, you can only have what you want by changing who you are. The Game of Life is set up with this purpose: that you discover who you really are. That mission, for you, can be accomplished only through your growing in consciousness—through your coming out of your box to become more than you were.

The key to having what you want is your transformation in consciousness. The purpose of this book is to lead you, step by step, through the nine steps of the transformation process so that you will have what you want.

Until one is Committed

If you are to follow the steps of the transformation process through to completion, you'll need to understand the importance of being totally committed.

The difference between wanting something and having it is in the choosing. But sometimes those who think they've chosen haven't really done so; they lack the total commitment necessary for having it happen. What they haven't realized, is that choosing to have something you want, is actually a BEING choice.

In order to BE the one who will have what you want, you must give up BEING the one who doesn't have it. This requires a transformation in consciousness, which probably won't happen without a commitment powerful enough to override the ego's resistance. Because they lack the necessary commitment, 60% will fizzle out in their attempt to change the quality of their lives. (At least, this was the ratio of failure back when I was seriously keeping track)

W H Murray, in his book, The Scottish Himalayan Expedition, had this to say about commitment:

BEING THE SOLUTION

He wrote:
> *Until one is committed there is hesitancy, the chance to draw back, always ineffectiveness. Concerning all acts of initiative (and creation), there is one element of truth, the ignorance of which kills countless ideas and splendid plans; that the moment one definitely commits oneself, then Providence moves, too. All sorts of things occur to help one that would never otherwise have occurred. A whole stream of events issues from the decision, raising in one's favor all manner of unforeseen incidents, meetings and material assistance, which no man would have dreamt would have come his way. I have learned deep respect for one of Goethe's couplets*

> **Whatever you can do or dream you can do, begin it.**
> **Boldness has genius, power, and magic in it.**

Providence takes over when you make a committed choice for a new way of BEING.

Taking charge of your thinking
Don't try to turn back the clock;
just wind it up again.

The greatest truth you could learn about life is:

we become what we think about.

Knowing this should inspire you to take charge of your thinking, to change the context, and then, the content of your life. In the next chapter, you will learn why we become what we think about.

The second greatest truth is:

what you have in life is a direct result of a BEING choice.

Knowing that, you should be able to see that you could change what you have by changing who you are BEING.

In fact, what you learn in Chapter III will change your mind forever about who you are.

3
IN THE IMAGE AND LIKENESS OF GOD

...what that really means

God, as man, in man, is man
--Science of Mind Textbook
Ernest Holmes

What happens if you don't know the rules

On a vacant lot one block from our home, my brother Bob played baseball for the first time. All he knew about the game was that you were supposed to hit the ball and run. On his first time up to bat, he hit a home run. The other players on his team yelled, "Run, Bob—run home!" And he did—all the way home.

I smile every time I think about that. Bob made this mistake because he didn't know the rules of the game. But what if life was a game and you didn't know the game's purpose or its rules? You wouldn't be touching all the bases either, would you? If that was the

BEING THE SOLUTION

case, what would be the odds against your winning the game, and would you be able to laugh about not winning?

Well, be prepared to laugh at yourself, because life is a cosmic joke, and the joke is on you. You see, life IS a game and you're probably playing it without knowing the game's rules or its purpose. I'd say that's a pretty large handicap.

But if you did know life was a game, had learned the rules, and understood the game's true purpose, you would be miles ahead of those who didn't know what you knew. What you learn from reading this book will make you a sure winner in the Game of Life, but only if you're really ready to be a winner.

Those who win big

Have you ever noticed that those who win big in the Game of Life play it like they had nothing to lose? What if I could show you how to change your self-concept and your perception of reality so that you could play from the powerful position of knowing that life was a game and you had nothing to lose? Would that interest you?

Your stake in the game of life is your self-concept,
not the stuff you hoped to win or feared you might lose.
--Darel Rutherford

Those who win big at the Game of Life know that the chips on the table, like Monopoly money, have no real value compared to who they are being and becoming as they fearlessly play the game. Helen Keller obviously understood that when she said,

Life is either a daring adventure or it's nothing!

To win at the Game of Life will require a change in the way you perceive reality—a change in your self-concept. This may sound like a big deal, but it's really not. Changing your self-concept is as simple as changing your attitude or your point of view about life. For example: changing your reality concerning wealth is nothing more difficult than changing your mind about how you will relate to money. I'll show you how later.

The Game of Life is set up so that you will have whatever you want as soon as you grow tall enough to claim it for yourself. And

IN THE IMAGE AND LIKENESS OF GOD

growing taller fulfills the game's purpose. This truth is based on a spiritual law that says you can have from life only that which belongs to you by right of consciousness. You will see why this is true when I share the following story of how you and I came to be playing this Game of Life without a clue that it was a game. By the way, you've heard this story before and weren't paying attention.

How the game got started

One day, God became bored and decided to play a game. Before long He realized that playing a game by oneself isn't that much fun. He solved that problem by creating gods who would play the game with Him.

He created those gods in His own image and likeness, and he called his creation mankind (see, told you you'd heard this story before). Then, God, AS MAN, proceeded to play the game, and once again, the playing just wasn't much fun. The problem with playing a game as a god is that you couldn't loose, and if you couldn't lose, the game wouldn't be a challenge.

To make the game interesting, God had man forget that he is a god. He said, "Now, he'll play, thinking he has something to lose. His fear of losing his life, his dignity, his job, or anything else he values should make the game fun."

"Man will play the Game of Life with the power of a god who doesn't know he has the power. Man will create his own reality, becoming a victim of those circumstances, without a clue that he is the creator of his own chaos. Playing the game under these new rules should make the playing a great deal more exciting and very interesting." Notice that this game plan makes your life and mine a cosmic joke.

Guess what that makes you

You've heard different versions of this story many times over. If you haven't accepted the reality of the presence of God in you, you were not really listening. If you had been paying attention, thinking it through, you would have already realized that being made "in the image and likeness of God" makes you an individualization of God.

This doesn't make you God any more than a drop of water is the ocean, but that drop of water has all the same attributes as the ocean. As an individualization of God, you have the same attributes as

BEING THE SOLUTION

your creator in your own sphere of life, with creative powers you haven't begun to imagine or use wisely.

The first of the nine steps out of your box

...was to *find your personal power*, the power of choice. I said I would show you that you have the power of the Universe behind your ability to choose who you will be. You may or may not appreciate this interpretation of scripture which, by the way, reads:

> *So, God created man in His own image,*
> *in the image of God created He him;*
> *male and female created He them*
> --Genesis 2:27 KJV

I've just reminded you that you have power by pointing out the source of your power—I say reminded you, because you've heard this truth over and over again, in one form or another all your life. Up until now, you've chosen to ignore it, because having the power of God in your sphere of life hasn't fit your concept of reality. Your ego doesn't want you to learn how powerful you really are, because that knowledge would destroy the illusion that you are a victim of your circumstances. Isn't it time you gave up your powerlessness in favor of finding your power?

A clue:

You will discover your power by proving it to yourself!

You can ignore your power, denying that you have it, but you can't make that power go away. You've been using it all your life, choosing who you will be, being and becoming that choice, yet totally unaware that you have this great power.

One of the strangest attributes of this power is that sometimes *it works by seeming not to work.* Those who seem to have no power have used the power to create their own powerlessness. The helpless got that way by choosing to BE victims, powerless to help themselves.

A paradigm shift?

For years, we've been flirting with, but avoiding direct reference to the idea of God, in man, as man, because the subject was, perhaps too profound a truth—too far outside our belief system. But now, in checking self-help best-seller lists, I find, almost without

IN THE IMAGE AND LIKENESS OF GOD

exception, the words "spiritual" or "soul" in the titles. It seems obvious to me that the world is ready for the paradigm shift in consciousness that will allow humankind to finally experience the spiritual truth in BEING human.

You are a human BEING, created in the image and likeness of God, with the God-given power to make BEING choices. At some level of consciousness, you know who you are; at another level, you are resisting that knowing. The time has come for you to acknowledge your power and put it to work to your advantage. It's time you played the game, with the knowledge of who you really are.

Ernest Holmes, founder of Science of Mind, author of the Science of Mind textbook, said it this way: *God as man, in man, is man.*

The value in being discontented
*The soul of God is poured into the world
through the thoughts of men*
--Ralph Waldo Emerson

The idea that God experiences Himself in and through you **as you** may rattle your cage a little or a lot, depending on your current belief system. The Game of Life is set up so that you gradually become aware of the presence of God in you, as you. You will find this internal power by using it to create a better life for yourself. You will find your power within yourself, but you will make that discovery only in the process of choosing out of your box.

Your purpose in life is to discovery your power, and that discovery can only happen outside the box. The discontent you feel over current circumstances is your invitation to use your hidden power—to choose out of your box!

Until you've proven your power to yourself by demonstrating it, your new relationship to God will be merely an intellectual understanding. To really know this truth for yourself, you must experience it—proving it to yourself in being and becoming more than you were.

The power to create your own reality

As a human Being, you have the power to BE—the power to create your own reality and the power to choose whom you will be in that reality. What you may not have realized is that once you choose,

BEING THE SOLUTION

the Universe is set up to provide you with everything that belongs in your life by right of that choice.

You've been using your God-given power all your life, creating new realities to suit your life as you've grown in consciousness. You've also created your current reality by choosing who you would be in that reality. You now have everything that belongs in the reality of your choice. The only thing missing, up to now, is the realization that you created your reality with a BEING choice.

Still not laughing?
When did I realize I was God?
Well, I was praying and I suddenly realized
I was talking to myself.
--Peter O'Toole, The Ruling Class

All this time, you've had the power to create your own reality and have not given yourself credit for having that power. Do you see the humor in that? You have used your great power to put yourself into a box and you're stuck in that box, because you don't get that you created the box you call reality.

You endure circumstances you don't like, seeing yourself as a victim, only because you haven't allowed yourself to see that you created those circumstances. That's the joke, and I notice you are still not laughing. Well, you may not want to hear this, but if you could laugh at yourself about having misused your great power all these years, it would mean you "got it," and "getting it" is the real point of the Game of Life.

The cosmic joke
Ignorance is a voluntary misfortune.
Italian Proverb

The joke is that, as an individualization of God, you have the power of the Universe behind your "I am" statement, and you've used that power to render yourself powerless. If you could be a casual observer, step back, be objective, and view your life from the outside looking in, you would laugh at your predicament. Laughing at yourself gives you back your power.

At the core, you are God individualized. On the surface you're playing a role and that role is a joke as long as you continue to see yourself trapped in it. So, ask yourself which of the following statements fit you.

- You pray negative prayers and complain that God didn't answer your prayers. "I am poor" is a prayer; you chose your reality and now you're living it. God DID answer your prayers. That's the problem, and that's why it's funny.
- Your push others away and complain that nobody loves you.
- You frown at the world and wonder why nobody's smiling.
- You wait for your ship to come in when you didn't send one out.
- You search for happiness when being happy is simply matter of choice.
- You defend your current reality, even though it doesn't give you what you want from life.

If any of the above victim stories fit you, the first step in solving your problem is to laugh at your predicament. When you can see the humor in it, you have found your way out.

Who would you be BEING?

You will find the solution to most problems in your answer to a simple question that goes right to the heart of the matter. That question:

*Who would you be BEING
if that were no longer a problem?*

To test this question out, think about your worst problem. Got it? Now, ask yourself that question. *Who would I be BEING if that were no longer the problem.* Notice that the question takes you right past the reasons for your problem to its solution. Think about this! If you allowed yourself to BE as powerful as you really are (Being God individualized), the problem would simply dissolve and disappear.

For example: I know someone who had a powerful fear of speaking in public. Her question would have been, *Who would I be BEING if my fear of speaking in public were no longer my problem?* She chose a new BEING statement that would take her beyond that fear. Then, she joined Toastmasters; six months later, she won a division speech contest.

BEING THE SOLUTION

My wife was deathly afraid of drowning. Her question would have been, *Who would I be BEING if I were no longer afraid of drowning?* She made up her mind to overcome her fear, took swimming lessons, and solved her fear of water. Another example question that would fit a great many people is, *Who would I be BEING if money were no longer an issue?*

If you think about it you can probably come up with many such examples of someone you know solving their problem by changing who they were BEING relative to their problem. So I repeat the question, "Who would YOU be BEING if you no longer had that problem?" Really give this some serious thought!

All the power you'll ever need

Your purpose in this Game of Life is self-discovery. To accomplish that mission, you will continue to use your creative powers over and over again, each time gaining power, until the day when you "get" who you really are—an individualization of God. You'll "get it" in the process of proving yourself to yourself.

You see, God gave you and I the power to choose who we would BE, and that power is all we will ever need to create the reality of our choice. I know this simple truth seems a little hard to believe, but your only real job in this Game of Life is to choose and re-choose who you will BE. God's Law of Correspondence will take care of the rest.

You might want to notice that you've already done that. You've chosen who you would be and already have everything that belongs in your life by right of that choice.

The bait

Oh, I know there's a lot of stuff you want that you don't have, but those goodies don't really belong in your current reality; they don't fit in with who you are now BEING. That stuff you want is outside your reality, baiting you to come out and get it.

That's right! What you want from life, what you don't have, will always be outside the box. What you call reality is built around your self-concept. You built that reality by saying "I am" and completing the sentence in so many ways that you wouldn't believe it—until you begin to pay attention. So, you might want to look back over your life and ask yourself what "I am" statement you've used to create your current limited reality.

IN THE IMAGE AND LIKENESS OF GOD

To learn the answer, you might want to monitor your own thoughts and words. Take time out to notice how many times a day you say or think, "I am," each time reinforcing status quo. (Your mind chatter keeps you in the box.) When you think thoughts like, "I'm poor;" "I'm unlovable;" "I'm not good enough," that's the creative maintenance power of your subconscious at work.

What most men pray when they pray to God
is that two and two may not make four
--Russian proverb

Is that your final answer?

In God's game show, when you use your power to say, "I am poor," the game show host (God) says, "Is that your final answer?" When you say "Yes," God says, "You got it," and what you've gotten for yourself is a direct result of your "I am" statement.

Each time you catch yourself making an "I am" statement—and you do this hundreds of times each day—ask yourself what you've created with that thought and if that's really who you want to be.

You say, "I'm sick and tired of this job," and then you sit back and wonder why you are always sick and tired. When you "get" that the pattern of your thinking created the box in which you live, you will begin to see how powerful you really are.

"Why me, God?"

When I was a carpenter years ago, I carried a lunch box to work each day and ate my lunch on the job site. One of my lunch companions constantly complained about
"These damn peanut butter and jelly sandwiches."
So, I asked him,
"Why don't you have your wife fix something else?"
He answered,
"I don't have a wife. I make my own sandwiches."

You think that's funny? The most important thing you could get from this story is that you fixed your own lunch. You did that when you chose who you would be. You did that when you chose how you would think, act, and react to the circumstances in your life. If you are tired of peanut butter and jelly sandwiches, fix a different lunch. Make a new choice about who you will be, and one day soon, you will open your lunch box to find a gourmet meal.

BEING THE SOLUTION

God did not intend that you be poor, only that you have the power to choose who you would be, and reap the consequences of that choice without His interference. It's up to you to discover your power and choose who you will be, and it is God's guarantee that you will get to experience life from whatever point of view you've chosen. You live under a spiritual law, The Law of Correspondence, that reads like this:

What you have in life
must correspond exactly to who you are.
--Darel Rutherford

That powerful law, dependable as the law of gravity, guarantees that you will have from life whatever belongs to you by right of consciousness.

In the next chapter you will be given a way to picture the Game of Life so that you'll have a better understanding of how the game works and where you stand in it.

If you can find the God inside of yourself,
you can find the God inside everybody.
--Stephen Levine

The task before you is nothing
compared to the great force behind you.
Ralph Waldo Emerson

4
THE GAME BOARD
...for The Game of Life

*You can almost never win
what you think you can't afford to lose.*
--Darel Rutherford

Your stake in the Game

Many years ago, I remember shooting craps with a man who owned the company for which I worked as a carpenter. His strategy for winning was to double his bet every time he lost. I don't recommend that strategy, but it worked for him. He almost always won because those he played against were betting what they couldn't afford to lose. Please get that his greatest asset in the game was his winning attitude!

BEING THE SOLUTION

What you're betting in the Game of Life is your concept of reality—and that's only a perception.
--Darel Rutherford

If you can play life's game with no attachment to the status quo, no fear of giving up your point of view, you'll win. If you can't afford to give up that idea in favor of better one, you may not move ahead to the next level of the game, and you'll lose. You'll lose, because your bet in the Game is something you've decided you can't afford to lose. To win at the Game of Life, detach yourself and move on to the next level.

Creating a game board

You and I have been playing at this Game of Life, completing the cycles of life's game board without a clue that a game was in process. We've passed GO time after time in our lives, without once noticing that we've been past this same point before. We've lived our lives, totally unaware of the game and its true purpose.

In order to have a better idea about how the Game of Life works, let's create an imaginary gameboard. To get the picture, remember how you played Monopoly as a child. You had your own uniquely-shaped piece that you moved according to the number of spaces indicated by your roll of the dice, and every time you passed "Go," you got $200.

Our imaginary Game-of-Life board will be spiral-shaped, like a road circling a mountain. The spaces on this gameboard will be circles instead of squares, and each trip around the cycle will take you to a different level in the Game of Life. So that you will better understand the illustration on the next page, I will explain the steps involved.

Destroy Attachments: In this step you will detach yourself from whatever holds you back.

Start: This is where you will create your vision of a new and better reality.

Transformation: Here, you will choose a new way of BEING in the new reality.

THE GAME BOARD

BE: For this step, you will practice BEING the new you in the new reality.

DO: Then, you will be DOING what must be done in order to have.

HAVE: At this point you would be having what you wanted from life. But this is the end, not the beginning. To make it to the next level you must, again detach yourself from your having.

The Game Board

To give you an overview

My intention in creating this game board is to give you an overview—a new way of looking at your life so that you'll see where you've been and where your trips around the cycle are taking you. Keeping this game board in mind, you will come to understand the game's true purpose.

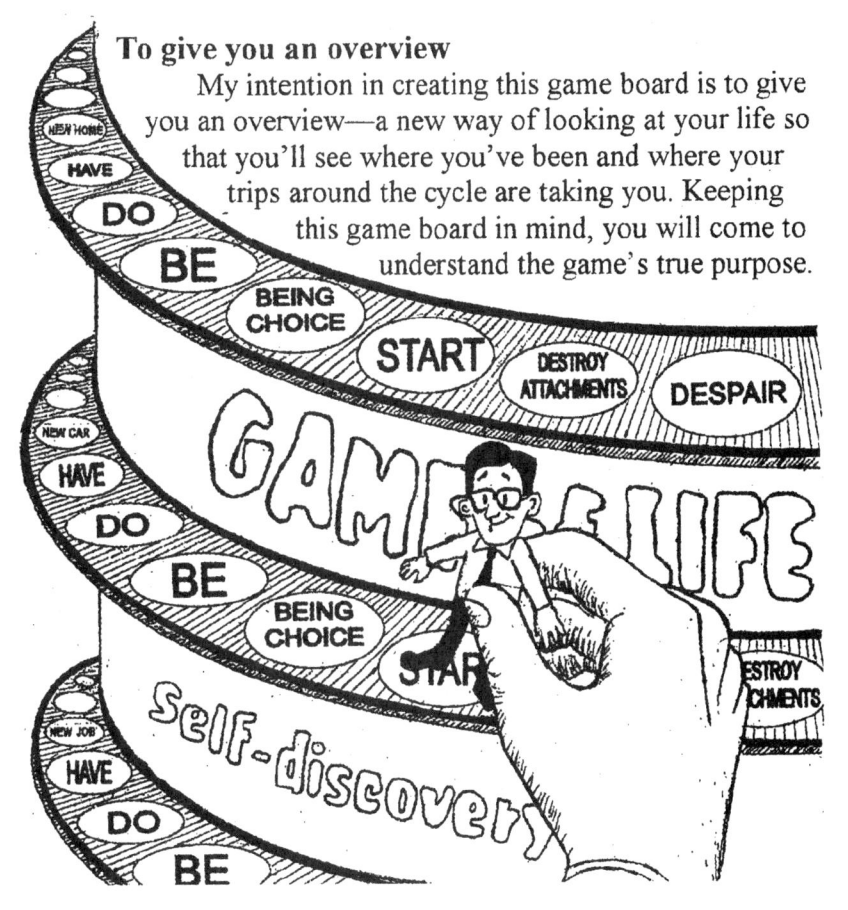

- 43 -

BEING THE SOLUTION

When you can accept this overview of your life, you'll better understand the process that will move you to the next level of consciousness, where you get to have what you want from life.

Each trip around this spiral-shaped gameboard represents a level of consciousness, and at the beginning of each gameboard level we find a circle marked "Transformation." In life's game, transformation is like GO in the game of Monopoly. The rules in the Game of Life require that you make a new BEING choice (pass GO) in order to move to the next level of consciousness.

In this Game of Life, your self-concept (your perception of yourself) will determine the shape and size of your piece. And the size of your piece (your level of consciousness) will determine at which level you can play the game. You can't play the game without a piece (you need your ego to play the game) and you can't pass Go (be transformed) until you expand the size of your piece (grow in consciousness). Get the picture?

The purpose of the Game

One of the problems most students of metaphysics have with the idea of becoming rich is that they think of themselves as being on a spiritual journey that would be side tracked by choosing to be wealthy. I agree that the purpose of life is not about becoming rich.

Instead, our true purpose in life is that we discover who we really are. But becoming rich in all ways is an important part of the self-discovery process. I'm here to tell you that the journey out of poverty into a life of abundance is a spiritual journey. You can't change from a poverty consciousness into a prosperity consciousness without increasing your awareness of that greater power within you, thereby fulfilling life's purpose of self-discovery.

It is in being transformed that we discover who we are. We grow in consciousness by choosing to BE the one who can handle whatever problems we face. Then, by rising above the problem, we become a living demonstration of that choice. Your job in the Game of Life is to choose who you will be and then to master that role, experiencing life fully from that point of view.

THE GAME BOARD
To win at the game of life, maintain this overview—

My reality is nothing more than a point of view.
When I change my point of view, my reality will change

    To play in the game and win, you must understand that your purpose is to discover your true identity as God individualized. You do that by making new BEING choices and then by being and becoming that choice (growing into the role).

    Playing out the role is important; you must allow the time to grow into the role you've chosen. But to win at the game, you must maintain an overview that allows you to see that it's your ego, not the real you, playing out the role. You are not your ego. You are the one who wrote the script; ego merely plays out the role as you've written it. And when you want something you don't have, you must be aware that a transformation in consciousness is the only way you can have it. You'll be writing a new script by making a new BEING choice.

Not about having

    You must know that you can't play at the next level of the game until you give up your attachment to the level you will leave behind.

The beginning and the end
reach out their ends to each other
--Chinese proverb

    Each time around the cycle, you will be trading in your old piece in order to play at that new level. You can't have what you want without being transformed. When you keep the purpose of the game in mind, you will know that the winning at each level was not your gain in material wealth or in achieving a desired end, but in your transformation in consciousness.

    If you're like most of us, your awareness of the presence of God in you is an intellectual understanding, not an experiential knowing.

We are wiser than we know
--Ralph Waldo Emerson

    You won't really know who you are experientially until you prove it to yourself in the being and becoming process—until you can

BEING THE SOLUTION

feel it and know it in your heart and be excited about the new you. You can only find your power by using it, each time, with a new level of certainty about who you are.

Up till now, you've used your power unconsciously. Up to now, you've misused your power and reaped unwelcome consequences. All of this because you didn't know the rules of the game. As you can see, you've been playing the game with a gigantic handicap.

You can't win if...
- You don't know you're playing a game
- You don't know the purpose of the game
- You don't know the rules

Nature delights in punishing stupid people.
--Ralph Waldo Emerson

The Consequences of being ignorance:
...examples of not winning

- If you think you're dumb, you are.
- If you think you are ugly, you are.
- If you believe you are powerless, you are.
- If you think you're a victim, you are.
- If you believe the rich are the bad guys, they are.
- If you expect to be poor, you will be.
- If you think there's no way out, there isn't.

Ignorance is voluntary misfortune
Italian proverb

Ironic, isn't it?—that we can be so powerful and yet so unaware of our power. Because you have the power, whatever you choose to believe becomes your reality. Your problem is that you haven't a clue that you have that power, and that you've used your power to create the swamp in which your alligators live—the ones that keep biting you in the rump.

From nature expect no punishment
...we reap only consequences.
--Darel Rutherford

THE GAME BOARD

The game is set up so that you must reap the consequences of your choices. You must live with the alligators until you choose to pull the plug and drain the swamp.

What it takes to win

To win, you must learn to play at life as if it were a game, having a winning attitude as you play, because you have nothing of real value to lose. To win, you must keep in mind that you are an individualization of God with the power to create your own reality. Your mission is to find that power within yourself and feel powerful! You will be creating new realities for yourself from time to time in order to grow, for it is in growing that you win.

Winning requires an overview that allows you to know that you are not your game piece, that you are the one rolling the dice and moving the piece. Winning comes from knowing you are not your ego and from being in charge of your life. Winning comes with knowing that nothing of great value is at stake with each roll of the dice other than giving up your current concept of reality in favor of your growing in consciousness.

The game is played in four stages.
1. A new BEING choice gets you past GO and starts you down the path of a new cycle in the game.
2. The next stage of your trip around the cycle is the being and becoming part, where you work at becoming the one who will have what you wanted.
3. The third stage of your trip around the cycle is the having part. Contrary to popular opinion, HAVING is the end of the cycle, not the beginning.
4. The fourth and most difficult stage of your trip around the cycle is taken when you manage to detach yourself from whatever you've become attached to in your current reality. Destroying your attachment is the thorniest part of the game. Just know that you can't stay attached and fulfill the game's purpose.

One must learn how to lose
before learning how to play.
--Mexican proverb

BEING THE SOLUTION

These are the rules of the game.
- To win, you must become more aware of who you are.
- A new round starts with wanting something you don't have.
- Your desire for more causes you to rediscover your power of choice.
- You must choose to BE the one who will have what you want.
- You must choose a new way of BEING in that new reality.
- You must play out whatever role you've chosen to play.
- You develop your new reality through being and becoming.
- You suffer the consequences of poor choices and learn from your mistakes.
- You must pass GO (be transformed) in order to play at the next level.
- You must be transformed in order to have what you want from life.
- You must trade in your old piece in order to play at the next level.
- To move on, you must become detached from the old role you were playing and all that stuff you've accumulated.
- The winning at each level is your transformation in consciousness.

Well, now you know you're playing a game; you know the purpose of the game, and you know the rules. You also know how powerful you are. Putting that knowledge to work means exercising your power of choice. Now that you know all of that, are you ready to choose? Probably not.

In the next chapter, you'll learn what stands between you and choosing out of your box.

5
YOUR SELF IMAGE

...the mental blue print running your life

Your Self-Image

*Raising the bar on your self-worth
changes the blueprint that shapes your life*
--Darel Rutherford

You created that box

When I came to the conclusion, as a four-year-old, that nobody loved me, I created the box I would call reality for many years to come. No one got into my head to help me arrive at that conclusion. I did it all by myself, <u>to</u> myself!

Looking back at that episode in my life, I can smile when I think what a dumb conclusion that was. But I can also appreciate the fact that I might not be writing this book if I had not created that problem so that I could grow my way out of it. The lesson you should be learning from my victim story is that I created my own box. My loveless self-image was the mental blueprint that ran my life for years.

BEING THE SOLUTION

The conclusion you should draw from this is that you also live in a box that you created. As long as you continue to deal with the problems in your life as the victim, you will be stuck in that box. As soon as you realize that you chose that victim role, you will be on your way out of that box.

The second of the nine steps to a new reality is to:
accept that you chose what you have.

In other words, you need to understand that you live in a box of your own creation. If you refuse to see that you created the box, you'll never find your way out of it.

Raising the bar

In some high-jump sports, the bar is raised to a new level each time the competing athlete successfully makes it over the previous bar height. In the Game of Life, our self-image sets the level for our quality of life. Our self-image is the concept we have of ourselves, an assessment of our qualities and personal worth. Raising the bar on our self-worth a notch or two allows us to play the game at the next level and have the life that goes with playing the game at that level. You live in a box; I live in a box; we all live in a box.

There's no reality except the one within us
--Herman Hesse

So, what is a box?

Your box is your self-image as it relates to your current concept of reality. It's your perception of who you are—your way of relating to whomever and whatever you've made significant in your life. But what you call reality (your box) is merely an illusion built out of nothing more concrete than your attitudes, opinions, points of view, and conclusions about whatever you've chosen to make significant. By choosing a point of view (taking a stand) on anything, you are essentially deciding who you will BE relative to that or any similar circumstance or condition. By choosing how you will relate to life, you've created your self-image.

By choosing who you will BE, you've created your box. Nothing wrong with having an opinion, or coming to a conclusion, except that, once we take a stand on anything, we tend to forget that it's just an assumption. We consider our opinion as fact, convinced that our

YOUR SELF-IMAGE

point of view is the way life is, and then we're stuck with that as our reality. Once that concept of reality becomes real to us, we're boxed in and there's no way out, or so it seems.

The field cannot be well seen from within the field
--Ralph Waldo Emerson

Being human means you have a point of view, and because you have a point of view, you live in a box. That's just the way the game is set up. You create a box, call it reality, and then you get to experience what it's like BEING you in that reality. You will remain in that box until it becomes too uncomfortable to stay. To come out of your box, you must choose out by changing your mind about who you will BE in a new reality. You'll find the power for that change of mind when you admit to yourself that you put yourself into that box and decide that you're ready to choose out.

Outgrowing your box

The Game of Life is set up so that, from time to time, our once-comfortable box becomes uncomfortable and confining. After a while, even a feather bed no longer feels cushy. Discomfort forces us out of our box, demanding that we build a bigger, more comfortable box.

Fulfilling life's true purpose (self-discovery) requires growing our self-image. Spirit in us mandates this growth in consciousness. To stay on track with our expanding consciousness, we must, occasionally, pass Go (be transformed). That means trading in our old game piece in favor of a larger, more self-aware piece (enhanced self-image) so we can be allowed to play the game at the next level.

We do have a choice in the matter of whether or not we come out of our box.

We can hide out in fear, surviving in discomfort,
or we can bravely create a new, more comfortable box.
--Darel Rutherford

As individualizations of God with amnesia, we will find our true selves only through expanding our concept of reality. When we enlarge our point of view about life, we've changed our consciousness (self-concept) and have built a bigger box. What you want from life that you don't have will always be outside the box. If you want what you want bad enough, you WILL come out of your box to get it.

Resolve and thou art free
--Henry Wadsworth Longfellow

The box, defined:
- Your box is your point of view about life appearing real.
- It's your attitude about life reflected back at you as your reality.
- It's your expressed opinion about everything you've made significant.
- It is your perception of yourself relative to everything else in your reality.
- It is your self-concept being verified as your experience of reality.
- It is your perception of reality made to appear authentic by your ego.
- It is your self-worth setting a limit to what you may have in life.
- It is the perceived reality of your self-imposed limitations.

A box example

As a kid, I believed I was dumb. My lack of self-confidence made me terribly shy. Back then, that was my perceived reality (my box). How did I experience that reality? On my way to school, each day, I'd pretend to be looking for something on the ground so I wouldn't have to face the people I met along the way. I would have had nothing to say to them, anyway. The advantage of keeping my eyes on the ground: I found all the money the other kids lost on their way to school.

For my first six years in school, I proved the reality of my inferiority with poor grades. Notice that my not-smart-enough self-concept during those early years made bettering my grades impossible. As long as I continued to think I was dumb, I could never allow BEING smart into my reality.

What I want you to see in my being-dumb example is that the problem was never real. I was not dumb. My problem existed only as a perceived reality.

YOUR SELF-IMAGE

*The solution to your problem
is in making a new BEING choice.*
--Darel Rutherford

The way out of my being-dumb reality was to change my perception of myself. How did I do that?

A seventh-grade English teacher had me diagram a sentence she didn't think could be diagrammed. When I surprised her by doing it, she praised me so highly in front of the class that I finally decided maybe I wasn't as dumb as I thought. With that conclusion I made a new BEING choice.

The solution to ANY problem can only be found through a change in who you are BEING relative to what only seems to be the real problem.

In So, Why Aren't You Rich, I told a story about a young lady who lived in a box called, "I'm a klutz." When a seminar leader asked for volunteer klutzes, she won first place, by failing to catch the tennis balls thrown to her.

The seminar leader told her, "We're going to try an experiment. I'm going to throw this tennis ball to you. Don't worry about catching it; just tell me which way the ball is twirling." Three times, he threw the ball. Each time she made a one-handed catch and told him the direction the ball had twirled. After three easy, unconscious, one-handed catches in a row, the instructor said, "I thought you said you were a klutz!"

She was shocked when she realized that the seminar leader had tricked her into catching the ball by directing her attention away from her self-concept of being a klutz. In that moment, the light dawned and she came out of her "I'm-a-klutz" box.

So, what does a box look like?
Like this:
- *I'm not smart enough.*
- *I'm not good enough.*
- *I'm a klutz.*
- *I'm a victim.*
- *I'm not loveable.*
- *I'll always be poor.*
- *I don't like my job, but can't quit.*
- *I'm in a rat race.*

BEING THE SOLUTION

- *I don't like my situation, but it's safe.*
- *I'll never have enough money.*

So, what does your box look like?
- ....
- ....

The way out of your box
is a rebellion against your self-imposed limitations.
--Darel Rutherford

So, how did you create that box?

In the first chapter, I shared my story of how I followed my brother to school, got chased back home, and created my nobody-loved-me box. I've shared this childish erroneous conclusion with you for two reasons: one, because I want you to see how kids arrive at dumb conclusions, and two, because I suspect that you live in a box created by a conclusion no less foolish.

You may not remember the incident or the conclusion that put you in your box, but there is one. If you are not rich in some way, it's because you reject prosperity in that form the same as I rejected love—because it doesn't fit into your box.

The young lady in the klutz example accepted her role when her father jokingly kidded her about stumbling over her own feet. She bought that label and wore it until she was tricked out of it; she lived her life BEING a klutz. Notice that she wasn't a klutz, she was BEING a klutz. Notice that BEING graceful was the solution to her klutz problem.

Whatever your problem,
you, BEING the solution, will solve it
--Darel Rutherford

My father had what some people called a sharp tongue. He was good at putting people down. I've always had this notion that my inferiority complex came out of being put down by my father. I'm not saying he did it to me. I'm saying that's who he was and I bought into it. He didn't get inside my head and make me feel inferior. I did that to myself. If you can see that I created my own box, you should also be able to admit to yourself that you created yours.

YOUR SELF-IMAGE

We create our own box by:
- Arriving at conclusions that may, or may not, have been so.
- Accepting someone else's point of view on something.
- Rejecting their point of view and choosing the opposite.
- Or just by having a point of view.
- Reacting to life (choosing whom you would be under those and similar circumstances.)
- Having an attitude about life (good or bad).
- Convincing yourself that you were right about all of the above.

Looking back at my life, I am actually grateful for the emotional hole I created for myself as a kid. My need to escape that misery gave me the power to find my way out of the box. Being powerfully motivated, I climbed a little farther out of my box than most people seem to climb.

Your desire to have a better life must be powerful enough to get you past your ego's resistance to change.
--Darel Rutherford

Being in a box is no big deal, unless. . . . .
1. You forget that you created the box in which you live.
2. You think there's no way out of the box.
3. You want out, but can't seem to find your way out.

The Game of Life is set up so that you will live most of your life as your ego (in a box), temporarily forgetting who you really are. You read, in the last chapter, that God, to make the game interesting, had man forget that he is a god.

The final obstacle is the belief that there is an obstacle.
--Papaji

You will remember (again) who you are each time you come out of your box to expand your concept of reality.

Each coming out will give you a sense of power, a feeling of well being difficult to describe. When you're reborn into a new reality, your new self-awareness gives you a grand and glorious feeling. Your new box will have a much better view of life, but it's still a box.

BEING THE SOLUTION

*Habits are to the soul
what veins and arteries are to the blood,
the courses in which it flows.*
–Horace Bushuell

It's ego's job to maintain a reality made out of nothing more substantial than attitudes, opinions, conclusions, and a point of view (your perception of what's real.) That reality will remain intact for as long as you continue to believe that there's no way out of that particular box. Even when you want out of your box, ego will find a way to make your desire seem like a part of your box.

*Wanting something is what we do from inside the box;
having that something is an outside the box experience*
--Darel Rutherford

That's why wanting out of your box is not enough. The only way out of your box is to choose out.

Why you have forgotten

Determined to keep you confined in the box you call reality, your powerful ego will maintain your illusion of reality by hiding the fact that you created your own box. Ego knows that once you remember having created your own reality, you will know that you have the power to create a new one. Ego maintains the illusion of powerlessness to keep you in the box.

*Ego's greatest fear is that you will discover
just how powerful you really are!*
--Darel Rutherford

Having what you want from life will require a change of heart, a transformation in consciousness. Actually, this only means you've changed your mind about who you will BE. But for the ego, a change of mind is a bigger deal than a simple mind change.

For instance, if you decided today that you were fed up with your job and wanted to quit, your ego would react in fear to that decision. The decision to quit was a transformation in consciousness because you changed your mind about yourself as related to the job. Your ego will be trying to get you to change your mind and stay with that job, because it fears the change in consciousness required. Your ego sees transformation as having to die in order to be reborn into a new consciousness. You can see why your ego does not want you to remember that you created your own box.

The creative process in man works like this: God gave you and I the power to choose who we would be in this world—the power to create our own reality. And He, also, gave us our ego as the means by which we would experience the reality of our choice. Ego does its job of maintaining our perceived reality by screening out everything that doesn't fit.

When you make the decision to change the quality of your life, the odds against your success are considerable, unless you are aware of ego's screening process and know how to deal with it.

Why you think there's no way out of your box . . .
- For your ego's self-concept to survive, there can be no other reality, and when there's nothing outside the box, there seems to be nowhere to go, no way out.
- Seeing your way out would destroy the illusion you call reality.
- Your ego doesn't want you to be transformed.
- Your ego IS the box in which you live.

How do you get out of your box?
Getting out of your box is a nine-step process. A chapter will be devoted to each of those nine steps. In this chapter you're learning to accept that the reality you're experiencing right now is, in fact, the reality you chose.

When you decide to take a cross-country trip in your car, the first thing you'll look for on the map is your present location. If you don't know where you are, you'll never find your way to where you want to be. What you should be getting from this chapter is that where you are now is where you chose to be.

BEING THE SOLUTION

REVIEW:
 Step one: In chapter three, you learned how to take the first step out of your box by realizing that you have the power to choose. As an individualization of God, you now know that you have the power to create your own reality.
 Step two: In this chapter, you've realized that you used your power to create the box you're in now. And you know that you are not stuck in that box, because you can exercise that same power and choose again.

To get out of your box:
1. You must want out so bad you can taste it.
2. Then, create your vision of what that bigger, better box looks like.
3. When your desire is white hot, choose that better box.

 Remember, your choice is not really about having what you want, as it seems to be; it's about choosing to BE the one in that vision of a new reality.

Coming out of the box
 As a boy, I dreamed about what life might be like if I no longer felt inferior. I read every self-help book I could find that might help me THINK my way out of that box. Gradually my vision of being self-confident began to seem more and more real to me—more believable.
 In other words, my hope became a belief and then a conviction. You must believe in the possibility of a new reality before you can choose it.

> *A dream is a figment of your imagination--a pipe dream,*
> *until you take it outside your box and make it real*
>   --Darel Rutherford

 At some point in that transformation process (that's what it was), I made a solid choice to BE self-confident. Choosing a bigger box only seems to be about choosing something new that you must DO; it's really about choosing to BE the one who can DO whatever is required,

YOUR SELF-IMAGE

naturally. Once I chose to BE that self-confident person, things began to happen to demonstrate that I really was, living in a bigger box.

A pat on the back by a teacher made me realize that I wasn't as dumb as I thought. I needed that praise to get me over the hump, but I could not have been receptive to that compliment had I not, first, opened myself to that possibility by choosing out of my box. As soon as I realized I wasn't dumb, I my grades went from just barely passing to "A's" and "B's".

In my new reality, I made many new friends. I was truly living in a larger box! That's the way the game works. What shows up in your reality comes to you because it belongs there. The Universe is set up to provide you with everything that belongs in the reality of your choice.

In fact, it's already done that for you. You've made your BEING choice, and you now have everything that belongs to you as a result of that choice. So know this: What you want that you don't have IS AND WILL ALWYAYS BE outside the box! You can only have what you want, by choosing to BE the one to whom it belongs.

He who chooses a the beginning of a road
Chooses the place to which it leads.
--Harry Emerson

> **Once Your Vision becomes A BURNING DESIRE you will choose to BE the one in that vision**

6
HOW TO KNOW WHAT YOU WANT

…by thinking out of the box

Don't Want
1. Don't like this neighborhood
2. Don't like my job
3. Don't like living alone

Want List
1. To own my own home
2. A good job that I like
3. A loving relationship

The question here is,
Who would I be BEING if I knew what I wanted?

How can I know what I want?

During a coffee break in a motivational seminar, Robert Barnes, a frustrated attendee, asked me, "How can I know what I want? Is there some special process for deciding what to want?" He continued, "I've been reading self-help books and attending workshops forever, taking almost every seminar available, but nothing seems to help. I think that's because I don't know what I want. So, tell me, how do I find out what I want?"

I answered, "That's easy, Robert. First, make a list of everything you have in your life that you don't want. Then make a want list that would cancel out every item on the don't-want list."

What makes Robert's question most interesting is that almost everyone, if they would admit to it, has the same question They don't know what they want and don't know how to figure it out. The question is doubly interesting because it isn't the real question. The question behind that question is, "How can I know what I want when I don't really know who I am?" The answer to that question is, you'll know who you are when you know, for sure, what belongs in your life and what doesn't.

BEING THE SOLUTION

The third of the nine steps out of your box
...is to *know what you want*

If you don't know what you want
If you don't know what you want from life, it's because you don't know who you are. Therefore, becoming clear about what you want and don't want from life could very well be the most important thing you could do for yourself, in terms of finding your true self.

*Knowing what you want from life and then choosing it
takes you yet another step closer to knowing who you really are!*
--Darel Rutherford

When you know who you are, you'll know what belongs in your life; if you don't already have it, you WILL choose to have it.

So, how will you know who you are?
You will know who you are now by observing what's happening in your life right now, by accepting that the content of your life is there as the result of a previous BEING choice. Everything you have in your life is there because it belongs with you; it fits who you've chosen to BE.

So, now might be a good time to take inventory of the circumstances, conditions, and relationship unhappiness you have in your life that you could do without. Allow yourself to see that those problems exist because they fit who you are BEING. Now, ask yourself who you would be BEING if your problem were no longer there. Again, notice that this question takes you right past your perceived problem to BEING its solution.

*You will know who you are
as soon as you've given yourself the power
to say "no" to what you don't want*
--Darel Rutherford

When a problem is not the problem:
One time my business, DAR TILE, was losing money faster than I had ever made it. My suppliers had raised my material costs, and my union employees had received a negotiated pay increase. My

HOW TO KNOW WHAT YOU WANT

problem: my larger customers had me convinced that I would lose their business if I raised my prices. I believed them, feared losing their business, and did nothing as my company headed toward the brink of financial disaster!

As I sat on my front porch one Sunday morning, I worried about what to do about my failing business. I sat there reading <u>Think and Grow Rich</u>, hoping to find a way out of my dilemma. I stopped reading from time to time, thinking about the possibility of closing the doors of my business forever. Then, halfway through Napoleon Hill's book, I finally got his point, a philosophic truth that would forever change my life.

That message: *we become what we think about.*

When I finally understood the profound significance of that simple truth, I had an immediate transformation in consciousness. In that instant, I changed my mind about who I was.

I couldn't wait

I woke up the following Monday morning, so fired up with enthusiasm that I couldn't wait to get to work and share my new attitude about life with my employees.

I didn't need to say a word. They took one look at me and said, "What the hell happened to you". The change in me was that obvious. Some of you have read this story before in <u>So, Why Aren't You Rich?</u>, but in a slightly different context. This time I'd like to use this example with a different lesson in mind. I want you to see that my problem, as I perceived it, was never the real problem.

The real problem was not in my circumstances, but in whom I was BEING relative to those circumstances. What seemed to be the problem was only the effect of the real problem. The real issue here was with my point of view about it. When I changed who I was BEING (my point of view), the problem no longer existed.

In that first week after my transformation, I raised prices for all my customers. I lost only one. Had I approached those customers with fear in my heart, I'm certain that I would have lost many more of them. My new self-confident presence convinced them that my price increase was absolutely necessary and unavoidable. Please note that their acceptance of the price increase resulted from who I was BEING as I presented my case, not from what I said to them.

BEING THE SOLUTION

The lesson here

The lesson in this example: your problem, as you perceive it, is never what it appears to be; the real problem is in who you're BEING relative to the perceived problem. The solution, therefore, will always be a change in who you are BEING.

Notice in the previous example that I had a clear picture of my problem—so clear that I couldn't see past the problem to its solution. From my point of view, a solution didn't exist. I wanted out of the problem, but I had no clue about how to solve it. The answer to my problem came with the massage, we become what we think about. *From that, I got, loud and clear, that I could change who I was BEING and the problem would no longer exist!*

All I knew prior to this revelation was that I had a serious problem and wanted a way out. Notice that who I was being at the time, could not say what I wanted; I could only say what I didn't want.

*Knowing what you want from life begins
with knowing what you don't want in your life*
--Darel Rutherford

To get value out of this example, you must see that you can't choose a solution to your problem because the problem belongs with who you are BEING. You can't know what you want (the solution) until you allow yourself to see that it is who you are BEING that is causing the problem. Once you've latched on to and chosen the BEING solution to your problem, you will know for sure what you want—what really belongs with your new BEING choice.

You were taking inventory

If you don't like what you see in your life, you need to know that you can create a different reality with a new BEING choice. The hidden bonus here, is that you will grow in stature, in terms of how you perceive yourself each time you give yourself permission to raise the bar on your standard of living. Knowing what you want begins with knowing what you don't want and in allowing yourself to want life to be better.

Why you don't want to know what you want

Who you are BEING, your ego, is threatened by your wanting something outside the box. It knows you can't change what you have in

HOW TO KNOW WHAT YOU WANT

life without a BEING change. Notice that ego's resistance to change is the main reason you don't know what you want. Ego survives by avoiding BEING changes. In case you've forgotten:

Ego is our self-concept, functioning in and as our individualized adaptation to our perception of reality.
--Darel Rutherford

If you don't know what you want and don't want to think about it, chalk up another win for your ego in its determination to maintain status quo.

Looking at why you don't have it

If you are not as rich as you want to be in some way, it's because you have some sort of barrier to becoming rich. Your barrier can seem like a solid wall when, in fact, it is nothing more serious than your point of view about why you don't already have what you want.

Your most important barrier to becoming rich is the one that prevents you from choosing that better life—the one that puts BEING RICH outside your box. Once you've chosen to be rich, the barriers that confront your BEING change will be less important, because by then, you would have become sufficiently motivated to overcome those barriers.

The Box Puzzle

Solving the puzzle on the following page has helped a great many people realize that the solution to their problems was outside the box. Even if you've seen this puzzle and worked it before, do it again. It will change the way you're thinking about your problem.

NOTE: I suggest you work the puzzle on a piece of scrap paper or in the BEING WORKBOOK so that the next person reading this book won't see your solution.

INSTRUCTIONS: CONNECT ALL NINE DOTS WITH ONE CONTINUOUS LINE CONSISTING OF FOUR STRAIGHT LINES

• • •

• • •

• • •

BEING THE SOLUTION

Clue: Working this puzzle will help you begin to think outside the box, which is the only place you will find the solution to your lack of wealth. See the end of chapter for the puzzle solution.

BEING RICH

> This is your
> box
> Notice that
> " BEING
> RICH" is
> outside the box

The solution will be outside the box
    Any decision requiring a new BEING choice is an outside the box decision. Therefore, the solution to your most serious problems will always be found outside the box. In other words, if who you were BEING caused the problem, then a change in who you are BEING will solve the problem.

The problem's effect always shows up inside the box; the problem's solution will ALWAYS BE outside the box
--Darel Rutherford

The next time you're faced with a problem, ask yourself,

Who would I be BEING, and what would I be doing, if this problem were no longer a problem?

    By asking yourself this question, you are allowing yourself to imagine yourself outside the box where the problem will no longer exist because it doesn't belong in your reality.
    This sort of thinking (outside the box) gives you back your power, puts you back in charge of your life, where you'll know what you want from it. Now that you've regained your power of choice, you can choose to BE the one who no longer has the problem.

How to know what you want

I am always amazed at the number of people, like Robert Barnes who don't know what they want. How can I come to know what I want?, is a question quite frequently asked. The following exercise will answer that question.

WANT/DON'T WANT EXERCISE:

Divide a lined pad into two equal columns. In the left-hand column, make a list of the things and circumstances in your life that you really don't want. When you've finished your don't-want list, make your want list in the right-hand column, listing what you want opposite what you don't want, so that each want cancels out an item on the don't-want list.

What I don't want in my life	What I want in my life, instead
1. I don't like this neighborhood	1. To own my own home
2. I don't like what I do for a living	2. A good job doing what I like
3. I don't like living alone	3. To have a loving relationship

Now you know what you want. Prioritize this want list, and begin to think about who you would need to be BEING in order to have the top items on your list BE your reality.

Flip a coin

If having what you want conflicts with another commitment or desire, you may have trouble deciding which one to choose. A good way to solve this dilemma is to flip a coin; heads you do and tails you don't. No, I'm not kidding! This is a great way to make a decision if you will pay attention to how you react to the flip of the coin!

When you don't like the decision, when you react negatively to the result of the coin flip, choose the other option. If you feel good about the decision made by the coin flip, go with that. The idea is to go with the heart. If it feels right, do it; if it doesn't feel right, you still know which way you need to go. When your intention is to go with your heart, you will see coin flipping as a great way of helping you arrive at the right choice.

BEING THE SOLUTION

Raising the bar on your self-worth

The minute you become clear about what you really and truly want in life you will begin to feel good about yourself in a way that triggers a change in your self-worth.

Actually, the process of changing your self-worth often starts with wanting something you don't have, wanting it so bad you can taste it, and then giving yourself permission to choose to BE the one who will have it. Choosing to BE the one living in your dream house or driving your dream car raises the bar on your self-worth.

Your self-esteem (pride in oneself) increases when you make it okay to have that new car, that new house or even that new dress. That's why women love to shop. When you can allow yourself to have something you've always wanted, you've raised the bar on your self-worth a notch or two.

But a self-image boost from a new purchase only works if you've finally <u>earned</u> the right to have something you've always wanted, and have chosen it because it belongs with you. "Earned the right," means you've saved the money or you have adequate income sources to pay for your purchase.

The shortcut that doesn't work

Don't fall into the credit-card trap of assuming that it's possible to spend your way to prosperity. Spending money you don't have for the purpose of instant gratification makes you poorer, not richer. Overextended credit has the reverse effect, by actually diminishing your self-worth.

It's a big mistake to assume that having something you want, by whatever means, will somehow transform you into being the person you've always wanted to be. This line of reasoning errs in assuming that the having somehow changes one's self-worth. To understand and use the creative process with purpose, you must see HAVING as the effect, not the cause, of BEING rich.

If you can accept HAVING as the result of a BEING choice, you will know why elevating your self-worth is the key to HAVING what you want from life. BE DO HAVE is the only true workable order of creation. Once you accept this premise, you will come to see BEING as the solution to most of your problems.

HOW TO KNOW WHAT YOU WANT

Knowing what you want is only the first step

Once you know what you want from life, the next, and most important step, is in choosing to BE the one who will have what you want from life.

If you have a problem that keeps you from having the life you want, ask yourself this question: *who would I be BEING if that were no longer a problem.*

By right of consciousness

The Game of Life is set up so that you can have from life, only that which belongs to you by right of consciousness. In fact, one rule of the game, The Law of Correspondence reads:

What you have in life
must correspond exactly to who you are.

If you are to have what you want from life, you will need to make a new choice about whom you will be in that new reality. Each time you raise the bar on your self-worth a notch or two, having what you want from life, you grow spiritually. Once you choose to be rich, you will find that the transition from poor to rich requires a powerful change in consciousness.

Self-discovery, your true purpose in life, can only happen outside the box, and that's where you'll also find whatever else you want from life. I understand why coming out of the box scares you, and I know that's why most of us never venture out. But, as always, facing your fears is the only way out of your current situation.

Puzzle Solution:

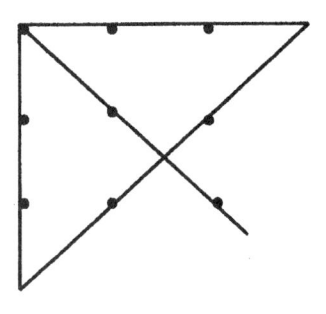

YOU ARE NOT YOUR PIECE

Your Piece

This is YOU →

As you play at The Game of Life,
keep this in mind-
you are not your piece;
you are the one rolling the dice,
moving the piece.

7
CREATING A BURNING DESIRE

...the prime ingredient to your success

EMPOWERED VISION = BURNING DESIRE = BEING choice

*If you don't know WHY you want to be rich,
you can bet the farm it will never happen for you.*
--Darel Rutherford

Not okay to want

J.M. (we'll call her Jeanie) wrote, "You keep telling us that the prime ingredient for success is a burning desire. I can't even imagine what it's like to have a burning desire. I remember my mother telling me I was being greedy when I asked for stuff I wanted—that I should be content with what I had. The message I got from her was that it's not okay to want, so I don't think I've ever allowed myself to have a burning desire for anything."

Jeanie, you'd be surprised how many people like you have the same *not-okay-to-want* story to tell. But I seriously doubt that you have never had a burning desire. I think you may have had that degree of hunger for a change in circumstances many times over in your life. But in terms of wanting "stuff," you're stifled. That's because you've been self-programmed not to want. With that sort of reality script, wanting something passionately would not fit your existing program. But Jeanie, you CAN rewrite the program.

*Every human mind is a great slumbering power
until awakened by a keen desire and by definite resolution to do.*
Edgar F. Roberts

BEING THE SOLUTION

The intention of this chapter is to help you turn up the heat under your want list until your desire for those lifestyle changes reaches the boiling point, motivating you to act. Once your desire heats up, it becomes the powerful motivator for moving you to choice, out of your box and on your way toward living your dream.

The fourth of the nine steps out of your box:
...*create a burning desire* **for the life that you want.**

Her burning desire

If you accidentally brushed your bare leg against the red-hot exhaust pipe of your Harley Davidson motorcycle, as a friend of mine recently did, you'd be highly motivated to move. You might say my friend had a burning desire to escape the source of her pain.

Any situation you face in life that causes enough discomfort will motivate you toward changing those circumstances. If you'll look back over your life, you will remember many such instances when you were motivated to take appropriate action. For the purpose of this discussion, let's label your call to action a burning desire.

Just know that without a powerful reason for coming out of your box, you could remain in *Wantsville* forever. The intention of this chapter is to show you how to convert your want list into the burning desire that will move you to commit to a BEING change.

When you want it this much

In seeking an example that would help you understand the importance of a burning desire, I'm reminded of the story about a man seeking wisdom who asked a monk to enlighten him. The monk responded by taking the man out on the lake, where he instructed him to jump out of the boat. Then, when the man tried to get back into the boat, the monk pushed his head under the water and held it there for quite a long while.

The man came up fighting mad, sputtering and gasping for air. Angrily he asked, "Why did you do that?" The monk answered, "When you come to me wanting a spiritual awakening as desperately as you wanted air just now, I will give you enlightenment.*"*

When you seek a solution to your problem as desperately as that man wanted air, you'll have no trouble with finding your way past the problem to its solution. And having chosen your BEING solution to

CREATING A BURNING DESIRE

that problem your Inner Light will just naturally shine brighter. With each new BEING choice you'll find further enlightenment!

Enlightenment is seeing that the world you've created inside your head doesn't really exist, except as a fabrication in your mind.
Jim Dreaver

The mission of this chapter is not to find a way to make you desperate, but to bring you to the point of desiring that new reality with the same degree of high-powered determination that you would have if you were desperate. The attitude you seek to acquire is not one of desperate need, but one of enthusiastic anticipation.

Enthusiastic anticipation

The world is filled with a multitude of wishful thinkers who want stuff they will never have, because they haven't learned that the number-one step toward having the life they want is a BEING step. Until they realize their mistake and take that step, they'll be among the multitude who are trapped in wanting a life they'll never have,

As previously discussed, knowing what you want won't get it for you. To have it, you must first choose to BE the one to whom it belongs. Because you have a powerful ego, determined to resist any BEING change, you will remain trapped in your current reality—until you find your way past that resistance. The key to opening the door to a better life, the key to finding your way past the resistance, is your burning desire for that change.

Genius is the power of lighting one's own fire.
John Foster

If your life is to be any different than that of the multitude stuck in *Wantsville*, you must convert your want list into a desire that will be powerful enough to move you to choice. Once you've made your new BEING choice, your burning desire will turn into enthusiastic anticipation. What we're looking for here is a way to turn up the heat under your desire, fanning the flames, until your desire becomes the powerful motivation you must have if you are to take the BEING step.

All human activity is prompted by desire.
Bertrand Russell

BEING THE SOLUTION
A trained elephant

You are stuck in *Wantsville* because that's the place in consciousness that, for the moment, best represents your perception of reality. You haven't allowed yourself to seriously consider the possibility of having your life be better, because that reality is outside the vision that runs your life (your concept of reality). To develop your burning desire, we will be changing that vision.

But first, let's look at how your concept of reality got created. To get the picture, think of your subconscious mind as an elephant, trained at an early age to stay within a twenty-foot circle. The elephant's training was accomplished with a ten-foot chain attached at one end to its hind leg, and at the other end to an iron stake. After many futile attempts to get outside that circle, the elephant's reality became a twenty-foot circle.

Maybe, as with Jeanie, someone helped you establish the outer boundaries of your reality by telling you that it wasn't okay to want. Your subconscious mind, like the elephant, is bound by a vision of a reality that won't allow you to see or think outside that circle. If we can change that vision and make it seem real, we can build the fire under your desire that will motivate and move your elephant to break out of the circle. Let's look at an example of how an elephant's vision might get changed.

The four stages of idea development

Each new reality you create will go through four stages of development:

1. The first stage is called *inspiration.* Inspire means "to breathe life into." In this step we would be inspired by the possibility of life getting better—picturing our life in a new way, outside the circle. This is when the light dawns for the elephant, and she begins to think about those peanuts in the popcorn stand at the carnival's main entrance. This is the beginning of a vision of what life might be like outside her circle. The elephant's natural hunger for peanuts and its vision of enjoying the eating inspire this vision.

2. The second stage in the development of an idea is *desire.* The elephant's vision of eating peanuts becomes clearer and clearer, so powerful now that she can almost taste the peanuts. Through the visualization process, the elephant's appetite for peanuts has become a *burning desire* to have them.

CREATING A BURNING DESIRE

3. The third stage in the development of the elephant's vision is *enthusiasm*. At this point, the vision seems real. This is where the elephant sees herself eating the peanuts and enjoying the experience. This is the stage of vision development where the idea of freedom, in a reality outside the circle, replaces the old vision of reality. This is when the elephants chooses to BE the one outside the circle eating peanuts changing its attitude from wanting to **enthusiastic anticipation.**

4. The fourth stage in developing an idea (vision) is *action.* That's when the elephant breaks her bondage from the old reality of a twenty-foot circle and begins her move out of the circle toward the popcorn stand and the peanuts she enjoyed in her vision.

Like a trained elephant

Your subconscious mind, like a trained elephant, runs your life because that is its job. But your elephant can only go so far, and then it's stopped, controlled by a vision of reality that looks like a twenty-foot circle.

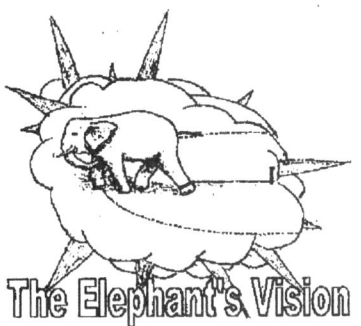

The Elephant's Vision

The elephant can see outside the circle and maybe imagine what it would be like out there, eating peanuts, but it can't go there. It is controlled by the memory of many leg-bruising attempts at freedom, while charging full speed to a sudden and painful stop at the end of an unforgiving chain.

You don't remember those sudden stops? That's when you were told that you were not good enough, fast enough, or smart enough to do what you dreamed you would do. You finally got the message, didn't you? You've been reminding yourself about those limitations ever since. That's your twenty-foot circle.

BEING THE SOLUTION

*The only limit to our realization of tomorrow
will be our doubts of today.*
-- Franklin Delano Roosevelt

The invisible chain

Take another look at what binds you. Notice that the chain is not really there. Someone or something convinced you that the chain would stop you, and you bought into that limitation. In Jeanie's case, the chain was *it's not-okay-to-ask*. This chain was a mother's limiting concept of reality becoming attached to her daughter.

The chain that binds you is a figment of your powerful imagination built out of nothing more powerful than your concept of reality. You won't need to remove that chain, because you will be replacing it with a new vision of yourself being happy, outside that circle, BEING free. To break out, your subconscious mind (the elephant) will need you to supply it with a new vision. Changing the quality of your life is that simple. It begins with a vision.

Your new vision will begin when you get ***inspired*** with the possibility of having what's just outside the circle. The more you think about having it, the more you will allow yourself to ***desire*** it. When your desire turns from wanting it to believing that you can have it, your desire becomes a determined intention and then finally shows up as powerful ***enthusiastic anticipation***. You will have chosen to BE the one who will have the life you've always wanted.

His twenty-foot circle

S. K., a RICHBITS subscriber who lives in India (we'll call him **Sam**), wrote, *My problem is in approaching girls and speaking with them. I just don't know what to speak and keep on smiling shyly. I have wanted to go on dates since I was in school, but just couldn't do it.*

Sam's concept of reality, that girls are not attracted to him, is the vision that runs his life. You must see that Sam's picturing of his relationship to girls creates his experience of that reality. Because Sam's vision of reality is built around wanting, having can't enter that picture. Actually, Sam is a handsome young man who would just naturally attract girls if he could only trade in his current boy/girl relationship vision for a new version.

One of life's greatest truths is ***what we believe creates our reality***. The problem is that most of us bet our lives that the exact

CREATING A BURNING DESIRE

opposite is true—that reality creates our beliefs. We tend to believe only in what we can see, and we have hard evidence to support that belief. Unfortunately, for as long as we believe only in the evidence of things seen, we'll be stuck in a life based on "that's just the way it is."

A vision runs your life

One of life's greatest paradoxes is that:

*What shows up in our lives
is merely the effect of what we believe.*
Darel Rutherford

The real truth is, "stuff" happens because we believe that it will, because we expect it. Most of us have based our concept of reality on the "seeing is believing" philosophy. To find your way past that B. S. (Belief System), you must know that your life is run by a vision, a concept of reality that can be easily replaced with a new vision.

If Sam continues to believe only in the hard evidence, that girls are not attracted to him, he will remain trapped in that luckless experience. To find his way out, Sam must finally come to realize that his life is run by a vision—by a concept of reality that will persist until he creates a new vision for himself. What you must see for Sam is that he must replace his *desperately-wanting* vision with a vision of *already having*.

In Sam's new vision, he would be handsome, friendly and outgoing, with many girls seeking his company. They come to him because he makes them feel pretty, interesting, and wanted. He no longer seeks or needs to seek a relationship with girls. They now seek him out.

This vision would become reality for Sam after having taken the four steps of developing the idea that he could change his relationship to girls. The first stage would have Sam being inspired with the possibility of having girls want to be in a relationship with him. Stage two in building his dream would have Sam believing in its possibility to the point of having a burning desire for it. In stage three, Sam adds the power of enthusiasm to his vision, eagerly anticipating BEING the one in his vision. In stage four he takes action and asks the girl for a date.

BEING THE SOLUTION

*"Enthusiasm" is derived from a Greek word
and it means, "God in us."*

So, what vision runs your life?

Perhaps it's time to take a look at the vision that runs your life. The quality of your life will depend on that vision and the attitude you've attached to it.

Actually there are two ingredients to your vision that will determine the quality of your life. One is your concept of reality, your vision, and the other is your attitude about life. A change of attitude is a BEING choice. Your vision determines the content of your life; your attitude controls the quality of it. To change the quality of your life, you must take charge of both your vision and your attitude.

The life you experience will be a representation of your concept of reality and a reflection of your attitude about it. Your attitude is the power behind your vision. Find your attitude about life in the lists below and you'll know what powers your vision. Are you positive, neutral or negative?

1	Positive	Optimistic	Powerful	Involved	I can	Proactive
2	Neutral	Pacifistic	Listless	Disengaged	I don't care	Inactive
3	Negative	Pessimistic	Victim	Dissenting	I can't	Reactive

In looking at the above lists, how would you rate Sam's vision? Was he powerful, listless, or being the victim? How did you rate your vision, as a 1, 2 or a 3?

Your vision is your motivation

If you've rated yourself as a 2 or a 3 in one of the above lists, you must know that it's your attitude about life that keeps you boxed into a reality that no longer serves you. To find your way out of that box, first know that your current vision, your concept of reality, determines your attitude. Your vision is your motivator. Now take a look at where your current vision has taken you and ask yourself if that's where you want to be.

This chapter is about acquiring the burning desire that will motivate you in making a new BEING choice. Your new vision will create that burning desire. Once you see the light at the end of the tunnel, the way out, your attitude will turn from negative to positive,

CREATING A BURNING DESIRE

from reactive to proactive. But to create your motivation, you must first change the vision

She came out of her box

I had lunch with P.K., a friend I hadn't seen for a while. We'll call her Polly. The light in Polly's eyes and the smile on her face told me she'd had a transformation since we'd last met. I asked what had happened in her life to bring about such a great change in her self-confidence.

Polly shared that she had joined a group of individuals dedicated to the expressed intent of keeping each other on purpose in life. In a later chapter you will learn how to set up your own support group. One of the commitments made by the members of her group was to acknowledge ten people each week. What a wonderful and empowering idea!

When I saw what a different person Polly had become, no longer the *people-think-I'm-stupid* person she once complained of being, I was really excited and happy for her. I am also enthusiastic when I think about how that exercise would be a wonderful way for you and I to find our way out of the box and grow our own consciousness.

I've been using the "pay a compliment ever chance you get" trick ever since Polly gave me the idea and it works wonders for my attitude and that of the recipient of my praise. Like yesterday, I said to someone I see frequently, "Wow, you ought to wear that blouse every day! It matches the color of your blue eyes." She beamed all over, obviously made happy by my compliment. If you could have seen the effect my compliment had on her, you'd pick up the acknowledging habit as well.

Those who worry about what others think, are being self-centered. Polly worried that people thought she was stupid; Sam worried that girls would not like him. If you are one of those who has serious concerns about what others are thinking, the truth is:

They are not thinking about you.

I'll tell you what most of them are thinking: they're thinking about themselves and maybe wondering what you're thinking. Knowing that, you can help them in the process. Ask them questions about themselves and really listen. Think about them instead of yourself. Make it your intention to help them to like themselves and your worry about what they're thinking will simply dissolve and disappear.

BEING THE SOLUTION

Being self-centered tends to keep you in your box;
acknowledging others takes you out of your box.
--Darel Rutherford

Out of your box, making a difference
The difference this exercise will make in your perspective on life will amaze you. Changing who you are BEING from rich to poor is as simple as changing your perspective.

EXERCISE: Acknowledge ten people a week for one month and notice what a difference it makes in how you feel about yourself. Notice how this changes your vision of reality, increasing your own personal power. Looking for the good in others, being there for them, takes you out of your self-centeredness—out of your box.

You will begin to know who you are
When you are making a difference in their lives.
--Darel Rutherford

The triple benefit in doing this exercise:
- One, you'll be pleasantly surprised at how many friends you'll make.
- Two, you will be amazed at how much more you like yourself while in the process of making others feel appreciated.
- And three, you will have found your way out of your box.

How does that get you out of your box?
If your *I need their approval* box suddenly becomes, *Wow, I don't need their approval, they need mine!* You've moved from powerless to powerful. That's coming out of your box in a big way.

Acknowledging people may not seem to be a grand and glorious purpose for your life, but it's something you could easily do that would really make a difference in their lives and in the way you feel about yourself. It would also accomplish our purpose for this chapter: to get you motivated and out of your box. This exercise is guaranteed to change your self-concept.

And now that you're out or your box, making a difference, give yourself a pat on the back and choose to give yourself your heart's

CREATING A BURNING DESIRE

desire—whatever your new self-image will allow you to choose. Your limitation in life was your self-worth. You've just changed that. Now that you're worthy of more, you will choose it.

An exercise in creating your dream
So, now that you're outside the box, making a difference (or even if you're not making a difference), let's talk about what you want from life. What does being a success mean to you? If you were being as successful as you've always wanted to be, what would that look like, feel like? Who would you be BEING? What would you be doing? What would you have that you don't have now? The obvious answer:

*Being successful means
being able to live your desires and dreams.*
Darel Rutherford

But you may not have a dream! The problem with being stuck in a box is that you may not have allowed yourself to dream, or if to dream, not to dream big. If you're like most people, you haven't thought much about what your life would be like outside the box. You haven't dreamed about enjoying a richer, fuller life, because up to now, it hasn't seemed possible (the twenty-foot circle).

To help you find your way out of your box, I will be reminding you again and again, that you are an individualization of God with the power to create your own reality—any reality you choose. The reality you've created with that power is the box in which you are now confined. You've thought yourself into that box. You CAN dream your way out of it.

Every thought you think has the power to free you or put you back in the box. If you want out of your box, you must first imagine what life could be like outside the box. It's time to dream, and as long as you're dreaming, dream big! This powerful vision will create the burning desire that will be the prime motivation for your new BEING choice.

A new lease on life
Remember the new light in Polly's eyes and the smile on her face? When you make a new BEING choice, you've just signed a new lease on life. Like being reborn, from that point on, your life will become a whole new exciting adventure. Your new BEING

BEING THE SOLUTION

commitment gives you a sense of personal power that makes you feel unstoppable. Your new self-confidence is exhilarating.

In one moment, you've transformed yourself from a powerless victim of unhappy circumstances into a powerful individual who is now fully in charge of the rest of your life. The experience is not unlike being reborn, as in, "I was blind and now I see." It feels great to be back in charge of your life.

Your new lease on life begins with a vision of what life might be like outside the box.

So, how do you create a new vision?

Are you ready to begin the four-step process for creating your new vision? The four steps are:

1. **Inspiration:** allowing yourself to think about how life could be better
2. **Desire:** allowing yourself to want that solution passionately
3. **Enthusiasm:** developing a self-confident expectation for that desired end
4. **Action:** choosing your new way of BEING based on that vision

Twenty reasons

My friend M. D. in England, (we'll call him Mark) mentioned several times in his email messages to me that he wanted to be rich. He had read my book, So, Why Aren't You Rich?, and we had talked often on the phone. He wanted counseling. Our phone conversations went on for over a year; I could see nothing happening that would indicate that Mark was serious about becoming rich.

Finally, I decided that it was time to find out if Mark was sincere, so I asked for this commitment. I suggested that if he was in earnest, he should create a list of twenty reasons why he wanted to be rich. He agreed.

A week later, Mark sent me ten reasons, claiming that ten was all he could come up with. I replied that only ten reasons proved to me that he wasn't really serious about wanting to be rich. Mark agreed to complete the list of twenty.

Soon after completing his list, opportunities for becoming rich opened up to him. Mark now has two exciting and very promising get-rich projects working, either of which could make it happen. One of those ventures was already in process, but he was treating it like a

CREATING A BURNING DESIRE

hobby, not as a business enterprise. He hadn't seen the possibilities in it for making him rich, until he committed to becoming rich.

*We won't hear opportunity knocking
until we're ready to open the door for it*
--Darel Rutherford

The other get-rich project, a brand new one, occurred to him only after he opened up the door to the possibility of being rich. Unless we're ready, willing and seeking it, we can't see opportunity, even when it knocks on our door. Until Mark had his twenty reasons written down, he just wasn't committed to the BEING change that would make him financially independent. Like Mark, when you are adequately motivated, you will choose to be rich and that commitment will start the ball rolling in your direction..

Create a list of twenty reasons
For this exercise, we will use the term "rich", meaning rich in consciousness. In our friend Sam's case, he would build his list around the benefits of being in relationships with girls. In your case, in place of the word "rich", substitute whatever you think you need to make your life whole and complete. If your problems are financial, the word "rich" will fit your needs perfectly.

Whether or not you become rich in the way that will fill your needs most will depend on how galvanized you are toward that end. To implement and empower your motivation, think about all the reasons why you want to be rich.

Exercise:
Find a ruled pad; create a list of twenty reasons why you would want to be rich in that way. This list will be the twenty real benefits you would expect to gain from being rich.
As I said at the beginning of this chapter, if you don't know WHY you want to be rich, it can never happen. But once you've written those twenty reasons down, you will know why you want to be rich.

This exercise will be difficult for some, because this sort of thinking is outside the box and uncomfortable if you're not powerfully motivated. For now, don't worry about your lack of motivation. Just allow yourself to think about how fantastic your life would be if your needs were filled. We will be using some of those twenty reasons to create the vision that WILL motivate you.

So, stop reading! Put down this book, get out the pad and write down your twenty reasons. Do it NOW! If you are serious about becoming rich, don't stop with ten reasons; let your imagination run wild; make your full list of twenty. Dare to dream.

Prioritizing the list

So, now your list is complete! Great! Pat yourself on the back. My experience is that those who complete the list will go on to become rich; those who don't will fizzle out in the attempt. You've just taken yourself out of the ranks of the poor in consciousness and set yourself on the path toward that better life you've always dreamed of having!

Now, review your list and prioritize it. Once you have your reasons listed in order of their importance, take the top two benefits and visualize what your life would be like if you had those benefits in your life. Think about who you would be BEING if that vision were now your reality.

If you've passed up the exercise, I suggest that you go back and do it, now!

Building a fire under your why

Now that you know why you want to be rich, it's time you built a fire under that desire, fanning the flames until they're white-hot! When you want that benefit so much you can taste it, you will make your new BEING choice. From that point on, your new vision is on your way toward becoming your reality (if you can manage to stay out of the box.)

Remember, your job here is to create the vision of a new reality and maintain it until you're motivated enough to make your BEING choice. Even then, you've still got a ways to go—your ego must accept that vision as the new reality. Your elephant must buy into the new vision before it can go the direction you want it to go!

Like quitting smoking

As I've said before, coming out of your box is one thing; staying out is another. Most of those who come out don't stay. Coming out of your box is like quitting smoking. It's easy to quit. I quit seven times before I made it stick. The last time I quit was the day I realized

CREATING A BURNING DESIRE

that I had three cigarettes going at one time. That's when I finally realized that I wasn't having a smoke. The cigarettes had me.

Finally seeing the extent of my addiction to nicotine opened my eyes to a bad cigarette cough, filthy ashtrays, and the foul smell of stale smoke in my home and office. That's when I began to think about the health benefits of quitting (my twenty reasons). As soon as I sold myself on those benefits, I had my motivation to quit. I was out of the smoking box and free! *Please get that I had not just chosen to quit smoking, I had chosen to BE a non-smoker.*

To empower your reasons for being rich in the way that fills your need, you will put your imagination to work on the vision of yourself living that better life. Imagine what your life would be like if you were already living life abundantly. The process is called visualization.

Imagination is not a talent of some men but is the health of every man.
Ralph Waldo Emerson

Now let's create your visualization

You've just created a list of the twenty benefits you would hope to gain from becoming rich. Take a look at each item on your list and imagine yourself enjoying the fruits of your wealth, whatever that may be for you. Remember to phrase your vision in present time consciousness, putting yourself into that picture. Imagine how you would feel if you were experiencing that benefit NOW.

If an ocean voyage were one of the twenty benefits you listed, you might see yourself walking the deck, feeling the sun on your face, enjoying the cool ocean breeze gently blowing your hair. You might be remarking to your companion about the wonderful service in the dining room and the fantastic seven-course meal you had just eaten that evening.

Find a place that sells used magazines; look for pictures that would help you picture life as it would be if you were living your dream. Find pictures that represent each of the twenty benefits on your prioritized list. Cut out those pictures and paste them up on a solid backing or poster board as a collage. Hang that collage on a wall in a prominent place and use it to help you empower your visualization of life as it WILL BE when you're living your dream. In that vision you will be enjoying those twenty benefits of being rich.

BEING THE SOLUTION

As you see yourself in your new vision, where would you be living? What kind of car would you be driving? What would you be doing instead of working? Your collage will help you visualize what your life would be like living your dream of being rich in whatever way fills your greatest need. The prime ingredient to YOUR new reality is the BEING choice motivated by your vision.

With your vision, you have converted your desire into "enthusiastic anticipation."

...enthusiasm;
nothing great was ever achieved without it.
Ralph Waldo Emerson

Speaking your dream exercise

Try this! One proven way to empower your dream is to stand in front of a mirror and tell yourself what your dream reality would look like. Or find a private place, close your eyes for one minute, and speak your dream aloud. Tell yourself what you would want your life to be like if it was perfect. Speaking your word with enthusiasm is a powerful way to activate your dreams.

The speaking-your-dream exercise is even more powerful if you can find someone else who also wants to share their dream and participate in this exercise. When you pair up to do the exercise, you speak your dream, while your partner in the exercise writes it down. Then you trade places.

While writing your dream, think of it as the script for the role that you intend to play in life, and then begin acting out the script! Your success in life will eventually depend on your coming to know who you really are. Your self-concept expands to new dimensions each time you take charge of your life and begin living your dream.

Your empowered vision
will motivate your new BEING choice.

Unless you know why

Remember my friend Mark in England? Mark kept telling himself that he wanted to be rich. He had all of the usual *how-to* questions, like *how do I become rich? How do I choose?* He was stuck in wanting to be rich, frustrated for almost two years while nothing happened. Then Mark created his list of twenty reasons why. Out of those twenty reasons came the vision that moved him to make his BEING choice. Now, he's on his way and unstoppable!

What you must see from this is that, even with all his wanting, Mark could never be rich because he hadn't chosen to BE. The gap between wanting something and choosing to BE the one who will have it is so wide that most wannabes will never have the life they want. What they lack is a burning desire powerful enough to move them to bridge the gap and make a new BEING choice.

In this chapter you learned how to create the burning desire that would move you to make the BEING choice. The BEING choice is the action step we talked about in the four stages of idea development. The next chapter is about choosing to BE rich.

Your true vision
for
BEING WEALTHY
is not so much about
SPENDING MONEY
as it is about
ATTRACTING WEALTH

ATTRACTING WEALTH

8
CHOOSING TO BE RICH

...your fifth step out of the box

Once you accept that you've chosen what you have, you will have found the power to choose again.
--Darel Rutherford

Not sure if you've chosen?

Corley, one of my RICHBITS subscribers, wrote, *"I'm serious about wanting to be a millionaire, but I'm not sure I've really chosen to be. How will I know for sure that I've chosen?"* (To get value out of Corley's question, ask yourself if you've actually chosen to have whatever it would take to make your life whole and complete)

My answer to Corley, *"If you had decided to go to New York or San Francisco, for a week's vacation, how would you know for sure that you had chosen?"*

You'll know you've chosen if you've ordered your plane or bus ticket, made reservations at your favorite hotel and perhaps, started a list of what to pack for the trip. In other words, you would have made a move in the direction of your chosen destination!

Corley, if you have truly chosen to be a millionaire, you will have made some sort of move in that direction. You would be excited about your up-coming trip to Millionaire Row. You would be dreaming about living the good life there, and you would be checking out some of

BEING THE SOLUTION

the paths you might take that would get you there. In chapter twenty, you'll learn how to create multiple streams of residual income that will make you wealthy.

If you haven't made your move

If Corley's problem is your problem, if you think you've chosen but haven't made a move in that direction, if nothing's happening, you probably haven't chosen. If you had really chosen, you would have come alive with enthusiastic anticipation of achieving your new goal in life. If you don't, yet, feel that new burst of energy, you might want to go back to chapter seven and light a fire under your enthusiasm.

The fifth step in finding your way out of your box:
Choose to BE the one who will have **what you want from life.**
Remember, choosing to have what you want is a BEING choice.

The intention of first seven chapters of this book were to bring you, step by step, to the point of choosing to BE whoever you need to be to have the life you've always wanted. If you've faithfully followed the first four steps, you should be certain, by now, about what you want. You should know that you have the power to choose it, and be bursting with enthusiastic anticipation for having it. With that level of commitment, you would be choosing it without a moment's hesitation.

If you haven't, yet, chosen your new reality, the question you should be asking yourself is, "Has what I've read, so far, moved me to the point of choosing to BE the one who will have that better life I've always wanted? Have I really chosen?"

Life is about choice

The Game of Life has been set up, so that the path toward finding yourself requires a conscious, determined decision, from time to time, to BE whoever you would need to BE in order to have your life BE the way you want it. Following your decision to BE, you will be proving yourself to yourself by choosing to DO whatever you need to DO for as long as necessary for HAVING life BE that great.

To go from poor to rich, you must first emphatically resolve that you will no longer be poor, and then, with powerful determination, choose to experience BEING rich. Your transformation begins with choosing to BE rich and continues with the process of BEING and BECOMING rich. When you can see that you are actually doing something with the expressed purpose of making you richer, you will know you're on the right track—that you've actually chosen to be rich.

> *Doing is BEING in action.*
> *Without the DOING, the BEING is only a pipe dream.*
> --Darel Rutherford

Being and becoming

The being and becoming process might best be explained by the example of planting two different types of seeds in your garden. Let's say you plant tomatoes and cucumbers. Notice that the tomato seed takes a different set of ingredients from the soil than does the seed that produces a cucumber vine, yet the soil in your garden is the same for each of them.

Choosing to be rich is like planting a "I'm gonna be rich" seed in the garden of your mind. Once you've chosen to be rich, everything that belongs with your new choice becomes available to you in the form of opportunities. You'll find opportunities to save money, to invest your saved money, and you will find ways that you could increase your income. These are new options, new choices you must make on your way toward becoming rich.

But there's still choices to be made

Choosing to be rich does not, automatically present riches to you on a silver platter; it only provides you with opportunities. These new possibilities are a sort of test in the Game of Life, a way for you to learn whether or not you are truly serious about becoming rich. If you can't choose and get excited about one of these opportunities offered, you must conclude that you are not serious about becoming rich.

After the initial choice, you must still choose again and again in the being and becoming process. There will be an new choice to make each time you come to a fork in the road, each time an opportunity for becoming rich becomes available. If you have truly chosen to be rich you'll have no problem choosing appropriate opportunities. Like the tomato seed knows what it needs to grow a tomato plant, you will automatically know what belongs with the new you and what doesn't.

If you are not being and becoming rich in all areas of your life, including growing spiritually, it's because you haven't been playing the game the way it was set up to promote your growth, and you probably haven't been aware that life's true purpose is self-discovery. And if that be the case, you are, presumably, not sure what it is that you are trying to prove with your life. In fact, you most likely, haven't noticed that you had a choice in the matter of who you would be.

Choices are not always what they seem

God gave you and I the power of choice, and we've been using that power all our lives, totally unaware of the true significance of our choosing. In most cases, we make the mistake of assuming that our choices were about deciding to have what we wanted. But, that's not what really happened, in your moment of choosing to buy a new car.

When you went looking at new cars, you thought you were only trying to decide which make and style of car you wanted so you could pick your favorite color and order it, but that probably wasn't true.

When you told that car salesman you were just looking, what your really meant was, that you hadn't really made 'having that new car' okay with yourself. Think about that. If you'll think back to how you acted, once you'd made it okay to have that new car, you'll remember that it took you about ten minutes to decide on the make, color and style.

The most important step

In most of your major decisions in life, you've taken and then overlooked the most important step in the process of choice. Before you can choose which car to buy, you must first choose to BE the one who can have a new car. And often, after taking the BEING step, we tend to forget that we've taken it, because our ego doesn't want us aware that we have the power to change our minds about who or what we will be.

Whenever it's time to choose something you seriously want from life, you would be wise to remind yourself that the real choice is in choosing to BE the one who can have it. You gain a great deal in personal power each time you, consciously, make a new choice about who you will BE. You empower yourself each time you say, "I'm worth it!"

Why we can't choose

If you are stuck in your current reality, if you can't see that you could have chosen differently, you'll need to take another look at your other options. Other ways to go will show up for you if you are open to the possibility! We pretend there's no way out, because we don't want to have to choose and take the responsibility for our choice. There is <u>always</u> a way out.

Each time we're faced with some form of confront, challenge, or circumstance we don't like, there are always three options: we can choose to give in, fight or run; when faced with the need for a decision we can, say yes, no or maybe. When the phone rings, we can choose to answer it or not; the list of options available can go on and on.

> *Life is about making choices,*
> *and choosing is a self-discovery process.*
> --Darel Rutherford

Choosing not to choose

Even when we think we're not choosing, we're choosing—not to choose. When you're reacting to life's circumstances, you're choosing who to be. Each of those choices seems to be about choosing what to DO, when, in fact, each and every choice is a decision about who to BE when faced with that condition in life. Each time you act, react, give in, fight or run you are choosing a way to BE, either creating or maintaining the pattern for your life.

Sometimes we don't choose for fear of the consequences, and sometimes we don't choose because we haven't a clue that we had a choice in the matter. But there's always a choice. If you're not choosing, you're choosing not to choose, which is choosing!

Life has a habit of confronting us with circumstances designed to move us to the point of choosing, so that in choosing, we come to know who we are. You see, that's the only way you will discover who you are—by rediscovering your power of choice—by choosing. Try it! Notice how powerful you feel just knowing that you have given yourself the right to choose.

And then you might want to consider your choices as the true measure of your consciousness.

How do I choose?

When I suggest that becoming rich is just a matter of choice, the question I hear most is, "How do I choose to be rich?" The problem with that question is, there is no "HOW" when it comes to choosing. You just choose. Or maybe I should say, you choose or you don't. To see why I say that, imagine yourself at the Baskin Robbins ice cream counter with 31 flavors from which to choose. Now, ask yourself, "How do I choose?" Silly question isn't it?

Or imagine yourself at the end of a diving board looking down at the swimming pool; then ask, "How do I jump." If you're asking your coach, "How do I get from the end of the diving board into the pool," that's another silly question. Obviously, you just jump, head first, feet first, or belly first with a big splash. Or you don't jump and cop out by asking a silly question, like, "How do I jump?"

The real question, here, is to choose or not to choose—or as Shakespeare might have said it, the real question is,

to BE or not to BE the one who can choose.

Pretty wise man—that Shakespeare. He was asking the right question way back then. I wonder how many heard what he was really saying?

By their choices shall ye know them

The actual quote in the bible reads, *by their fruits shall ye know them.* This is just the reverse way of saying that what you have in life must correspond exactly to who you are. In other words, who you are (your self-concept) determines what you can have, therefore, what you have tells us who you are—or better yet, tells, YOU who you are.

I like to take that observation a step farther. I pay close attention to your choices. I will know who you are when I see what you choose for yourself. You see the game is set up so that you and I can only choose that which belongs to us by right of consciousness. If it were otherwise, there would be no need for us to grow, and that would defeat the purpose of the game.

Consciousness

I'm using the term, 'consciousness' as a measure of one's concept of reality as it relates to being self-aware and in charge of his or her life.

In other words, **CONSCIOUSNESS is**:
- A measure of your being aware of the presence of God in you.
- The degree to which you're aware of your power to create your own reality by exercising the power of choice.
- The degree to which your concept of reality no longer limits you.

- Your self-concept as it relates to your self-esteem and your self-worth.
- A measure of your ability to side-step ego's resistance, to think outside the box.

*That stuff you want, that you don't have
is on the next level of the game board (consciousness).*
&
*You will only be allowed to claim it
when you grow tall enough (in consciousness) to reach it.*
--Darel Rutherford

The sad part about not being able to choose is not that you won't have what you want; the real tragedy in not choosing, is that you won't know who you are, and haven't realized that your purpose in life is to choose and find out.

You've already chosen

So, do yourself a big favor; take a long hard look at what you have in life, and accept the fact that what you have, sends a message, loud and clear, about who you are being. Who you are, really, is an individualization of God; who you are being, is a whole other story. Knowing who you are, gives you the power to change who you are BEING!

So, take the next logical step toward changing your circumstances. Take full responsibility for what you've created. For instance: if you're unhappy about some happening in your life, accept the fact that you chose unhappiness as your way of responding. When you 'get' that you chose what you have, you have just replaced your victim role with a more powerful position of being responsible for your own feelings. With this exercise, you've regained the power to choose to be happy!

You have chosen who you would BE, and what you have now is the result of that choice. Who you are (your self-concept), was no accident, and you are not the victim you perceive yourself to be. Your parents didn't make you who you are. You did that by acting or reacting—by choosing who you would be under life's circumstances. Your parents only gave you the body that houses your mind; you alone, decided what to put into your mind.

BEING THE SOLUTION

We become what we think about; accept that truth, and realize that your thoughts created who you are BEING. You can blame your parents, blame your circumstances, blame whatever you want, but you are only kidding yourself. Your thoughts have made you who you are. No, one else got into your head to think those thoughts, you must take full responsibility for your creation if you are ever to find your way out of the box.

The context of your life will always determine the content. If you seem trapped by your circumstances, your entrapment is only an illusion. You will free yourself from bondage, when you realize that you can change the content by changing the context, and you ARE the one in charge of the context.

It's only an illusion

As long as you continue to believe that your reality is solid, locked in stone and unchangeable, you will find no way out of the box you've built for yourself. But once you can see your reality as a figment of your imagination, you will have found your power of choice and the way out.

Our realities, are each an illusion, built out of nothing more solid than attitudes, opinions and points of view. You and I were given the power to choose who we each would be, and the means by which we would experience that choice as our separate realities. Individual realities would not be possible if we didn't have an ego that performs the miracle of making our realities seem real.

Each and every one of us on this planet has the power to create his or her own reality, and we've each done that. The remarkable thing, here, is that while living under exactly the same circumstances, we can each experience life from a different point of view, each living our lives in entirely different realities.

Now that you're aware that your perceived reality is an illusion, you must know that your true reality is not in your circumstances, but in your attitude about those circumstances.

Changing the illusion
*Changing your reality
is as simple as changing your point of view.*
--Darel Rutherford

CHOOSING TO BE RICH

If you could flip a switch in your mind, and suddenly, see your condition of lack as a wonderful opportunity for growth, that condition could no longer be a problem. You would have changed your reality by merely changing your point of view, and changing your point of view changes who you are BEING.

Actually, it IS that simple! You can change your reality if you will change your attitude about it. The problem with changing your mind is that, as far as your ego is concerned, you are your point of view. If you change your point of view, your ego must die and be reborn into a new level of consciousness.

Your ego will do everything within its power to prevent you from realizing that your reality is just an illusion. Ego's survival depends on its ability to maintain status quo!

Always ready with the blinders

Our subconscious mind, acting as our ego, serves us by allowing us to experience life as our chosen reality. It maintains that reality (the illusion) by screening out everything that doesn't fit what we currently believe. To prevent our hearing anything that would upset our current B. S. (belief system,) our ego, always vigilant, stands ready with the blinders to prevent our seeing the truth and with earplugs to prevent our hearing it.

We are all blessed or cursed, as the case may be, with our own built-in resistance to change. The good news is that your current perception of reality is safe and secure, protected by your good friend the ego. The bad news is that you won't get the message I'm bringing you here, unless you can read it with an open mind—from outside the box you call your reality.

To get this message you will need to override your ego's resistance to your getting it.

The options are:

The best part about living a life that is merely an illusion is that we have the option, at any time, of changing that illusion. To change your reality, (create a different illusion) just change your perspective. Poverty in any form (lack of love, health, wealth, happiness or spiritual awareness) is an attitude, not the condition of lack it appears to be.

To transform the quality of your life, make the decision, right now, to change your perception (your concept of reality) about what you seem to lack. I say, seem to lack, because that lack is merely the illusion you choose to maintain.

BEING THE SOLUTION

What you lack in life,
is your perception of reality
made to appear real.
--Darel Rutherford

So, how do you change that reality? Your first step might be to totally reject the painfully unsatisfactory reality you now endure only because it's safe.

The power of no

When you find yourself in a Baskin Robbins Ice Cream Parlor trying to decide which of 31 flavors you will choose, your first job is to say no to all but one or two flavors. I chose a double dip cone with butter pecan and chocolate chip. What's your choice?

Only after you've said no to 30 flavors,
can you say yes to the one.
--Darel Rutherford

If you have trouble deciding which movie to see, or which restaurant to choose, you are among the majority who may never get to have what they really want from life. To have the life you want, you must be able to reject all other options to settle on the one.

To find your way out of your box, you must find the courage to say "no" to what you don't want. You must kick yourself out of the current nest before you can move into a bigger, better one. Those who have trouble making choices in life, will not have the grit to choose out of unhappy circumstances. They just don't know how to say "no."

Your "no" gives you back your power

In a contest between 'yes' and 'no', it would seem to many that 'yes' is the more powerful of the two. But I disagree! For my money, 'no' is the big winner, by far! When you're faced with a situation you don't like, and can find the courage to say *no* to it, you will be amazed at the power that gives you. Having found your 'no' power you will have found all the power you need to say 'yes' to what you do want.

In fact, learning how to say 'no' is an important part of finding yourself. By saying 'no' emphatically, you decide what does NOT belong in your life; by saying 'no,' you've declared who you are not.

CHOOSING TO BE RICH

When you're clear about what you don't want in your life, you will know what you want. When you know what you want, you'll know who you are.

If you are not pleased with your circumstances, you can change that state of affairs, by giving yourself permission to say, "no—I've had enough!"

The first step in the direction of living your dream is in saying 'no' to whatever seems to stand in the way of your living it. If you have a swamp full of alligators, you must pull the plug and drain the swamp before you can experience a life without alligators.

Where did the alligators go? Your swamp was an illusion created to maintain the reality of your perceived problem. The alligators disappeared because they were a part of that illusion.

You have the God-given power to create your own new reality. You do that every time you make a new choice about who you will be—or won't be.

The power switch

The governing principle that determines what your life will be like is this: *We become what we think about.* Your thoughts have greater power than you have yet imagined. That's true, only because you have not yet realized that you are an individualization of God.

The power switch that turns on that great power in you is "I am." And since almost every thought you think is an, "I am" thought, you unconsciously use your power switch hundreds of times each day. Even when you say, I don't like pumpkin pie, you are making an, "I am" statement. You are choosing who you will be relative to pumpkin pie.

So, changing the quality of your life must begin with the realization that each and every thought you think, throughout the day, has the power to keep you in your box or set you free. Those thoughts make you who you are. Isn't it time you took charge of your thinking?

Adding power to your thoughts

Some thoughts are more powerful than are others. The powerful thoughts you think are the ones to which you have attached strong feelings. A slight uneasy feeling is one type of worry; being afraid is a much more powerful thought because it has the emotion of fear giving it power.

On the positive side of the emotional scale, setting a goal without a great deal of enthusiastic anticipation is one thing; getting truly excited about that goal multiplies your chances of reaching it exponentially.

So, we might want to change that governing principle, *we become what we think about,* to:

> ***We become what we think about with passion.***

The power to keep you boxed in

If you will pay close attention to your thoughts, you will find that you think or say, "I am," a great many times each day. More importantly, when you feel fear, doubt, anxiety or concern as you think about your circumstances, you give negative emotional power to that thought. On the other hand, if you think about having what you want with enthusiastic anticipation (as you might feel when planning a vacation) you empower your thoughts with positive energy.

Because you haven't realized that your thoughts have great power, you have enslaved yourself by your own thinking patterns. Your habitual way of thinking about your situation is designed by your ego to keep you confined to your box. To exit the box, you must take charge of your thoughts and create new thinking habits.

As a prosperity coach I often hear people say "I intend to be rich," and then, the very next words out of their mouth will be some negative, "yeah but" or "what if" thought, designed to keep them confined in their box. All your thoughts are powerful! If you really want out of your box to stay, you must become your own thought monitor. You'll learn how you can be the negative thought monitor in a later chapter.

In the mean time, have you ever wondered why we all live in a box? You'll learn about that in the next chapter.

9
BEING TRANSFORMED

...means having what you want from life

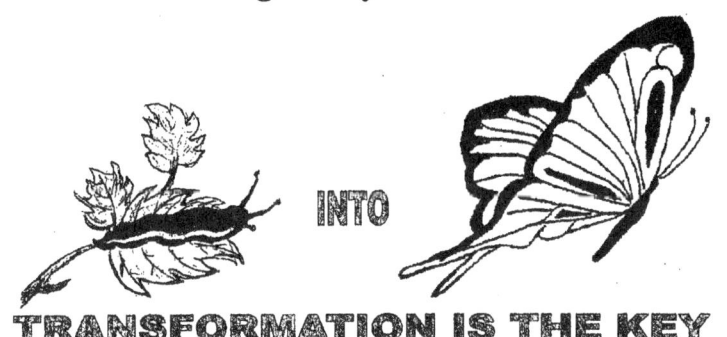

TRANSFORMATION IS THE KEY

*To change the quality of your life,
merely change the pattern of your thinking*
--Darel Rutherford

The magic in believing

Like most kids, I believed in magic. I remember playing at being a wizard, pretending that I could have whatever I wanted from life, instantaneously, at the flick of my magic-wand curtain rod. My magic still works, but not always with the instantaneous results I imagined when I was playing at being a wizard like Harry Potter. As kids, we all believed in magic. I'd like to give you back your magic!

The power behind your magic is always there
It needs only that you believe in yourself!
--Darel Rutherford

I happen to believe we're all Harry Potters who haven't gone to wizard school and have not yet learned how to work our magic. A great power is discovered in the process of changing our minds about who we will be and then in having that BEING choice made real! The trick is, in finally coming to see that we created our own reality.

BEING THE SOLUTION

Meet Harry Potter

In the first Harry Potter novel, The Sorcerer's Stone, by J. K. Rowling, Harry Potter spends most of his early years, almost always in trouble because of the strange things that keep happening in his life. Harry is often punished for happenings that he doesn't believe he caused. Harry's problem is that his magic works to cause the trouble, and because he doesn't know he's a wizard, he sees himself as the innocent victim of those happenings. Wouldn't you like to know why Harry Potter novels are so popular?

It's because, at some deeper level of conscious, we all know that we, like Harry Potter, are wizards. Like Harry, we keep creating strange happenings in our lives and suffering the consequences of our creations. And like Harry, we refuse to take any responsibility for having created the reality that we now endure with disdain. The Game of Life is set up so that we must, sooner or later come to know the truth about the magic power of our thoughts.

As individualizations of God, you and I have the magic power of being able to transform ourselves into BEING whoever we need to be in order to have our dreams made real! Our power comes with being able to choose who we will BE and then in having the means by which we may BECOME the one living our dream.

For the sixth step out of your box you must *change your mind about who you are and how you relate to the circumstances in your perceived reality.*

"Be ye transformed..."

Transformation truly is the key to having what you want from life, but being transformed sounds like such a big deal. It's really not. The transformation formula I'm about to give you seldom produces the immediate results you might expect from waving a magic wand. But the transformation that results from using the formula in this chapter is guaranteed when you follow the instructions and complete the exercise.

With this process you will transform yourself into the person who will have what you want from life. This may sound like wizardry, but it's not really magic. It's for real! The transformation process works because it's based on the principle: *we become what we think about.*

A principle is a law, a basic truth, a rule that you can depend on to work for you every time you use it as a basis for your decisions. You can count on it, because it will always be true. In mathematics, for example, you can know that 2 x 2 = 4, always. Another example of principle is the law of gravity. Because of it, you can go into your living room each morning and expect to find the furniture exactly where you left it the night before. The principle, *we become what we think about,* is as dependable as the law of gravity.

Transformation by choice is not a new idea. The disciple Paul had this in mind when he said, "Be ye transformed by the renewing of your mind". When using the transformation exercise as the process for the renewing of your mind, you have God's guarantee that the quality of your life will be transformed forever. The process works for you if your intention is clear and your desire remains strong.

BE DO HAVE, the true order of creation

For many years, I would have told you that the correct order of creation was DO HAVE BE. I believed then that you could change what you were DOING and resolve all your problems, but I was wrong! As mentioned previously, BE DO HAVE is the only correct order for creating your new reality. You must change who you are BEING before you can change what you are DOING; otherwise the attempted doing will fizzle out even before it gets off the ground.

Most self-help books would have you believe that if you do as they suggest you will have what you want from life. They imply that once you've had your reward from DOING as they suggested you would automatically be the person you'd always wanted to be. Not so! The first step toward a quality of life change is a BEING decision.

> *Don't pursue success;*
> *BE the one to whom it belongs and attract it.*
> --Darel Rutherford

Having what you want is not what makes you rich; what turns that trick is a prosperity consciousness that just naturally attracts riches. That prosperity-attracting consciousness is how you will be BEING when you feel prosperous. Rich is about who you are, not about what you have.

As a management consultant

For several years of my life, while managing my own business, I offered others my services as a management consultant. This was a

BEING THE SOLUTION

period of my life when I thought a simple change of procedure would solve serious business problems.

For instance, Joe Black came to me with serious cash-flow problems. I showed Joe how a change in his credit policy with slow-paying customers would increase his cash flow. I pointed out that having the resulting cash surplus available would allow him to purchase inventory for much less, and his lowered costs would double his profits. Joe and I both, thought that this change in his credit policy would be a great solution to his cash-flow problems. Joe was also thrilled about the prospect of doubling profits. But that cash-flow bonanza never happened for Joe because the new credit policies were never implemented. Can you guess why?

My solution for Joe didn't fly because I had offered him a DOING solution to what was actually a problem with who he was BEING. Joe couldn't change his credit policy because doing so would have required what, for him, turned out to be an unacceptable BEING change. It was too far out of his box. Joe just couldn't see himself as the hard-hearted, tough-minded credit manager he would have needed to BE, before he could dictate and maintain a firm credit policy to those slow paying customers.

As a consultant, I had not allowed myself to see that my clients' real problems were in who they were being, not in what they were doing. I gave excellent advice (in my opinion) when advising clients about what they could DO to solve their business problems. But in those days, I didn't tell them that they would need to change who they were BEING in order to take my advice—a serious mistake on my part! I hadn't learned that the creative process for mankind was BE DO HAVE, not DO HAVE BE.

The power of visualization

In Chapter Seven you learned: that using the visualization process to create a burning desire, would motivate your making a new BEING choice and having your dream reality come true. Here's another example of how well that works.

I read this story in the Reader's Digest about a man who spent considerable time in a POW camp. Every day, to keep his mind off the discomfort of being cramped up in a small cell, he visualized himself playing golf on his favorite golf course. He remembered, in detail, every fairway, every sand trap and each putting green on that golf course in his hometown.

BEING TRANSFORMED

Every day, while in that cramped cell, he played all 18 holes of that golf course, one hole after the other. For each hole, he chose the appropriate golf club and teed off. After each tee shot, he imagined himself walking to his ball and choosing his next club, depending on the length of the hole and how well he'd imagined playing his tee shot. With each hole, he chipped onto the green and putted. He kept score, and as you might have guessed, scored a little better than average for his visualized rounds of golf.

If I remember the story correctly, he was in that prison for over three years. When he came home, his first priority for recreation was to play a round of golf on that same golf course he had played in his mind for those years in prison. For his first real game of golf in years, he beat his best-ever-real score by two strokes. Such is the power of visualization.

In a visualization,
you are BEING the solution to your problem.
Darel Rutherford

Winning through visualization

Another visualization example: The daughter of a friend is a key player on a champion soccer team. Their coach is a management consultant, much wiser at consulting than I was. As a regular training exercise, this coach has each player on the team visualize BEING a star player on their winning team.

She teaches them how to visualize BEING winners—practicing winning moves in mind, before they are called on to DO the great plays that win so many games for them. Net result: their team has been division champion four years in a row!

Being a winner in life
is first a BEING choice and then your reality.
--Darel Rutherford

Doing is just 'being' in action

Once you are seriously considering the possibility of becoming rich, one of your first questions will be, "How do I do that?" In other words, "What do I do; what action step must I take to become rich?" I want to remind you again that 'rich" in this book means rich in consciousness. "Rich" means having whatever you think you need to

BEING THE SOLUTION

have your life be whole and complete. When I use money as an example, you need to substitute whatever for you will fill your greatest need.

If BEING financially independent fills that need, I'll show you how to create multiple streams of residual income in a later chapter. But knowing what to DO is not the first step in the becoming rich process. Choosing to BE rich is the first step. That's because rich is about who you are BEING, not about what you do or have.

I'm not trying to convince you that the doing is not an important part of the becoming-rich process. On the contrary, without the doing, the BEING rich can never really happen. What I'm saying is that the Doing follows the Being choice in the BE DO HAVE success formula. DOING is the becoming part of BEING—the action part.

As a prosperity coach, I often meet those who say they've chosen, but when it comes to the doing part of being and becoming, they fall far short. Most of these 'wannabes' actually believe they've made a new choice about whom they will be when they really haven't. Those who continually talk about what they're going to do, but never do it, are conning themselves about their intentions.

A man's action is only a picture book of his creed.
Ralph Waldo Emerson

An old-fashioned steam engine needed a full head of steam to climb a steep hill. Blowing your own whistle to impress friends is like blowing off steam. Bragging is sometimes so rewarding that it dissipates the motivation needed for climbing your hill. The time for deserving a pat on the back is AFTER you've climbed your hill and reached your goal. Once you've made your BEING decision, don't just talk about it, get on with the DOING part!

Unless you've bought your ticket

A dream without an action step is just a dream. No matter how much you dream it or talk about it, it's still just a dream. Until you take that first step down that yellow brick road toward your new reality, your dream is a fairy tale that can have no happy ending except in your dreams.

If you keep saying you intend to go to Disney World, but never get around to buying a ticket or packing a suitcase, I will know that your trip to Disney World was just something to talk about, never your real intention. Your intention was to dream and talk about it, not to do it.

*You'll know you're on your way to that dream reality
as soon as you've made your first move in that direction*
Darel Rutherford

If you sincerely intend to be rich, prove it, not to ME, to YOU, by making your move. A good first step, after you've prioritized your list of twenty reasons for becoming rich, is to do something, anything, to set the wheels in motion on the most important reason at the top of your list. Stop reading now, and ask yourself what that move will be and then make it!

Until one is committed

No matter how much you think you want something, nothing happens until you're committed. Being committed means being willing to:

DO whatever it takes for as long as it takes.

If you're not that committed, you're probably not serious about having the life style change you say you want.

Getting past your ego's resistance will require your powerful commitment to make it happen. You will have set the wheels in motion when you make that commitment. Once you are committed you will boldly act in some way to make it happen. That's when the power of the Universe gets behind your intention. The following quote is my favorite on the subject of commitment. It's worth repeating.

*Whatever you can do, or dream you can, begin it.
Boldness has genius, power, and magic in it.*
-- Goethe

The Transformation Process

Transformation truly is the key to having your life change to be the way you want it. So, how do you go about the process of transforming yourself into BEING the person you will need to be in order to have that quality of life change? The answer is simple: you merely change the pattern of your thinking.

BEING THE SOLUTION

Your habitual thought patterns and your beliefs make you who you are. Any thinking pattern that keeps you poor in any aspect of your life is merely a bad habit.

*We first make our habits
and then our habits make us.*
--Dryden

How do you break a bad thinking habit? Simple! Replace it with a new habit—create a new pattern to your thinking. Changing your thinking habits will change who you are. That simple change of mind is the transformation you seek.

Before you seriously attempt the transformation process, you must convince yourself that the process will work for you. To increase your faith in the process, I suggest that you copy the following affirmation on a 3x5 card, carry the card with you and read it aloud several times a day. Continue reading it until you are certain beyond a shadow of a doubt that changing your thinking will change your reality—read it aloud until you can get excited about having found the simple solution for changing your life style.

Your 3x5 card: *I know that my persistent thoughts eventually become reality for me. I will, therefore, concentrate my attention, for thirty minutes daily, on thinking of myself as The person I intend to become.*

Memorizing these words should give you a renewed sense of power and strengthen your belief in the transformation process. Speaking the words aloud will increase your determination to take charge of your life and to plan your future. Now, would be a good time for you to stop reading and create your own 3x5 card!

In Psycho-cybernetics, Maxwell Maltz, tells us that it takes about 21 days to change a habit. The transformation process is quite simple. By concentrating your thoughts for thirty minutes daily on thinking of yourself as the person you intend to become, you become that person in about 21 days.

If your intention is clear and your desire remains powerful enough to overcome your ego's determined resistance to change, your transformation is guaranteed.

The BE DO HAVE Exercise

Daydreaming about what we want is often a waste of time, because wanting it won't get it for you. The only way you can ever have what you want from life is by choosing to BE the one who will have it.

But once you've chosen to BE the one in your dream, you're on dangerous ground, because your ego will still be running on the old track. It will yet be busy defending who you were being before. Until the new BEING choice is accepted by your ego as your reality, it will be trying to get you back into your old box.

To win in the contest of wills between you and your ego, you will need to have a powerful commitment and a transformational process that will keep you on track until your ego buys into the new reality. So, how do you BECOME the one who will successfully DO what you would need to DO in order to HAVE what you want? The following exercise should start you down that path.

Exercise Instructions:

Find a ruled pad and divide it into three equal columns. Label the left column BE, the middle column DO, and the right column HAVE, as shown in the example below. Notice that I've numbered the columns as well as labeled them, and that the numbering goes from right to left.

3 BE	2 DO	1 HAVE
WHO YOU WOULD NEED TO BE	WHAT YOU MUST DO	WHAT YOU WANT FROM LIFE
IF YOU WERE BEING SUCCESSFUL	IN ORDER TO HAVE WHAT YOU WANT	THAT YOU DON'T HAVE
AT HAVING WHAT YOU WANT	DO THIS COLUMN SECOND	DO THIS COLUMN FIRST
Examples	Examples	Examples
be worthy of a pay increase	serve more people better	a salary increase
be a true friend	go places, meet people	good friends

1. Starting in the HAVE column first, make a list of everything you want from life that you don't have.

BEING THE SOLUTION

2. Once your HAVE list is completed, see if you can decide what you would need to DO in order to HAVE what you want; enter that in the middle column.
3. Now ask yourself who you would BE if you were DOING those things and already had what you wanted. Put that into the BE column.

The question here is, *"Who would you be BEING if you already HAD everything on your want list?"*

Twenty-one days to a new reality

Now that you've decided who you would need to BE in order to have what you want from life, how do you start the process of transforming yourself into that person? Remember the information on the 3x5 card that you committed to memory? Now you get to put that belief to work.

INSTRUCTIONS: On three new 3x5 cards, write I will concentrate my thoughts for thirty minutes daily on thinking of myself as . . . (see example below) Fill in three separate cards with the same information from your BE column. You'll put each of these cards in a different place to use as reminders. See card use instructions on the following page.

At the bottom of your three cards, write, *I will focus my attention on this, my dream...*(see example card). When you've completed writing out your commitment, make it official and strengthen your resolve by signing your name to it. This is important!

By signing it, you are making a solid agreement with yourself to change who you are BEING into the one who can have what you want from life. Unless you are totally committed to the idea of being transformed, your desire for that better life will most probably fall by the wayside before the process is completed.

MY COMMITMENT: I will concentrate my thoughts for thirty minutes daily on the visualization of myself as a millionaire, living with my loving family in the house of our dreams. I no longer work for a living because all of my income is residual. I now have all the time I need to do the things I never had time for before. How sweet it is!

I will focus my attention on this dream until it becomes real to me. I will then set about the process of being and becoming the one in my dream.

BEING TRANSFORMED

What I've written on the example card are my words; yours will be different, filled in according to your needs. Choosing to be a millionaire may be too far outside the box—may seem an unreachable goal for you. In that case, I suggest you choose an end result more suitable to your present image or self-worth. This is not my vision; it's yours!

If you need another example, you might consider:
- doubling your income
- finding a better job
- creating a loving relationship
- gaining in personal power
- increasing your self-worth

Whatever fills your greatest need should be the BEING statement written on your cards. The question to be answered in your BEING-change commitment statement is,

"Who would I be BEING if I ALREADY HAD what I want from life?"

Card use instructions:
- Tape one of your three cards to your bathroom mirror;
- Put one in your pocket or purse,
- Put the other on your desk or refrigerator.

Your commitment to yourself is to concentrate your thoughts for thirty minutes each day: seeing yourself BEING the successful person who already has what you want most from life. This process works better if you break the thirty minutes into three ten-minute segments, perhaps morning, noon and night. I suggest you do the last visualization just before you go to bed, so you can dream about it.

The words you've written on these cards can change your life, but when used only as an affirmation, they seldom work as well as when used in visualization. If you can see yourself living that better life in your dream reality, feeling as you would feel if you were BEING that successful person, your chances for transforming your life will be much greater.

When you try to change your reality through affirmations like repeating "I am rich" over and over again, when that's not really true for you—your ego says "Yeah sure", and your affirmation gets shot down before it even begins to fly. The ego tends to reject affirmations as untruths, but when you do visualization in present time consciousness, that vision won't be rejected by the ego's defense system. Why not?

Our subconscious mind can't tell the difference between the perceived reality and the visualization of a new reality.

What does a transformation looks like?

So, how do you know when you've been transformed? What does that feel like? How will your life be different after a transformation?

Being transformed can be a grand and glorious experience, especially if it stems from a revelation, a new sense of awareness that shows up as re-discovered inner personal power. This sort of transformation comes from finding the courage to face a problem and rise above it; it comes from finding your inner power in the process of choosing to be more than you were.

When you have this sort of transformation, you will just naturally need and want less sleep. You'll get up every morning, wide-awake, excited about the new day before you. You won't want to wait to get to work where you will experience BEING the enthusiastic new you that you've just uncovered. You'll feel unstoppable in everything you attempt; you will love life and enjoy what you're doing. That was my experience of being transformed, but all transformations do not necessarily follow this pattern.

When my daughter, Sherry, decided it was time to stop having migraine headaches, she was able to locate the source of the stress that caused her headaches and deal with it. When the headaches were gone, she said, "You have no idea how empowered I feel being back in charge of my life!" She was, quite obviously, elated and empowered by her transformation.

An immediate transformation

One Sunday morning, years ago while searching for a solution to the problem of my failing business, I sat reading Napoleon Hill's Think and Grow Rich. Halfway through Hill's book, I was transformed with a force that was not unlike being struck by a bolt of lightning. It was like, a bright light had gone off in my head.

I was in awe of the truth that had just dawned on me, and in that moment, I went from being fearful and despondent to being wildly

BEING TRANSFORMED

enthusiastic and excited about my future. What truth changed my life forever? *We become what we think about.*

My transformation was like going from darkness into the light! When you have this sort of transformation, your friends will take one look at you and ask, "Wow! What the heck happened to you, and where can I go to get what you have?"

Some transformations happen slowly

When I was a kid, a friend's mother had her son stand in a doorway every six months so she could mark his new height on the doorjamb. In this way, she kept track of his physical growth.

Sometimes our growth in consciousness can only be measured by looking back, by seeing who we were six months ago, compared to who we are now. For the slow transformations, we don't really see or feel the change happening. And afterward, the ego often wants to pretend that it didn't happen. Your ego doesn't want you to know that you have transformational capabilities.

A denied transformation

Not long after my wife did a life-changing seminar, similar to the Forum, I asked what she had gotten out of it. She answered," nothing;" and then in almost the next breath said, "and I want a new car!" in a determined tone and with a self-assurance that left nothing in doubt about whether or not she would have a new car. This was definitely not the same Betty from before the workshop. She had been transformed, but wouldn't allow herself to see that she had changed!

Before her transformation, I would have responded with, "You don't need a new car. There's nothing wrong with the one you have." Instead, I said, "Okay, what make, what color?" She came out of that workshop transformed but denying that anything about her was different.

You've been in the process of being transformed all your life, and my guess is that you've forgotten what it's like to be transformed. That's because most of your changes in consciousness were gradual and unnoticed. They happened slowly, like growing taller.

Being transformed simply means you've changed your mind about who you are. In most cases, your ego will pretend that you've always been this way. But sometimes, the change is too dramatic to ignore.

BEING THE SOLUTION
Transformation in a revelation

At the conclusion of one transformational workshop I attended, a Baptist Minister got up and, with tears in his eyes, shared with us. He said, "I've been preaching about God for 25 years. This is the first time I have known God."

What really happens in a transformation? You become more aware of who you really are, an individualization of God. You have just rediscovered your power by uncovering a greater dimension of your own being. It has been said that self-discovery is rather like peeling an onion. With each new revelation, you've just peeled off another layer of ego to discover the real you. And like with peeling onions, I'd be surprised if discovering your inner power doesn't bring tears of joy to your eyes.

Once you have been transformed by the renewing of your mind, you will be enthusiastically anticipating the being and becoming part of creating a new you. Enthusiasm, by the way, is derived from the Greek word "Entheos," which means, "God in us", or "inspired by God."

The best example of a transformation I know is that of the caterpillar waking up one day to discover that it has wings and can fly. Isn't it time you found your wings?

Do less, BE more

Once you're fired up with enthusiasm, you'll get busy building your new box, enamoured with whatever you will be doing to accomplish your mission. I suggest you focus your attention more on the BEING than on the doing.

Once you get your new box built, you will forget what it was like to be enthusiastic, alive and on purpose. You will put your ego back in charge, settle into your box safe and secure, (doing and having, not being), comfortable, not happy, and trapped again. Sorry. That's just the way the game is played.

You can stay at the winner's circle in the Game of Life if you will keep remembering that you are not your ego. You can find your way out of the need-for-security trap (the new box) if you will keep remembering that the purpose of the game is self-discovery. Keep knowing that you will only find your true self whenever you find the courage to step out of the box with a new BEING choice.

To stay alive in Life's Game, you will need to continually remind yourself that the Game is not about having, it's about BEING.

10
UNDERSTANDING EGO'S RESISTANCE
...puts you back in charge of your life

*With the power of negative mind chatter
ego will try, desperately, to get you back into your box,*
--Darel Rutherford

Mind chatter

From time to time, you will have second thoughts about your decision to change your life. In every weak moment, when your thoughts turn away from your vision to consider the possibility of failure, your ego will put fear in your heart. Don't fight the fear. Expect it. When you're feeling that fear, you will know that your ego is running the show and that it's time to put yourself back in charge.

That ego-resistance will show up in the form of the reasons why you shouldn't, couldn't or wouldn't complete your mission. When you, originally, chose not to be rich, you gave yourself what you thought were good reasons for that decision. You've been justifying your choice with those reasons, ever since. Now that you've made a new decision, those reasons will confront you in the form of mind chatter.

Mind chatter looks like:
- *But what if I fail?*
- *I could loose it all!*
- *I tried before and failed; what makes me think this time will be different?*
- *Is this just another one of my pipe dreams?*

Your way past the mind chatter, and ego's fear of change, is not to fight with your ego, but to understand its fears so that you will know how to deal with them. The idea is to get your ego working with you on building your dream.

Step Seven of the nine steps out of your box is:
Understand and learn how to deal with the resistance

Where we've come so far:
If you've done your homework, you have, so far,
- Rediscovered your power of choice
- Agreed that you chose what you have
- Decided what you want from life
- Created a burning desire for it
- Actually chosen to BE the one who will have it
- Begun the transformational process outlined in the last chapter

These are the first six of the nine steps out of your box to personal freedom. If you have not taken any one, or all of these steps, reading this chapter may help you understand why you haven't acted, so far.

If you haven't chosen to BE the one who will DO whatever you need to do to HAVE your life be the way you've always wanted it, reading this chapter may move you to the point of choosing. If so, you may want to go back and do the BE DO HAVE exercise again so you'll know who you'd need to BE to have your life be the way you want it.

UNDERSTANDING EGO'S RESISTANCE

Human bondage stems from ignorance

The root word in 'ignorance' is, ignore. According to Webster, **Ignore means**:
1. to refuse to take notice of.
2. to reject

We have the power of the Universe behind our "I am" statement. But we refuse "to take notice of" our power because acknowledging it would destroy the victim role we've chosen to play in life.

You have the God-given power to choose that better life for yourself. But by not choosing the life you want you live in bondage, exemplifying Webster's definition of ignorance! So, choose your way out of bondage with a new BEING choice!

Slavery by choice

As humans, ignoring the truth, we've enslaved ourselves to live lives that do not satisfy our needs, wants, and desires. We've chosen ignorance because we're afraid of the truth. We ignore this liberating truth because it doesn't fit our chosen concept of reality.

So, we live in a perceived reality made up of attitudes, opinions and points of view, which are designed to keep us in bondage. We experience our lives as egos determined to maintain our chosen viewpoint at the exclusion of all others to the contrary. We don't hear the truth, because we don't want to hear it.

We're in bondage, not because we're stupid, as in, lacking intelligence; we're in bondage because we are, either unaware, or uninformed of this truth. And our lack of enlightenment is not because the information has not been available to us, but because we've chosen to ignore it.

Ignorance of the truth,
is the root cause of human bondage
--Ernest Holmes

So, what truth have we ignored?

You've heard over and over again that you were "created in the image and likeness of God." You've chosen to ignore that truth or twist it to fit because it didn't agree with what you had already chosen to believe. When you were told that Christ said, "The kingdom of God is within you," you chose not to understand what that really means. When

BEING THE SOLUTION

you heard that Christ said, "that truth would set you free," you failed to ask, "what truth?" and "free of what?"

You are in bondage to a concept of reality designed to prevent you knowing who you really are. Your jail keeper is an ego, determined to keep you from finding your way out of confinement. You will have found the key to your cage once you accept the fact that your reality is nothing more or less than a point of view that can be easily changed.

You will be free of a concept of reality that doesn't work for you, once you rediscover your power to choose another reality. You will be free once you've proven to yourself that you are, indeed, an individualization of God with the power to create any reality you can give yourself permission to choose! To be free of bondage, you must become more aware of ego's defense system.

Ego is our self-concept, functioning in and as our individualized adaptation to our perception of reality.
--Darel Rutherford

Ego's defense system

Past workshop participants who fizzled out, were stopped in their tracks on their way toward living their dream of a better life. They failed in the attempt to make a life-style change, because they were unaware of, and therefore, ill-equipped to deal with their ego's defense system. Ego uses many tactics to keep us confined.

Whenever you think about the possibility of changing the quality of your life, your ego's first defense will be an attempt to talk you out of that notion. Ego uses mind chatter, self-talk, as its first line of defense against your making a new BEING choice. Once you've chosen out of your box, however, your ego will use fear tactics in an attempt to get you back into your box.

Lacking staying power

If you are now out of your box, congratulations! Hug yourself, and while you're in that position, pat yourself on the back! But coming out of your box is one thing; staying out is a whole other thing.

Many who venture out of their box don't have the courage or the necessary resolve to stay out. From my experience, about 60% won't have the essential staying power. Ego will use negative mind chatter or fear to chase the less-determined seeker of change back into

UNDERSTANDING EGO'S RESISTANCE

their box. In other words, even though you're out of your box, the odds are about 60 to 40 against your being able to stay out.

I'm saying 60% of those who commence the 21-day transformation process, learned in the last chapter, will find some silly excuse for not completing it. Sometimes, it's not even a conscious excuse. This chapter will change those odds by putting you back in charge of your life. You may have thought you were running the show, but if you're still stuck in that box, ego is obviously the one in charge.

Ego's reasons for fearing change

Although we lose sight of the process from time to time, the creative process in mankind is BE DO HAVE. It works like this: We choose who we will be and then, once ego accepts your new reality, it takes over to provide us with the experience of life from that new perspective. Ego's function in life is to maintain our chosen reality by screening out any and all ideas that don't fit.

Ego's main job in life is survival. And, since ego's maintained reality is made out of nothing more substantial than a preconceived notion about the way it is, it can't afford to have you changing your mind about what's so.

You'll find that changing of your point of view is a much easier task if you can think of your ego as an idea come to life—a perception of reality that's now in charge and being demonstrated as your life. For your ego to survive in and as that perceived reality, your self-concept and your Belief System must remain intact.

Ego's job is to keep that perceived reality intact. Ego's defense system is, for the ego, a life or death matter. When you try to change your point of view, your ego knows that it must die in order to be reborn into that new consciousness.

Why you did not choose to be rich

If you're ready to make a new choice about who you will be, let's review some of the beliefs and self-concepts that stood between you and choosing to be rich. Let's face it, when it became your time to choose between being rich or poor, you would have chosen to be rich, not poor, if your self-concept would have allowed it. But some belief or self-concept stood in the way of your choosing riches over poverty. So what idea caused you to choose what you did?

BEING THE SOLUTION

Here are some of the possible reasons why you may have chosen not to be rich.
- Your self-worth wouldn't allow it
- Rich didn't fit who you've chosen to be
- You were afraid that, in trying, you might fail
- Being successful might take you out of your box

Mind chatter comes in two types, self-doubt and BS (Belief System).

Self-depreciating mind chatter

My workshop participants, who chose out of their box, thought they were on the way to becoming rich. But sometime during the transformation process, they began to doubt their ability to pull it off. While their certainty was at half mast, ego slipped up behind them and whispered, "You can't do that because:
- *you're not smart enough"*
- *you don't have what it takes"*
- *you tried that once and failed"*
- *you've never followed through before, so what makes you think . . . .,"*
- *etceteras, etceteras.*

If you think you have never heard your personal devil (your ego) whisper in your ear, listen again. It's that little voice in the back of your head that keeps telling you why it could never happen.

My challenge to you

If you are not rich, it's because, at some point in your life, you chose not to be. Ever since you chose not to be rich, your ego has been busy keeping you in poverty, by defending your decision with mind chatter. If you don't believe that, I challenge you, right now, to think seriously about becoming rich.

I challenge you to check out the mind chatter, by making your decision, right now, with the full intention of becoming rich. (Unless you make this a commitment, your ego won't take you seriously, and you won't experience the resistance.)

Once you're committed, allow yourself to hear your ego's self-talk and experience the fear; that's your ego's defense system clicking in. Did you hear the "yeah buts," the negative mind chatter? You've been hearing that self-talk all your life. It's what keeps you confined in your box.

UNDERSTANDING EGO'S RESISTANCE

Irrational logic mind chatter

Your Belief System (BS) mind chatter will look like logic, but it's really not. It will sound like, "you can't do that because:
- *It takes money to make money, and you don't have any*
- *Rich people are snobs; you don't want to be one of them!*
- *Money is the root of all evil, therefore all rich people are bad!*
- *Having more than my share means someone must do without!*
- *It's just not in the cards for you to be rich.*

It doesn't matter that none of the above viewpoints are true; your mind chatter is who you are BEING relative to the idea of becoming rich. Those ideas are your chosen way to BE relative to having riches in any of its forms.

Your servant, not your master

You are not your ego! You are a spiritual being, experiencing a reality in a material world. Your ego serves you by providing the means by which you get to experience that reality. Ego provides you with that experience, by taking charge, by maintaining your chosen reality.

Once we turn reality maintenance over to our egos,
we tend to forget who is in charge.
--Darel Rutherford

Your ego is your servant, not your master. To be master of your fate, you must put yourself back in charge.

Back in charge

Now that you understand ego's fear of change, now that you're back in charge, now that you're being objective, you can deal with ego's fears as an adult dealing with a child. When you experience the fear (as your ego), step out of that role, take charge, acknowledge your ego's reasons for being afraid, and then switch your attitude from fear to faith, from fear to empowerment.

BEING THE SOLUTION

To rebuild your faith in yourself and in your new vision of reality, take time to remember how you felt when you first found the courage to choose that vision. Bring your thinking back to the benefits of being transformed. Find your list of twenty reasons for becoming rich and read those benefits aloud every time you have doubts. Rekindle the fire of desire that gave you the courage to commit to a better life in the first place.

Your battle with the ego will be won only if you maintain a clear mental image of yourself enjoying the success you wanted.

Until one is committed

You have the God-given power to choose that better life for yourself. By not choosing it, you ignore your power, exemplifying Webster's definition of ignorance! So, choose!

If you are ready to find a way out of your box, take a look at the three most powerful steps you must take:
1. Create a powerful vision.
2. Whet your appetite.
3. Choose to BE the one in that vision!

Ask yourself: Is your WHY powerful enough to take you past your ego's determination to maintain status quo? If it's not, work on your vision; see yourself already living the benefits of being in that bigger box. Once your vision becomes believable, make your new BEING choice.

Nothing really happens until you make the commitment. But, once you're committed, you can expect your new reality to be demonstrated by an ego with a new mission in life.

11
YOUR WAY PAST THE RESISTANCE

...the three minute Power Pause

A simple way to take charge of your thinking
and change the quality of your life forever

Moving past the barriers

As a self-made millionaire, presenting workshops from coast to coast, I have, for 35 years, coached and mentored workshop participants and clients in the process of finding and removing their barriers to becoming rich. Since writing, So Why Aren't You Rich? in 1999, however, I have discovered a more direct and effective way of moving participants past their barriers.

When someone tells me their victim story, I ask them,

Who would you be BEING
if that were no longer the problem?

That question takes the one with a problem, right past that problem to BEING its solution. The question has transformational powers because the solution to almost any problem will be found in a simple change of attitude about the problem.

To see the power in this simple question, you must accept that a change in the way you think and feel about your problem, changes it's significance. That change in the problem's importance does nothing toward solving the problem; it changes your relationship to the problem. It changes who you are BEING relative to the problem and the problem ceases to be a problem.

After the appropriate attitude adjustment
the perceived problem seldom needs fixing
--Darel Rutherford

Step eight of the nine steps out of your box:
Learn the secret to overcoming the resistance

Almost everyone has a problem. So what's your problem? In regard to that problem, my question for you is:

Who would you be BEING
if that were no longer a problem?

He was ready to quit!

When J. G. (we'll call him Jim) came to me for counseling, he was ready to quit his job. Upset with his boss, Jim said, "I love my job, but he's trying to make me over into a clone of himself. If I can't be me in my job, I'll have no choice but to quit!"

Jim was hoping I would tell him what he could do that would solve his problem with his boss. Instead, I asked Jim the BEING question. I said, "Who would you be BEING if you were receptive to being coached as the one who would, some day soon take over that business?"

Jim's shocked response: "Damn, this isn't about him! It's about me, isn't it?" I introduced Jim, to the Power Pause, a three-step process for bypassing his problem, to BEING its solution. Then, Jim used the Power Pause to change who he was BEING in his relationship to his boss. Six months later, his boss turned over the business to him.

Some kind of miracle?

Was Jim's good fortune some kind of miracle? Was it a coincidence that he inherited that business? Not really! Changing your way of BEING, as in how you are choosing to relate to the problem, can solve almost any problem you can name. That's because your real problem is not with the circumstances, but in your way of dealing with those circumstances.

As long as Jim continued to see his boss as a domineering, do-it-my-way employer, he could never have solved his problem. Any attempt Jim made to change his boss' way of being would have failed and he would have had to quit. To solve the problem, Jim changed the only thing he could change—his own attitude about the problem.

As soon as he allowed himself to see his boss' coaching as a blessing and an opportunity, not a threat, his whole future in that job changed instantaneously. In that moment, Jim had transformed himself into one who no longer had that problem.

If you choose to see Jim's solution to the problem as a change in what he was doing, you will have missed the point. The change that solved his problem was the change he made in who he was BEING relative to the perceived problem. You'll gain greater benefit from this example if you can see that Jim's perceived problem was never the real problem.

The solution to Jim's problem was never a change in the circumstances, but a change of perception about those circumstances—a change of attitude. I can just hear your mind chatter right now, telling you that Jim's example doesn't fit your circumstances. As you read the chapters devoted to the Power Pause solution to all types of problems, I think you'll change your mind.

The Power Pause, by John Harricharan

In all my years of teaching prosperity workshops, I've been frustrated with the number of participants that have crawled back into their boxes like scared pups, with their tails between their legs. I've since, discovered a cure for the fear that puts most of them back into their the box. It's called the "Power Pause."

As soon as I read The Power Pause, 3 Minutes, 3 Steps to Personal Success and Real Happiness, By John Harricharan, I knew I had found the solution to their fizzle-out problem. I now had the way to bypass their ego's fear-based mind chatter. In terms of simplifying my coaching job, what I found in John's book blew me away.

Transformation is the key to having what you want in life, and I had just found the perfect transformational tool. After reading The Power Pause, I had no choice but to call John Harricharan and ask permission to promote this powerful life-changing process in my

RICHBITS e-mail newsletter, and to teach the Power Pause solution in my workshops.

John, very generously, gave me permission to use The Power Pause any way I pleased, including the writing of this book. The Three-minute Power Pause is not my gift; it's John's gift to you through me.

Exactly what I'd been looking for

John's Power Pause allows you to change the quality of your life, by sidestepping ego's fears, changing the way you think and feel about your problem. Solving a problem, by changing your attitude about it, is rather like having the alligators disappear, because you've drained the swamp in which they lived.

Once you've used the Power Pause to solve a problem, you'll say as I did, "WOW! This is exactly what I've been looking for—*a simple way to take charge of my thinking and change the quality of my life forever.*

I've been offering the Power Pause Solution to my RICHBITS subscribers, ever since, and with remarkable results. I'll share those success stories with you in the next few chapters.

John Harricharan's Power Pause

The Power Pause is written in story form in a way that will inspire you to use the Power Pause as your way of handling fears and self-doubts. In case you hadn't noticed, your ego uses fear to rattle your cage and scare you back into your box.

In this great book, John has this to say about fear:

Fear seems to wait for the time when you are at your weakest. It picks your most vulnerable moments then jumps out to grab you by the throat. It lurks in dark corners of the mind, watching and waiting for an opportune moment to hurl itself full force at your shaken defenses

Also from John's book, see if this sounds like something that's ever happened to you:

Fear and anxiety had played on my emotions and before I knew it, I was imagining the worst possible sets of circumstances. Fear uses this method over and over to trap us.

YOUR WAY PAST THE RESISTANCE

John's Power Pause will show you how to avoid falling into ego's fear trap.

Although I'll be giving you the Three Step Power Pause formula for dealing with your fears, the power in that process will make a much deeper life-changing impression on you when you read about it in story form as John Harricharan has written it. You can buy John's book, The Power Pause from his web site: http://www.powerpause.com Just image what your life would be like without fear! You'll do yourself a favor when you buy and read John's book.

By these principles:

Power Pause success stories seem like miracles until you realize that those seeming miracles are merely the combined effects of applying the two basic principles that govern what we may, or may not, have from life.

Those principles are:
- *We become what we think about, and*
- *What you have in life must correspond exactly to who you are*

From these two principals you can extrapolate the key to the transformational process:
1. If what we have must correspond to who we are, it must, therefore, be necessary to change who we are BEING if we are to have something from life that we don't already have.
2. If we become what we think about, it must, therefore, follow that we could change who we're being and have what we want, by simply changing the pattern of our thinking

The conclusions you must draw from your acceptance of the governing power of these two principles are:
1. That your transformation will be the key to having what you want, and
2. Since you have the ability to change the way you think, you already have the power to transform yourself into BEING the one who can have whatever you want from life.

If you can spare three minutes

So, if I were to give you a sure-fire way to replace all your fearful self-doubts with positive, enthusiastic, anticipative thoughts, your new way of thinking would BE the powerful transformation in

- 127 -

consciousness necessary to having life be the way you want it. Make sense?

If you can spare three minutes every time you feel worried or concerned about your future, I'm offering you a simple way to change your thinking habits and become richer in all aspects of your life!

The Power Pause Steps

The Power Pause, is the perfect tool for replacing any form of fear thought with a new vision and the positive emotion you will need to empower it. But to get full value out of using the Power Pause, you must want something that is being threatened by your fear of not having it. That fear may not show up for you until you actually choose to have it.

The Power Pause is a three-step process that takes 3 minutes or less to complete each time you use it.

1. **Step One**, go to a peaceful place in your mind. Everyone can remember a time and place when they felt at peace. My peaceful place is a fishing hole. A picture of my ideal fishing hole hung behind my desk for years. I've never actually fished there, but every time I felt work-related stress, I put myself into that picture. Each time I imagined myself fishing there, I escaped the stress and found peace.

    Everyone has a place like that. Your peaceful place could be on the beach, listening to the waves rolling in, on a path in the woods communing with nature, enjoying a waving field of grass, or at the seashore, admiring a beautiful Hawaiian sunset.

    Think of your favorite place and go there in your mind. Be at peace for a full minute. This moment of peace may take longer to establish the first time you try for it, but having done it once or twice, you will find yourself at peace almost the moment you declare a Power Pause in the future.

    This moment of peace, intentionally, places a buffer between you and your fear thoughts.

2. **Step Two** of the Power Pause: Visualize your life as it would be if the reason for your fear no longer existed. Who would you be BEING and how would you FEEL if your swamp were drained and the alligators gone? Your intent in this step, is to capture the feeling

YOUR WAY PAST THE RESISTANCE

of well being you would have if your problem were solved, or no longer existed. You would be celebrating that victory.

In your vision, you are not looking for the solution to your problem; you've already solved it, and are FEELING the joy and satisfaction you'd, just naturally, experience under those circumstances. The important thing, here, is to empower your vision with the joyful feelings of a happy ending. Generate the good feeling you would have if the problem were solved and then experience that triumph with all the good feeling you can muster.

3. **Step Three:** Thank God, or whatever you call your higher power, for the problem already solved! Say, "Thank you, God! Amen!" Your vision is empowered; you've seen your problem solved, and now, you're thankful. It is important, in this step, that you feel a very strong sense of gratitude. An attitude of gratitude is the most powerful of all prayers.

The Power Pause is a three-step process for transforming the quality of your life. To change your life, you need only change the pattern of your thinking. You live in a box created by your thinking habits. Your thoughts make you who you are. Changing your way of thinking changes who you are BEING.

The Power Pause is the perfect formula for the simple solution to all problems. How do I know this? In all my 35 years of teaching the new thought philosophy, I've never seen anything work so quickly to change the quality of lives.

- Hattie Pembrook used it to convert her unhappy marriage into a loving relationship.
- Sherry Jaramillo used it to permanently rid herself of migraine headaches
- Marie Mays, after five years of struggling, increased her massage business by 33% in only one month
- Dolores Jackson, after two years living in poverty, used it to land a song-writing contract in the music industry and a new job in just one week
- Jim G. used it to change his attitude from "ready to quit," to "my boss retired and left me the business" in six months
- Rev. Toni LaMotta's transformation in consciousness landed her the minister's job in a church ten times larger than the one she left.

BEING THE SOLUTION

Three months after taking that position, she had increased attendance there by 55%, teaching these principles!

Impressed? You'll learn more about these Power Pause success stories in the following chapters. But for now, just know that each of the above had a major problem that was quickly solved when they used the Power Pause to change who they were BEING relative to their perceived problem.

The Power Pause works, based on the spiritual principle: *we become what we think about*. This simple visualization process, allows you to change who you are BEING in a way that cuts past your ego's natural resistance to that change. When you change who you are BEING relative to your perceived problem, your problem will simply dissolve and disappear.

How to use The Power Pause

Remember that the solution to Jim's problem began when I asked him the BEING question. I suggest you look at your problems in life one at a time and ask yourself that same question,

Who would I be BEING
if that were no longer a problem?

When you've figured out the answer to that question, build your vision for the Power Pause out of that BEING solution. Making a habit of using the Power Pause on a regular basis, changes who you are BEING by changing your attitude.

When you change who you're BEING,
you change what belongs in your life,
--Darel Rutherford

The first step in implementing the Power Pause habit, would be to make a habit of listening to your mind chatter, with the intention of dealing with your fears. Remember, when you have self-doubts, that's fear talking, not the real you.

Don't run or hide from your fears; be there for them; acknowledge them. Talk to your ego. Say, "I hear you but it's time to declare a Power Pause." If you are sincere about wanting that change, I suggest you pick a problem and test out the Power Pause as your way of solving it.

YOUR WAY PAST THE RESISTANCE

EXERCISE:
Allow yourself to think about the most troubling thing in your life right now. Got it? Declare a Power Pause;
1. Go to your peaceful place, and for a full moment, experience being at peace;
2. Then, visualize your life as it would be if the problem were solved. Experience the joy, the excitement, and the good feeling you would have if the problem were no longer a problem.
3. Finish the exercise with the attitude of gratitude; say, "Thank You God."

Did you experience having your problem solved?

The most difficult step for some is in being at peace when faced with a problem. During the peace step, you are not attempting to make the problem go away; you are not saying it doesn't exist; you are merely setting it aside for a moment of peace. You may want to practice the peace step until peace is an automatic and instant result of declaring a Power Pause.

Visualization is the most difficult step for some. We all had great imaginations when we were kids, but tend to give up that capability as we grow older. To make the visualization easier, some people need to begin with something more substantial than an imagined picture of success. We're out of practice when it comes to "imagineering" a new reality.

If that's your problem, find a place that sells old magazines; in thumbing through those magazines, you'll find pictures that will graphically depict your life as it could be, if your problem were solved. Cut out those pictures and glue them on a solid background to form a collage. Use the collage to help you create your Power Pause visualization.

Not without the intent

In order for the Power Pause to work for you, you must have a serious intention to create the new realty that will have the problem solved. You have your ticket to a new reality, guaranteed, if you will declare a Power Pause every time you have self-doubts, or fears about what's outside the box.

The solution to whatever problem you're having with life will always be found in a change in who you are BEING relative to that problem. The Power Pause is your way of creating the mental blueprint for that change in consciousness. But you must have serious intent before you will be able to create the blueprint.

A transformational tool

The Power Pause is a tool for transforming yourself into BEING the one who will have the life you've always wanted. The time for completing a transformation and the experiencing of material results will vary. Some transformations will be almost instantaneous and some will take more time.

Jim's transformation happened the moment he realized that HE, not his boss, was the problem. In his case, the Power Pause merely helped him perfect the new role he had chosen to play in the relationship to his boss. Notice that Jim's life was in crisis just prior to his change of attitude. If you are not hurting for the change, as Jim was, the transformation may take more time to develop.

The speed of your transformation will depend on the amount of discomfort you're experiencing in your current reality. For instance, if you were living in a rented house, up to your ears in debt, but wanting to own your own home, you may have to work a while on that vision before it becomes your reality.

One couple, who lived through that sort of discomfort, with a large family in a home too small, ended up in their new home in about six months. During that whole period, faced with all sorts of apparent reasons why it couldn't happen, she continued with the Power Pause, maintaining a vision of her family in that new home. But six-months later, the family moved into that new home.

Notice that the Power Pause doesn't change the circumstances until you have changed who you are BEING relative to the circumstances.

Acquiring the Power Pause habit

Now that you've done the Power Pause, you can do it again and again. Once you get the Power Pause habit, you won't have to search for a moment of peace; peace will come to you the moment you declare a Power Pause.

It should take you less than three minutes to complete this exercise each time you experience worry, doubt or fear. No matter where you are, or what's going on, you can take a moment to declare a Power Pause and cancel the stress you're feeling in that situation. By

YOUR WAY PAST THE RESISTANCE

this process, you are exchanging a bad thinking habit for a good one—replacing worrisome fear thoughts with positive happy ones.

The Power Pause is a being and becoming exercise, the perfect transformational tool. With the Power Pause, you create your vision of BEING the solution. If there's an action step necessary to solving your problem, the new you will know about that step and take it with confidence!

It's John Harricharan's Power Pause

I want to remind you that the Power Pause solution to problems comes to us, compliments of John Harricharan's generosity in allowing me to dispense it to you. Use it with confidence. It really works. I have noticed, however, that those who read John's book, seem to have more certain and dramatic results than those who haven't read his book.

Lori Blethen, one of my RICHBITS subscribers, put it this way:

" *The email summary of the Power Pause, as provided by you, was instrumental in my having purchased John's book. But the summary did not have the same transformational effect on my heart. John's words and the detailed story are divine and have a power that cannot be explained. Anyone interested in acquiring the Power Pause habit must purchase John's book.*"

I tend to agree with Lori. Although the Power Pause exercise works for anyone who uses it consistently, it seems to work better for those who have read John's book. There's a spiritual awakening in reading about it in story form, that doesn't necessarily happen with learning the simple formula.

What others are saying about John's book

Take a moment to read some of the comments others made about John's book.

Three steps?
It only takes three steps to solve problems, create wealth and feel happy? I didn't believe it either, until I tried it. Not only do the three steps work, but you can do them anywhere, anytime, for any situation---and in about three minutes! " --Joe "Mr. Fire!" Vitale--author of There's a Customer Born Every Minute.

"An amazing method"

"...What an amazing method the 'Powerpause' is! It pulls you in from the very first word! I highly recommend it to anyone who has stress or wants a more peaceful life." --Marlon Sanders Creator of the "Amazing Formula that Sells Products Like Crazy"

"Seriously amazing stuff!"

" It literally brought tears to my eyes. The "Power Pause" is a gift I shall never forget. And these words come from my heart." --Monique Harris Co-author with Ken Evoy of "Make Your Knowledge Sell

"Kudos..."

"From the moment fortunate readers of your material learn the simple Power Pause technique, they, for the rest of their lives, will be avoiding needless grief and anxiety while opening the door to a lifetime of peace and happiness. --Rick Beneteau Author of "The Ezine Marketing Machine,"

"I just couldn't believe..."

"I spent six years of my life and considerable money getting my Masters degree in Psychology/Counseling. I learned one of the most important strategies in how to take control of any stressful situation in one night reading your material. ... couldn't believe how simple and practical the 'Power Pause' is." --Gary LeMaster Psychologist, MO

"A skilled guide"

"A skilled and eloquent guide... a discovery of truth that we must all make sometime in our life." --Deepak Chopra, MD

Reading John's The Power Pause will inspire you and change the quality of your life forever.

In the next chapter, you'll learn the last necessary step to personal freedom and financial independence.

12
CREATING YOUR SUPPORT TEAM
...empowering your success

*They believe in me, because
I have believed in them and myself.*
--Darel Rutherford

You'll need a recharge

One night, when I parked my car, I left the car door slightly ajar. The dome light burned all night and, the next morning, I needed a jump-start to get my car up and running again. When you and I experience fear and self-doubt, we suffer a severe energy drain. Like a car with a dead battery, we've lost starting power. When we've temporarily lost our enthusiasm for our stated goal in life, we could easily end up back in our box. Without a jump-start from another power source, we might have to leave the car in the garage.

Everyone has moments in life when they feel like giving up. No one stays pumped up all the time. If you don't have someplace to go or someone to talk to when your self-confidence needs recharging or when your vision of that great new reality blurs, you will surely fail in your intention to change the quality of your life.

The Power Pause is not enough

Although the Power Pause is great for overcoming ego's mind chatter, it will not, in and of itself, be enough to keep you out of your box. You may be charged up with enthusiasm now, but emotional upset will drain your high-level charge from time to time. This chapter shows how you can get your go-power back in a support group.

Your desire for that better life has given you the necessary motivation for coming out of your box; the Power Pause has given you your way past ego's first line of defense, your way to replace fearful thoughts as they pop up. You're out of the box, but don't count that a win—not yet. Ego has a last line of defense! Your ego waits behind the scenes for one of your weaker moments when you've lost your enthusiasm.

We all have those occasional moments in life when, without any apparent reason, we're discouraged and "down in the dumps", emotionally drained. In those desperate moments, when we're filled with self-doubt and fear, ready to quit, we will need outside help to get us back on the fast track.

Fear is a kind of bell...
It is the soul's signal for rallying.
--Henry Ward Beecher

Reinforcement and encouragement

When you become discouraged and feel like giving up, your ego will sneak up behind you, zap you with fear, and throw you back into your box.

To survive this battle with your ego, you must find a way to fire up your enthusiasm and recharge your personal power.

You can do nothing effectually without enthusiasm.
Guizot

To win the game you're playing, you must have the reinforcement and the encouragement, that can only be found as a participant in your support group. My name for that support group is: "Powerpact."

WHAT YOU'VE LEARNED SO FAR

Step nine in finding your way out of the box:
...*Create a support group* to empower you when you need encouragement

So what is a Powerpact?

A Powerpact is a separate entity, a powerful force, called into being when two or more minds combine forces for a common purpose and mutual support. I call this new focused force in the universe a "Powerpact." Napoleon Hill called it a "Mastermind." It matters not what you call it, as long as you recognize it as a separate entity, a force to be reckoned with, a source of empowerment.

While doing research for <u>Think and Grow Rich</u>, Napoleon Hill interviewed the most successful businessmen of his time, asking each for their success secret. The powerful men he interviewed—men like Andrew Carnegie, Henry Ford, and Thomas Edison—all credited their success to the creative energy generated by the team spirit of their management groups, In my book, these power groups are "Powerpacts." A company's sales department is a Powerpact; a production department will be a separate Powerpact, and if the company is to succeed, the board of directors must be a Powerpact. Every winning team comes together as a Powerpact to find the team spirit necessary for winning.

Powerpact definition

"Powerpact" is a coined word made from two words which, combined, point to the fact that two or more individuals have made a pact to support and empower each other in being and becoming whoever they each need to be in order to achieve their goals.

A Powerpact is: the entity called into being
when two or more people of like minds come together
for a common purpose and mutual support

Bible defines the Powerpact

The concept of a Powerpact, by whatever name you choose to call it, is nothing new. Years ago, as a Science of Mind Practitioner, I called it a "Prayer Triangle". Call it what you will, it has been the empowering force, the real reason for all team successes for centuries. Christ created a Powerpact with his twelve disciples.

BEING THE SOLUTION

Maybe you will better understand the power generated in a Powerpact when you know the source of that power. Here's what the bible has to say about it:

Where two or three gather together in my name, there am I in the midst of them.
--Matthew 18:20

In my name

If these words of wisdom are to be accepted as words spoken by God, our next question would be, "So, what IS God's name?" When Moses asked God that question on the mountaintop where, he received the Ten Commandments, God answered, "I am that I Am." To really find your personal power, you will need to accept that God experiences the reality of a material existence in and through you as you.

"God, as man, in man, is man."
God's name, in you, as you, is "I AM."
--Ernest Holmes

The power switch

Because you are an individualization of God, you call that force into BEING each time you say or think 'I am.' Those two words are the power switch that you use to turn on God's power in you. That same power switch is activated in a big way when you form a Powerpact and say, "WE are a team." That power is activated, and your personal power is multiplied, when you combine forces with others for the purpose of mutual support.

Your God-given power lies in your ability to choose who you will BE in your chosen reality. A Powerpact is where you'll find the quality of support you must have if you are to achieve your new BEING goal. The Powerpact reinforces your ability to BE and become whoever you will need to be in order to accomplish your mission in life.

Only a few, truly understand their need for a Powerpact support group. Not many will appreciate the greater power for success generated by team support; yet, if the truth were known, it is next to impossible to achieve anything but mediocre success without one!

WHAT YOU'VE LEARNED SO FAR
The formula for a Powerpact is:

> *They will have faith in me because I have faith in them and in myself. Our combined consciousness reinforces and raises our individual levels of self-confidence and personal power to new and greater heights.*

It has been said, " behind every successful man is a woman who believes in him." That quote may have outlived its time. It might be more appropriate to say, "behind everyone who succeeds is someone who believes in him or her." The lesson here is...

*No one ever succeeds greatly
without the reinforcement found in having team support.*

You've found your way out of that box. The trick is to stay out. The odds against your staying out are greater than you might imagine—about 60 to 40 against! Unless you have a support group that will encourage you and reinforce your belief in yourself, you probably won't survive ego's determined, last-ditch effort to shove you back into your box. Without the benefit of a Powerpact, during one of those weaker moments when you feel like quitting, you probably will.

The Power Pause, discussed in the last chapter, is the perfect tool for dealing with occasional moments of worry, doubt or fear that will pop up when you think about your goal. For those times, using the Power Pause is like flipping a switch. In three minutes or less, you move from being afraid to being at peace, then to joyfully experiencing your success vision, followed by an attitude of gratitude. In those empowered moments, it will seem as though nothing can stop you.

During moments of self-doubt

Believe me, there will be moments when the Power Pause will not be enough. At times, you'll be dealing with something much more powerful than mind chatter.

*Our greatest foes,
and whom we must chiefly combat, are within.* --John Ozell

The time will come, in a moment of emotional let-down, when you'll be asking yourself what the hell you're doing out of your box.

BEING THE SOLUTION

During those periods of self-doubt, you will tend to believe that the safest place for you would be back in your box. And unless you have a support group to encourage you and reinforce your self-confidence, that's where you'll end up—back in the box.

> *The fearful Unbelief, is unbelief in yourself.*
> --Thomas Carlisle

If you are determined to stay out of the box, you MUST create your own Powerpact.

Your commitment to form a Powerpact

It would be natural, at this point in your reading, to say to yourself, "Wow! That's a great idea, I should form a Powerpact." But then you read on and never get back to doing anything about creating your Powerpact. After all, it's not comfortable to think about sharing our deeper thoughts and feelings with others. In fact, your ego will try to convince you that you shouldn't.

In my experience, most of those who think about forming a Powerpact never get around to it. So, if you are serious in your intention to be rich in all aspects of your life, you must first commit to the task of forming or finding your own support group—a Powerpact. To make your commitment solid, write it down on a 4x6 card, as in the following example:

MY COMMITMENT TO FORMING A POWERPACT

I understand that my personal power and self-confidence level will increase exponentially as a result of being part of a working Powerpact.

I will, therefore, concentrate my intention on forming my own empowering Powerpact. I will begin by finding two people of like mind who have a similar intention of growing their self-worth and their consciousness. I will seek, not so much to be supported, as to give support, knowing that as I give, so shall I receive.

I will commit this affirmation to memory and repeat it aloud three times daily, until my empowering powerpact is in force.

Signed_____

WHAT YOU'VE LEARNED SO FAR

Don't just think about it. Find your card or a piece of blank paper and copy this commitment down. Don't forget to sign it. Put it somewhere, like on your bathroom mirror, and read it aloud to yourself several times a day, until you're 100% committed to forming your own Powerpact. If you're serious about wanting a life-style change, you must do this for yourself!

Make your list, find your partners

So, stop reading now and create a list of people you would consider as possible partners in your three-party Powerpact. Find possible copartners who have a desire to change the quality of their lives. Talk to them, casually, about the benefits of participating in a Powerpact, but don't push it at this point.

So they'll understand the need for a Powerpact, you might want to loan them this book and have them read this chapter.

Your initial conversation with them would be to discern their level of interest, but not necessarily to invite them to be in your Powerpact. Don't agree to enter into a Powerpact with anyone unless you feel supported in his or her presence and feel certain that he or she will keep your sharing confidential. In fact, you might want to create some form of agreement that has you all on the same page in that Powerpact. Maybe something like the following:

Powerpact agreement

I choose to be in this Powerpact with _____ and _____, knowing that I will be empowered by the combined energy created by our coming together. I will listen with my full and undivided attention to who they are BEING, and I will fully support them in their being and becoming whoever they need to be in order to have their dreams made real. I agree that confidences revealed in this Powerpact will not be repeated by me to anyone outside our Powerpact. I will give our scheduled meeting times priority over all other schedule options.

Signed_____.

BEING THE SOLUTION
The power level

Your success in life will depend on the levels of:
- your personal power
- your self-worth
- your self-confidence

Your Powerpact support group will help you raise the bar on your self-worth so that you can reach greater levels of self-confidence and personal power, opening the receiving channel through which your good must flow.

If you have taken each of the previous eight steps out of your box, you will have already changed your mind about who you are. That change of mind was a transformation in consciousness. You committed to that change of heart when you came out of your box. In your Powerpact, you will be multiplying your personal power and empowering your completion of the transformation process.

In a Powerpact, you will find what's seldom found elsewhere in life—a comfortable space that encourages you to:
- be yourself,
- to like yourself,
- to know who you really are, and
- to grow.

That's a lot of yourself to find all in one place!

Your Powerpact members will see in you strengths and a potential which you have been unable to see for yourself, and once you accept their expanded viewpoint about yourself, your self-confidence will soar. You will have grown in consciousness. Wow! How can you not see the benefit in doing this?

The Powerpact Exercise

In every prosperity workshop, the most important thing we do is the Powerpact Exercise. This training exercise surprises most workshop participants, because they hadn't recognized their need for the type of support that can only be found in a working Powerpact. But once into the exercise, most of them do not want to end it when the time is up.

Participants are all somewhat hesitant at first to share their deeper feelings with strangers. But once they learn how being supported feels, they're hooked on the experience of having their own Powerpact.

WHAT YOU'VE LEARNED SO FAR
THE EXERCISE:

For this exercise, you would divide into groups of three to practice being in a Powerpact. In this practice session, you will be learning how to listen in a way that lets the other person know that you're truly hearing what they say. By really BEING there for the other person, you will see an immediate effect in them and you'll know what real support feels like when you're doing the supporting. When the favor is returned, you'll know how it feels to be really supported, acknowledged and encouraged.

Three to four minutes each

Each of the Powerpact threesome is given three to four minutes to introduce themselves, tell what they do in life, share what they want from life, and say what they think prevents them from having it. Then the other two, each, have one minute to support, acknowledge and encourage the one who just shared to go for their dream.

In a practice Powerpact, each will take your turn at introducing yourself in a way that the others will get some sense of what you do and who you are. If you have a problem you need to solve, or a want that needs fulfilling, you would share that problem or need with them. If you've made a new BEING choice that will solve your problem, you will share that commitment with them.

In short, they need to know who you are, what your problem is and, if you have a BEING solution, what that is. They need all of that in order to support you in BEING the one who no longer has that problem.

Most of us only half listen. Instead of really hearing what's being said, our thoughts are often focused on what we will say when it's our turn. When in a Powerpact, you must give them your full attention. Hear what they're saying with your head and your heart. Ask questions that will let them know you heard them loud and clear. Get to know who they are and be committed to supporting them in BEING the solution to their problem. When you're in the support mode, you will know automatically what to say to support them.

Let them know that you support their new BEING choice and that you believe in them. No phony compliments will work. They must know your support is sincere. They must be empowered with renewed confidence by your faith in them.

The support to be found in a Powerpact is
the space we give each other for BEING who we are. --Darel Rutherford

BEING THE SOLUTION

Why three, not more?

You can build a Powerpact with any number of people, but the ideal number is three. It seems that three people can come to a point of mutual agreement and support more readily than four or more. The bible message that promotes the idea of a Powerpact supports the number three, as well. Notice that the bible passage reads, "when **two or three** are gathered in my name...." It doesn't say two or more, as most people tend to misquote it.

The triangle is the most powerful of all geometric figures. Bridge builders use that form to build strong bridges; architects use it to design the powerful trusses that hold up your roof. The power of three works best in the relationship we're calling a Powerpact, because it seems to offer the greatest support for the other two in the support group.

Power from being supportive

It is most important for you to realize that your focus in a Powerpact is not so much to get support, as it is to give support to the others in your group. You'll get your support automatically if each of you has that supportive attitude, but you'll find that you are even more empowered by discovering how much you have to give while being supportive rather than while being supported.

*You will know who you are
when you know how much you have to give.*
--Darel Rutherford

The true purpose of your Powerpact is to provide the space for each of you to be who you are and to encourage you to grow into BEING who you want to be. To set the stage for listening, you need to hear your Powerpact partners' answer to this question: "As whom do you want to be listened to?" In other words, "Who do you want to be and how can we help you believe in yourself as that BEING transition?"

In response to that question from my Powerpact, I said, "I want to be listened to as the author of a new best selling book called, BEING, THE SOLUTION."

To be a good listener, you will need to see beyond your friend's self-imposed limitations, focus on their true potential, and then help

WHAT YOU'VE LEARNED SO FAR

them to see in themselves what you see in them—even when they can't see it at the moment. It's your job to make sure that each Powerpact partner likes him or herself more, when in this Powerpact with you.

You will discover that you have the power to empower others by believing in them and by building their self-confidence and their self-worth. You will be amazed at how powerful you feel while in the process of showing others their own power. As they are empowered, their increased personal power reflects back on you, empowering you even more. You may want to try this technique in all your relationships.

You give but little when you give of your possessions.
It's when you give of yourself that you truly give.
Kahlil Gibran

A space for the truth

Supporting the other person doesn't mean you accept and sympathize with their victim story. Your job is to empower them; being the victim is the opposite of being powerful. When someone sings their victim song to me, I usually help them out by playing my imaginary violin. My pantomime usually gets a laugh, and then we get down to the truth.

It has been said that "*the truth will set you free.*" Telling yourself that you are a victim makes you powerless to change the circumstances. If, as a member of your Powerpact, I can help you see the truth about who you really are, you will become the victor, not the victim. That's what I mean by support. Just make sure that your coaching is seen as support and not judgement. The idea is to see past your partners' victim stories to who they really are and help them see that for themselves.

A true friend is more to be esteemed than kinfolk.
--Cicero

A Powerpact is the space for the truth. It has the purpose of getting at the real truth of your being. If you are not ready for that level of truth, you're probably not ready to be in a Powerpact.

Our personal power is amplified when
people of like minds support our BEING intention.
--Darel Rutherford

BEING THE SOLUTION

Your power increases exponentially

Your personal power increases exponentially as a result of your participation in a supportive Powerpact. By exponentially, I mean, three to the power of three.

For example, let's hypothetically rate the personal power of each of the three individuals in the Powerpact. On a scale of one to ten, we'll rate each one at the power of three. Now, you might assume that the combined power force in the Powerpact is 3+3+3, or 9. But if my theory is correct, it comes out 3x3x3 or 27.

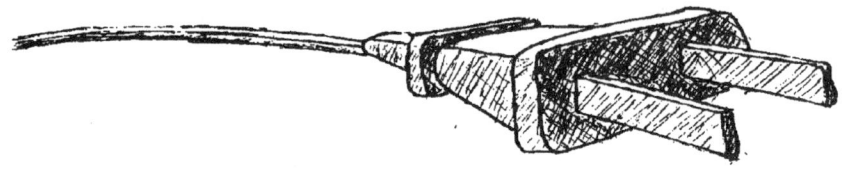

Being part of a Powerpact is like plugging into the power of the Universe.
--Darel Rutherford

I know this: a flashlight with three batteries puts out a beam of light much brighter than three times the light beam from a one-battery flashlight. As a part of a team, each member has available the combined power of the whole team, a power much greater than the sum of its parts. As part of a team, you have that team power available to use in your daily life.

Think about this! Your personal power is a measure of how much you believe in yourself. Your faith in yourself establishes your consciousness level, builds your self-esteem and increases your self-worth. Your self-esteem will skyrocket as a result of being in a really supportive Powerpact.

The source of the power in a Powerpact

Your life's purpose is self-discovery. You will find your true self only through exercising your power of choice to choose a new way of BEING. You will know a little more about who you are each time you give yourself permission to choose a new reality. You'll find your way out of the box only by exercising your power of choice. This is Spirit, in you, as you, choosing a new reality, not your ego.

When, as Spirit, you choose out of your box, you will know who you are; when you are being your ego, you will be stuck in the

WHAT YOU'VE LEARNED SO FAR

box. On your own, with sufficient motivation, you can easily find the personal power to choose out of your box, but that burst of power is not enough to keep you out. To remain out of your box, you will need to reinforce your personal power by tapping into the greater power generated by the joining of forces in your Powerpact.

When you form a Powerpact, the Power you find there will surpass your greatest expectation. ("...there am I in the midst of them.") Your true purpose in life is to find the spirit of God in you. You will find that power source while participating in a Powerpact, even if the others in your support group don't understand the nature or the source of the power they unleash!

Some powerful results

Over 25 years ago, Herb Beatty, Bob Williamson and I formed a Powerpact. We've been meeting almost every Friday for lunch ever since. Each of us owes a great deal of his personal success to being a participant in that Powerpact.

When we began our Powerpact, Bob worked 14 hours a day, 7 days a week, as a self-employed businessman, in the advertising business. He did great work for his clients, but made very little money at it. Back then, he lacked the kind of self-worth that would allow him to earn a respectable income.

Bob finally quit that business and went to work as marketing manager for only one client. His coaching made that client remarkably successful, and while there, Bob honed his management skills. Now, years later, Bob is a very successful management consultant for the mortgage banking industry, with clients all over the country. Much of his income is residual, coming from his percentage of the increased business his clients gained from taking his advice.

Bob now does much of his work from his home. He earns more in one week than he made in a year back when he was working 14 hours a day. He created all of that success on his own, but he gained a great deal of his increased personal power from participating in our Powerpact.

Dr. Herb Beatty, a struggling chiropractor when we joined forces as a Powerpact,. now owns one of the most successful chiropractic practices in town. He has also proven himself a successful businessman, investing his money to make more money. Herb would be happy to tell you about the increase in personal power he experienced from being part of our Powerpact.

BEING THE SOLUTION

My business, DAR TILE Company, grew and prospered as a result of whom I had become while a member of that Powerpact. I owe much of my success to the empowering support I received in it. When I sold DAR TILE for over a million dollars in 1978, I had over 100 employees who also shared in my success. They owned 25% of the company. My management Powerpacts within the company drove that success.

Some time ago, I entered into a Powerpact with the Rev. Dr. Toni LaMotta, and Rev. W. Hunter Roberts. Both lived in California— Toni in Alpine and Hunter in San Francisco. I live in Albuquerque, New Mexico. We communicated weekly via a three-way phone call.

When I did a workshop in Alpine, I offered to mentor Rev. Toni in the growth of her church. When we began our phone meetings, Rev. Toni was minister to a church with maybe 150 members and an average Sunday attendance of about 45. A year later, Rev. Toni accepted a position as the minister of a Sarasota, Florida church with 1500 members and a Sunday attendance starting with about 500 The last I heard, attendance had grown to 800 each Sunday.

The growth in consciousness was Rev. Toni's, but she credits the Powerpact for empowering that growth.

W. Hunter Roberts, the other member of our Powerpact is showing an equal level of growth in consciousness and has a fantastic project in the works that I'm not at liberty to divulge at this writing. I can tell you that she has doubled her income in the past year. When we joined in a Powerpact, she was talking about her project, but it wasn't coming together for her. Now it is! When you become a part of a Powerpact, you will change your mind about who you are, big time!

When I joined the Powerpact with Toni and Hunter, most of the conversation was about them and who they were being relative to their problems. Very little of each session was devoted to my intention for the Powerpact. Not that they weren't willing to go there; I just didn't have much to say about my intentions.

When I did share, I said my number-one goal, was to write this book, but in truth, the book wasn't being written. The two of them finally pinned me down to setting a deadline, and I obviously did that. Without that Powerpact, I would probably still be talking about my intention to write this book. Without that Powerpact, you might not be reading it.

One last example: I recently had lunch with a young lady who had been in one of my workshop Powerpacts. The light in P. K's eyes

WHAT YOU'VE LEARNED SO FAR

and the smile on her face, that day, told me the whole story about how much she'd grown in consciousness since I had last seen her. I've already shared her story with you in another chapter. What you need to know is that her new increased level of self-confidence was found as a result of her participation as a member of a Powerpact.

So, do yourself a big favor. Create your own Powerpact and find the personal power you'll need to change the quality of your life!

The Powerpacts in business

If and when you own your own business, you will find yourself creating different departments as the business grows. Each management team will be a Powerpact within the overall company Powerpact. Each Powerpact established will have a different focus intended to further the overall success of the business.

The employees of my company, DAR TILE, were all part of the company Powerpact, and each participated in other Powerpacts within the company. The sales force, the production department, and the office force, were each Powerpacts. The company's board of directors was another. Each Powerpact had a different agenda and a different stated purpose within the company, and each Powerpact became part of the whole in staff meetings (another Powerpact).

As a business owner, you will begin building Powerpacts, whether you realize that's what you're doing or not. And whether or not your business prospers will depend on the quality and the team power of your management groups (Powerpacts), the power to produce the results you seek.

A house divided

If you are a wise leader, you will realize the importance of the team spirit that comes into being as a result of joining forces in a powerful Powerpact. As their leader, you know that your number-one job is to develop and maintain that team spirit. You will also know when that team spirit is missing and the Powerpact is no longer effective. That Powerpact will lack harmonious agreement and the spirit of mutual support.

And if a house be divided against itself,
that house cannot stand
--Mark 3:24

BEING THE SOLUTION

A business Powerpact is powerful only if each team member believes in the other members and in their leader. The wise team leader knows how to build team spirit and knows that his or her main function is to focus the team's attention on the company goal and to empower team members, moving them individually and together toward believing in the team and each other.

If the team lacks leadership or team spirit, the team will most surely fail. If there's disharmony within the ranks, it's your job as their leader to make peace or to find the rotten apple in the barrel and throw it out. If the team lacks leadership, you may need to re-create yourself, perhaps by finding and participating in another Powerpact outside the business, empowering yourself as a leader. Most successful business leaders have their own support groups that were created by joining forces with other business leaders with similar problems and responsibilities.

Get off the plane!

On a Southwest Airline plane from Phoenix to Albuquerque, the stewardess made this announcement: "This plane is going to Albuquerque. If you're going to Hawaii, you're on the wrong plane." She was jesting, of course, but I think the example applies to a business. As the leader, you should be telling the disgruntled employee the same thing. "If you're not going where we're going, get off the plane!"

Life works by agreement, and life stops working for you when there's disharmony and disagreement. Whether you are in business or not, you will find the power for your success in life in a Powerpact.

In the next chapter, you'll get to see what you've learned so far.

13
WHAT YOU'VE LEARNED SO FAR

…has no real value until you put it to work.

LET'S SEE WHAT YOU'VE LEARNED

*Knowledge is power, but only when
applied to solve your problems*
--Darel Rutherford

The odds have changed

I'm frustrated when my workshop participants fizzle out in the becoming-rich process. Even knowing why so many don't permanently make it out of their box hasn't helped me change those odds much—until now. I'm happy to say that, thanks to the Power Pause, those odds are changing!

In the last twelve chapters, I've given you nine steps to take; I've shown you your way out of your box and the power tools that will keep you out. With a powerful desire for that better life, you WILL overcome ego's resistance and enjoy your new life outside the box. But what you've learned so far will be theory only for you, until you've formed a strategy for putting it to work—until you've taken the action step and actually used this knowledge to change the quality of your life.

What you do speaks so loud that I can't hear what you say.
--Ralph Waldo Emerson

Let's see if you are one of the determined few who will help me improve the odds. Let's see IF what you've learned, so far, has **really** given you the power, the drive and the determination to change your reality from poverty to riches.

If you're still telling yourself, "I'm already rich," you may want to go back to Chapter One and check your score on the rich/poor test again. Remember, if there's anything you lack that you think would make your life whole and complete if you had it, you are poor. Isn't it time you faced up to that lack as a problem needing a solution?

Until you admit to having a problem,
you will do nothing to solve it.
--Darel Rutherford

So, why aren't you rich?

The average person will have five barriers standing between him/her being able to choose to be rich:
1. A belief that he or she doesn't have a choice in the matter of being rich or poor.
2. Ignorance of the fact that his/her ego will resist any change attempted.
3. His/her fear of whatever is outside the box—success or failure.
4. A low level of self-esteem or self-worth—a poverty consciousness.
5. A mind-set or a thinking pattern designed to keep him or her poor.

All five of these barriers will come into play when you consider the possibility of choosing out of your have-not box. In the first twelve chapters, I've given you a step-by-step course of action for finding your way out of that box to personal and financial freedom. Those nine steps will get you past the first three barriers on this list. In the following chapters, I'll be showing you how to raise the bar on your self-worth and to change your mind-set concerning wealth.

Barrier Quiz

To find out if you really know what you think you know about what you've learned so far, I'll be asking you questions. Your answers will tell you what you know for sure; you'll find my answers in the last half of this chapter. This quiz is not about my giving you the answers again. It's about you knowing the answers and being able to apply them

WHAT YOU'VE LEARNED SO FAR

in solving your problems. If you find you don't know an answer, I suggest you go back and read the appropriate chapter again.

Don't cheat yourself by looking at my answers before you've thought about what your answer would be. As Emerson once said, "Don't read me a quote; tell me what you know." You really need to know what you know for sure, what YOU believe for sure. If our answers don't agree, that's good—at least you're thinking! Now, you'll know what you believe compared to what I believe. And you might want to go back and reread the applicable chapter to see if you could consider changing your mind about what you believe.

Before you take a hard stand on any difference of opinion, you might want to consider the fact that what you have believed up to now is what got you to where you are now. If that's exactly where you want to be in life, don't even think about changing your mind. But if you're not happy with your circumstances, you might want to think over your position again. Changing your mind is the first step toward changing the quality of your life.

Review: Chapter One

Being rich is more about who you are than about what you have. You are rich if you have everything you need to make your life whole and complete, and you're poor if there's something you want from life that you don't have. If you are not rich, it's because you chose not to be, and your reason for that choice has become a barrier to having the life you want.

There is no reality except the one contained within us.
---Hermann Hesse

QUIZ INSTRUCTIONS:

Find a ruled pad; write, *Barrier answers* at the top of the page. This will be the label for your answers to the first set of questions about what you've learned from the material in chapter one. Following those you'll find questions about what you've learned from each subsequent chapter, and each question set will be labeled so you can identify your answers with mine. I suggest that you don't look at any of my answers until you've answered all the questions yourself, to your own satisfaction. I won't be grading your answers. Instead, you will be grading both yours, and mine based on your current concept of reality.

BEING THE SOLUTION

Remember, the purpose of this book is to make you richer in all ways by changing your concept of reality.

Barrier Questions:
If you once believed that you didn't have a choice in the matter of being rich or poor,
1. What have you learned in reading this book, that gives you the power to choose to be rich?

If you've tried and failed to change the quality of your life,
2. What have you learned about ego's resistance that puts you back charge of your life?
3. What source of empowerment will you use to get you past those weaker moments when you feel like retreating back into your box?

Almost any form of lack points to a self-worth problem:
4. Which power tool that I've given you would work best for changing your self-worth?

Your current income is the effect of your chosen relationship to money:
5. What do you suppose would be your first step in changing your relationship to money?

Review the Nine Steps
The key to self-discovery and to having the life you want is a transformation in consciousness. In Chapter Two, I've given you a list of the nine steps that must be taken if you are to transform yourself into BEING the one who can have your life be the way you've always wanted it to be. So what are the nine steps to that transformation again?

Be ye transformed by the renewing of your mind
    --The Apostle Paul; Romans 12:2

QUIZ INSTRUCTIONS:
Label your next answers *The Nine Steps*. Then list the nine steps.

Review: Know that you have the power to choose
In chapter three you learned that life is a game, the purpose of which is to discover that you are an individualization of God. You learned that the game (the self-discovery process) is set up so that you must make a new choice about who you will be if you are to have what

WHAT YOU'VE LEARNED SO FAR

you want from life. Let's see what you've gotten out of reading chapter three.

God enters by a private door into every individual.
--Ralph Waldo Emerson

QUIZ INSTRUCTIONS:
Label your answers: *Where is God? answers*

Where is God Questions
1. To what degree have you accepted the reality of the Presence of God in you?
2. How will this make a difference in your life?
3. How will you prove the Presence in yourself, to yourself?
4. How will you know that you know this truth?

Review: The Game Board
In Chapter Four, you learned that you and I have been playing at The Game of Life all our lives without a clue that a game was in progress. My imaginary game board illustrated in Chapter Four, gave you a better picture of how the game works so you could finally come to see life as a game.

*Do not take life too seriously;
you'll never get out of it alive.*
--Elbert Hubbard

QUIZ INSTRUCTIONS:
Label the next set of answers *Game of Life answers*

Life is a Game Questions
1. What makes life a cosmic joke?
2. Have you really accepted the fact that life is a game?
3. How has that changed your life?
4. What advantage do you gain over the other players by knowing life is a game?
5. What are our handicaps to winning the game?
6. What is the real purpose of the game?

BEING THE SOLUTION

Review: Knowing what you want

Knowing what you want from life is obviously the first step in the process of having it. As I explained in Chapter Five, making this important decision is an important part of the self-discovery process. In fact, you can only know who you are when you've allowed yourself to see that:

*The true measure of your self-worth
is in what you have given yourself permission to choose.*
--Darel Rutherford

QUIZ INSTRUCTIONS:
Label your answers *Knowing what you want answers*

Knowing what you want questions
1. So, what do you want from life? Do you know?
2. What conclusion can you draw from realizing that you don't know what you want?
3. What stands between you and knowing what you want?
4. What's the best exercise for coming to know what you want?

Review: Develop a burning desire.

Most workshop participants who doubled their incomes from what they learned in my workshops had a burning desire to change the quality of their lives. If you are to be rich **in all ways**, you will need to whet your appetite for becoming rich. If you are serious in that intent, you will have created your 20 reasons for becoming rich.

*Every human mind is a great slumbering power
until awakened by a keen desire and by definite resolution to do.*
--Edgar F. Roberts

QUIZ INSTRUCTIONS:
Label your answers, *Burning desire answers*

WHAT YOU'VE LEARNED SO FAR

Burning desire questions
1. What should we conclude if you were not able to come up with 20 reasons?
2. What's the real benefit of creating 20 reasons for becoming rich?
3. What step can you take that will make those 20 reasons more than wishful thinking?

Review: Choosing to be the one
Wanting to be rich won't get it for you, as we discussed in Chapter Seven. If you want the abundant life bad enough, you will choose to be the one who has it. So, what's between you and choosing that better life?

> *When you have a choice and don't make it,*
> *that in itself is a choice.*
> --William James

QUIZ INSTRUCTIONS:
Label your answers, *Choosing answers*

Choosing to be Questions
1. Define "Rich" and "Poor."
2. In The Rich/Poor Exercise, how many ways did you rate yourself poor?
3. What's the determinative difference between the rich and the poor?
4. What's between you and choosing to be rich?

Review: Transforming yourself
Having what you want in life requires a transformation in consciousness. I've given you the formula for a transformation in Chapter Eight. It's a simple process that takes thirty minutes a day for 21 days. If you are serious about becoming rich you will have already begun the process. When will you complete it?

> *Everyone thinks of changing the world,*
> *but no one thinks of changing himself.*
> --Leo Tolstoi

BEING THE SOLUTION

QUIZ INSTRUCTIONS:
Label your answers, *Transformation answers*

Transformation Questions
1. What spiritual truth makes the transformation process work?
2. What spiritual law determines what we can have in life?
3. Why does it take 21 days to complete the transformation?
4. Why do so many fail to complete the transformation process?
5. Will you faithfully do the work, every day, for 21 days?
6. If no, why not?
7. Are you ready to re-commit?

Review: Understanding the resistance

By now you know that your ego does not want you being transformed. And because you understand the reason for that resistance, you will know how to deal with it. Knowing this puts you in control of your life.

Convictions are more dangerous foes of truth than lies.
--Nietzsche

QUIZ INSTRUCTIONS:
Label your answers *Understanding resistance answers*

Understanding Resistance Questions
1. Why does your ego resist change?
2. How does the ego make its resistance to change known to you?
3. What powerful second line of defense will ego use to get you back in your box?
4. Why does knowing this put you back in charge of your life?

Review: Overcoming the resistance

You learned in Chapter Ten that most of the ego's resistance will be in the form of mind chatter. And you've been given the perfect tool in Chapter Eleven for canceling out the negative influence of the

WHAT YOU'VE LEARNED SO FAR

mind chatter. With that tool, you will replace your negative thoughts with your vision of a new and prosperous reality.

Your life is what you make it.
--Marcus Aurelius

QUIZ INSTRUCTIONS:
Label your answers *Overcoming resistance answers*

Overcoming Resistance Questions
1. How will you become aware of ego resistance?
2. What power tool will you be using every time you need to overcome that resistance?
3. Describe the three steps for the Power Pause.
4. Explain why those steps work.

Review: Setting up the support group
You've learned in Chapter Twelve that ego uses fear as its most powerful weapon against change. The odds are 60 to 40 that you will end up back in the box if you don't have a Powerpact to help you past those moments when fear and self-doubt have you ready to quit.

It is one of the most beautiful compensations of this life that no man can sincerely try to help another without helping himself.
--Ralph Waldo Emerson

QUIZ INSTRUCTIONS:
Label your answers *Powerpact answers*

Support Questions
1. Define a Powerpact.
2. Why does everyone need a Powerpact?
3. What's the bible's definition of the Powerpact?
4. What source of power comes into BEING in a Powerpact?
5. What's the ideal number of partners for a Powerpact?

QUESTION ANSWERS
Note: I've answered these questions in the first person, as I imagine you might have answered if you had gotten the message intended in each chapter.

Barrier answers
1. I've learned that being rich is about who I am, not about what I have. And since I am an individualization of God, I have the power to choose who I will be, **and I choose to be rich!**
2. When my ego buys into a self-concept, it becomes that idea. When I change my idea of self, the ego must die and be reborn into the new idea of self. Understanding that I am not my ego allows me to change my mind about who I will be. I can now deal objectively and effectively with my ego's resistance to that change.
3. Only in a Powerpact will I find the kind of support and the empowerment I will need to get me past those times when I feel like quitting.
4. Every time I'm feeling unworthy, I could declare a Power Pause to visualize having what I want from life and feeling good about it.
5. I must realize that my current attitude about being rich keeps me poor. In order to change my relationship to wealth in all its forms, I must be open to another way of looking at who I am BEING relative to whatever I seem to lack.

The nine steps
1. Rediscovering my personal power—my power of choice
2. Accepting that I chose what I have
3. Knowing what I really want
4. Developing a burning desire for it
5. Choosing to BE the one who will have it
6. Transforming myself into that person
7. Understanding my built-in resistance to change
8. Learning how to overcome that resistance
9. Establishing the support I need for when I get discouraged and feel like quitting

Where is God? answers
1. I understand, intellectually, that God lives in and through me as me, but to know this experientially, I must prove the Presence in me by exercising my power to choose and then to experience the new reality I've chosen.

WHAT YOU'VE LEARNED SO FAR

2. I will be rich in all aspects of my life, enjoying every moment of it, because I will be living in the moment, being the one in charge.
3. I will prove the Presence in me by being and becoming all that I can be, by really making a difference.
4. I will know that I know this truth when my knowing has moved from my head to my heart.

Game of Life answers

1. I have the power of the Universe behind my "I am" statement. I haven't used that power to set myself free, but rather to enslave myself. I see the joke in that and am laughing at my silly predicament.
2. Not yet, but I'm thinking seriously about life as being a game of self-discovery, and I'm open to changes that would make life more enjoyable.
3. I see now that I'm not a victim; I'm in charge of my own destiny.
4. I will be able to win big in the Game of Life, because I now see that there really never was anything of real value to lose.
5. I wasn't winning because I didn't know the rules:
   My handicaps in winning at the Game of Life were:
   - I hadn't realized that life was a game.
   - I didn't know life's real purpose.
6. The real purpose of the game is that I discover who I really am: an individualization of God

Knowing what you want answers

1. I haven't decided what I really want from life, but I'm working on it!
2. I assume not knowing means I don't really know who I am.
3. I'm not sure, but it's probably a self-worth barrier.
4. I will first make a list of what I don't want in my life, and then I will make a want list that will cancel out the items on the don't-want list.

BEING THE SOLUTION

Burning desire answers
1. If I couldn't come up with 20 reasons for wanting to be rich, I'm obviously not as serious about becoming rich as I thought.
2. By coming up with 20 reasons, I will have developed the motivation strong enough to get me out of my box. I can prioritize that list and focus on the benefits I want most.
3. By visualizing myself enjoying the benefits of those 20 reasons, I will be transforming myself into BEING the one in my dream.

Choosing answers
1. I am rich if I have everything I need to make my life whole and complete and I am poor if there's anything I want from life that I don't have.
2. There are several areas of my life in which I could stand to be much richer.
3. The rich chose to be rich and the poor chose not to be. The only reason I lack anything is because I've chosen to be one who doesn't have it.
4. Who I am now, the poor me, doesn't want me to be rich.

Transformation answers
1. The transformation process works because we become what we think about.
2. The Law of Correspondence says that what I have in life must correspond exactly to who I am.
3. Changing who I am simply means changing my thought patterns (my habitual way of thinking). I understand that it takes 21 days or more to replace a bad habit with a good one.
4. Many people fail because their ego zaps them with self-doubt and fear, throwing them back into the box before they can finish the process.
5. _____?
6. Well, the car wouldn't start…or the cat had kittens? Any dumb reason will do as long as I'm making excuses.
7. Come to think about it, it's time I took charge of my life. Yes! I'm ready to commit!

WHAT YOU'VE LEARNED SO FAR

Understanding resistance answers
1. Changing whom I am, which is a transformation, means that my ego must die in order to be reborn in consciousness. It does not want to die.
2. My ego uses mind chatter to keep me in my box.
3. My ego uses the self-doubt and fear to scare me back into my box.
4. Understanding my ego allows me to be objective in solving my problems. Reminding myself that I am not my ego puts me back in charge of my life.

Overcoming resistance answers
1. To take charge of my thinking, I will listen and be aware of the mind chatter.
2. When confronted with doubts, worry or concern, as I think about what I want from life, I will declare a Power Pause, replacing those thoughts with a vision of living my dream.
3. Step one of the Power Pause is to go to a peaceful place in my mind and experience being at peace. For step two, I will feel as I would feel if I had no doubts and was living in my dream. And for step three, I will thank God for having answered my prayer.
4. My moment of peace creates a buffer between my self-doubts and me. The visualization works because my subconscious mind does not know the difference between the vision and reality. If the vision is repeated often, it becomes my reality. Adding feeling empowers my vision, and saying, "Thank you, God," makes the vision an answered prayer.

Powerpact answers
1. A Powerpact is formed when two or more people combine forces with the intention of supporting each other in being whoever they each must be to have what they want from life.
2. If we are to rise to our full potential, we all need to grow in consciousness, discovering who we really are in the process. The support in a Powerpact multiplies personal power, allowing us to find our way home sooner.
3. According to the bible, God said, "Where two or three are gathered together in my name, there am I in the midst of them"

4. By this definition, the source of the increased power to be found in a Powerpact is the spirit of God being demonstrated through me, as my new-found enthusiasm for life.
5. The ideal number for a Powerpact is three. The power I will find in a Powerpact comes from mutual support and a unity of intention. Our chances of reaching a consensus of agreement are much greater with three than with any other number of participants.

Well, there you have it. Your answers to those questions will not, necessarily, have been the same as mine, nor should they have been. And if you were to read this book a year from now, your answers won't be the same as they were today. That's because you will not be then who you are now.

But by answering the questions, you will have come to know yourself a little better. You will begin to know who you are when you know what you believe. Knowing who you are empowers you by giving you back your power of choice. As you exercise your power of choice from time to time, you will come by degrees to know who you are—a little more aware each time you venture out of your box.

When you really know who you are, you will have won the game!

Until then, the Game of Life is about being transformed by the renewing of your mind. You now have all the power tools you need to speed up the transformation process. In the following chapters, we'll be discussing some ways you might put what you've learned, to work in your life.

If you have decided to change some of your answers after reading mine, congratulations! You have transformed yourself by simply taking this quiz seriously.

In the next chapter you will learn how your BEING choice (your self-image) has set a limit on what you may or may not have in life.

14
SOLVING SELF-IMAGE PROBLEMS
...with the Power Pause

Self-confidence Vision

*You can never get the right answer
as long as you're asking the wrong question*
--Darel Rutherford

Mary's problem

"*Who has a relationship problem they'd like to share with us?*"

This was the question a relationship counselor asked of the group taking his relationship seminar. Mary volunteered, and shared this problem:

"I have a co-worker who thinks I need advice on how to do my job. She keeps leaving these unwelcome notes on my desk to point out what she thinks I did wrong, with suggestions on how she thinks I should be doing it. She's not my supervisor and deeply I resent her constant critical notes. What can I do to solve this problem?"

BEING THE SOLUTION

Mary's problem sounds very much like a relationship problem when it's actually a self-image problem. If Mary had a powerful self-image, she would have easily handled the problem the first time it happened. She's now asking the seminar leader for a doing solution to a problem that must first be solved with a BEING change.

Your BEING choice (your self-image) has set a limit on what you may or may not have in life.
---Darel Rutherford

Change the blueprint
The most important discovery you could ever make in life would be to realize that your self-image is the mental blueprint for your life. How you picture yourself BEING in your chosen reality determines what you may or may not have from life, and your self-concept sets the pattern for how you will deal with life's circumstances.

Sow an act and you reap a habit.
Sow a habit and you reap a character.
Sow a character and you reap a destiny.
Charles Reade

If you think you're dumb, you'll get grades in school to prove it. If you think you're unlovable, you'll push away those who try to hug you. Your self-image has set the limits; the die is cast; your lot in life is fixed until you make the second most important discovery in life:

You CAN change your self-image.

Yes, you have the power to redefine your self-concept. You can change the blueprint that runs your life! If you didn't know how to make changes in it before, you do now. I've given you the perfect tool for the job. It's called a Power Pause!

A shortcut to solving your problem
When I first read John Harricharan's The Power Pause, I knew I had found the short cut to solving most personal problems. Once I decided to write this book (with John's permission), I knew I would need living examples of Power Pause problem solving! I offered to send

SOLVING SELF-IMAGE PROBLEMS

the three-step Power Pause formula free to RICHBITS subscribers who would share their problems and report their Power Pause success stories.

The response has been great, and I'll be sharing their problems, solutions and successes with you. I've separated problem types into four categories and devoted a chapter to each.

Problem types:
- Self-image or self-worth problems
- Relationship problems
- Health problems (Yes, even health problems)
- Prosperity Consciousness problems (as in how we relate to money)

In sorting out the problems submitted, I found that deciding the category into which some examples should be placed was not always easy. That's because every problem we face is really about who we have chosen to BE (our self-concept) as we relate to the problems of health, wealth and relationships.

Let's talk about Mary's problem as an example of someone seeking a relationship solution to what was actually more of a a self-image problem. Mary attended the relationship workshop, hoping to learn what she should be DOING in order to be more assertive. She complained about the coworker who continually left critical notes on her desk. She wanted advice on how she should deal with this person.

As I see it, Mary's question ("What should I DO to solve my problem?") was not the right question. She asked for a DOING suggestion when the appropriate question would have been as follows:

*"Who would I be BEING if
my co-worker's critical notes were no longer a problem?"*

Before we get into possible Power Pause solutions to Mary's problem, let's look at some of the possible ways her problem might be solved with a new BEING choice..

Possible DOING solutions for Mary:
- Mary could choose that, the coworker's notes would no longer disturb her peace of mind. By assuming a so-what attitude, she will have taken away her coworker's power to influence her feelings one way or the other.

BEING THE SOLUTION

- Mary, empowered by a new level of self-confidence, could confront her coworker and make a new agreement with her so that she no longer felt free to criticize, or...
- Mary could accept the coworker as a mentor, thank her for the good advice, become best friends with her. Then her new friend would no longer feel the need to criticize.

Any one of these three solutions could eliminate the problem, and there would, of course, be other possible DOING solutions. What you must see here is that each solution requires a change in who Mary will BE relative to her perceived problem.

With the above solutions in mind, I think you will also see that telling Mary what she should DO to deal with the coworker would not have served either her or the coworker. Mary would have been happy with what-to-do advice, and she might even have found the courage to act on it, but the doing part would have been out of character for her without a change in who she was BEING.

We have problems for a reason

The most interesting thing about having a serious problem is that it has become a grave problem only because we've made it significant. We've given our problem the power to disturb our peace of mind. If and when we take our focus off the problem and choose to BE its solution, we take away the problem's power, giving the power back to ourselves.

For Mary to get full value out of her coworker problem, she needs to rise above it. Mary has made the problem significant, and only she, can make it insignificant. Mary can only solve her problem with a BEING change.

You and I tend to look for a change in the other person or a change in conditions as the only possible solution to our problems. That solution will never happen until I change who I am being relative to my perceived problem! In any situation I face, I can control only me, and that's really the only control I need. If my problem is to be solved, I am the one who must change first.

So, how does Mary solve her problem?
Mary's visualization:

Mary needs to visualize her life, as it would be when the problem no longer exists. She must BE the one in that vision. She will

SOLVING SELF-IMAGE PROBLEMS

feel as she would if the problem were no longer a problem. To do the visualization, she doesn't need to find a solution to the problem; she needs to choose to BE the one without the problem. Once she no longer needs the problem, it will simply dissolve and disappear because of who Mary has become. Mary's vision will depend on which BEING choice best fits who she chooses to BE.

For example: Mary might visualize herself BEING and feeling powerful, amused and smiling when she finds the coworker's note on her desk, laughing at her previous reaction to finding one of those "nasty notes" She's now happy that she no longer feels the need to react. She tosses the note in the round file—unread.

*Life is really simple,
but we insist on making it complicated.*
--Confucius

It's not magic...

It's power—the power to choose who you will be. Once you make your new BEING choice and become fully committed to that choice, the Universe will provide the rest. The thing you must do to change the world you live in is to choose who you will be in that new reality. As Confucius has said, Life really is that simple, but we make it complicated by looking for a "if-I-could-only-change-them" solution to what's really our self-image problem.

Although a change in the way Mary chooses to deal with the problem would be a DOING solution, the real change needed will be in who she is BEING. If she decided to be assertive and tell her coworker to stop with the notes, she would need to muster the courage to do that. Being courageous would require a new BEING choice for Mary.

If she decided to ignore the notes, to not care, and to just toss them, she would need to reach a point of not caring what her coworker thought or wrote. This solution would also require a BEING change in Mary.

If Mary decided to thank that person for the good advice and make her a good friend, that would probably require the biggest BEING change of all three solutions.

No matter what our problem category, the solution to it will boil down to the same thing: a change in who we are BEING relative to whatever seems to be our problem.

BEING THE SOLUTION

Perhaps one of the examples in this chapter will fit your situation and allow you to see past your relationship problem to BEING its solution. It may help to remember that the solution to your problem will always be in choosing out of your box.

A Self-image problem

J. T. (we'll call him Jason) wrote,

> *My most pressing problem is a lack of self-esteem and personal belief in myself. Although I've been told by most people I come into contact with that I help them a lot and make them feel good about themselves, I'm the one in a perpetual state of low level depression. I am constantly listening to motivational tapes, and I choose every opportunity to take motivational seminars, and yet I still have an incredible amount of self-doubt and fear. I am a recovering alcoholic for 18 years, so I think that may have a lot to do with my problem.*

My answer to Jason:

Jason, you don't own the patent on having low self-esteem. Most of us have, or once had, a self-esteem problem. Most of us are in the process of successfully growing our self-confidence. As one of those self-doubters, I started life deeper down in that negative self-image hole than most, and had farther to climb to find real self-confidence.

Today, I'm actually grateful to a father who undoubtedly helped put me in that emotional hole with his frequent verbal put-downs. Looking back on my life, I can see that I've climbed the self-confidence ladder to a higher level of self-worth than I might otherwise have reached. If I hadn't started my climb from so far down in the well of self-doubt, I might not have had the powerful motivation I needed to find my way out. I only wish I had known, back then, about the Power Pause solution to self-worth problems. It would have made the climb out of my box so much quicker and easier.

My problem: I had taken my father's criticism to heart and made it part of my self-talk. The solution to my problem (although I didn't know it then) would have been to simply change the pattern of my thinking.

SOLVING SELF-IMAGE PROBLEMS
Jason's Power Pause Logic;

If you're like Jason, your problem stems from your habitual way of thinking about yourself—your self-talk. And your way out of that hole is simply to side-step your self-doubting by replacing your negative *I'm-not-okay* self-talk with a vision of a new confident you.

The question to ask yourself, all you Jasons, is:
*"Who would I be BEING if
I no longer doubted myself or felt depressed?*

How would you be acting; how would you be feeling; what would you be doing if you were BEING joyfully self-confident and sure of yourself?

A Jason's Power Pause Visualization:

In your visualization you will see yourself BEING totally self-confident and self-assured. You are feeling as you would feel if you hadn't one speck of self-doubt. In this vision, everyone you meet is inspired by your presence. They are awed by who you are BEING. You are the perfect example of self-confidence and self-esteem. You bubble over with enthusiasm, really feeling good about who you are. Everyone you meet each day walks away from that encounter empowered and feeling good about themselves because your self-confidence and enthusiasm for life is catching. Knowing that you are making a difference in their lives inspires you to even greater levels of self-confidence!

How does it feel to be that powerful? Capture that feeling! The power behind your Power Pause visualization is in the feeling you put into it. Allow yourself to feel joyful and enthusiastic as you paint that winning picture of yourself. That feeling of well-being has the power to bring you out of your hole; using the Power Pause to maintain that feeling will keep you out.

Feeling good about yourself is the key to changing your self-image. Declaring a Power Pause every time you hear self-doubting mind chatter will change the pattern of your thinking, and your changed thinking will automatically change who you are. You will have used the Power Pause to change the mental blueprint that has been running your life.

BEING THE SOLUTION

Fear of sales/promotion

Dr. P. N. G. (we'll call her Nancy) wrote:
> *I'm afraid of dealing with the sales/promotion of the products—even products that I whole-heartedly believe in.*

Dr. Nancy refers here to a top-quality high-potency nutritional supplement, one proven superior to most others on the market. As proof of its quality, Nancy has available clinical proof that these supplements made a significant difference in the wellness of people with a large variety of serious health problems. Yet she is afraid to recommend this health-enhancing vitamin supplement to her patients. Why? In some circles, it is considered unethical for a doctor to profit from the sale of products to a patient. The logic in this ethics problem escapes me, but Dr. Nancy has bought into it big time..

Dr. Nancy has received sufficient coaching on the possible DOING solutions to product promotion. None of that coaching has or will work for her until she changes how she perceives herself in the doctor/patient relationship. She'll need to choose a new way of BEING before she can successfully recommend these exceptional products to her patients.

Dr. Nancy's Power Pause logic:

Dr. Nancy, as a doctor, you are absolutely certain that this product would make a big difference in your patients' health and in the quality of their living, yet you hesitate to tell them about it. You'd rather let them continue to suffer with their health problem than risk being unethical. You may need to rethink that logic.

This is especially true since I know that you could arrange for your patients to receive these superior vitamins direct from the manufacturer. They could obtain the vitamins at the lowest possible wholesale price, and you would also receive a commission (residual income) for as long as your patient continued to use the product. That would be a win for both you and your patient. How could your patients object to that...especially if they had the same opportunity to earn residual income by recommending the product to friends?

A Power Pause visualization for all like Nancy:

--See yourself offering alternative solutions to your patients' health problems—problems that can't be solved

SOLVING SELF-IMAGE PROBLEMS

> *through chiropractic adjustments. In your visualization, your patients would read about the amazing restored-health benefits others had from using the product and immediately be anxious to try it. They read about this in your waiting room from a notebook filled with many such improved-health examples. In this vision, you are not selling: they are asking YOU how they may obtain the product!*
>
> *Every day, your patients are thanking you for providing such a simple solution to their health problems. Each of these grateful patients is recommending the product to their friends. Each week, you feel more prosperous as you deposit your commission checks. Many of your patients boast that their vitamins are now free because their commissions more than cover the cost*

The solution to your fear-of-selling problem is to change your BEING vision into one of recommending a great product to patients who deserve to know about it. The Power Pause is the appropriate tool for maintaining that vision until it becomes your reality. With this tool you will rewrite the blueprint that runs your life. Visualization works because your subconscious doesn't know the difference between your perceived reality and your vision. Acquire the Power Pause habit so you can maintain that vision until it becomes your new reality.

If you will, persistently replace your fear of recommending the products with the vision of happy, healthy patients, your fear will fade away and disappear. You will also find that you like yourself for having helped patients find true health. And you will soon see residual income as the means by which you will retire and live comfortably the rest of your life. Faithfully paint that picture for your subconscious and that retirement income must eventually become your reality.

Take your problems out of the basket

H. P. (we'll call her Harriet) wrote:

> *There are so many things I am interested in that it is difficult to focus in on a major goal. At fifty-seven years of age, I still haven't got it together. At one time my goal was to be a motivational speaker, and I have done some of that for a few years. I've wanted to write, and my children are very precious to me.*

BEING THE SOLUTION

Harriet's Power Pause logic:

If age seems to be your handicap, know this, I'm 79 years old, and I still haven't gotten it all together, either. Actually, I did get it all together once, and then I couldn't remember where I put it! :-) When you're not sure where all the pieces go, it sometimes helps to laugh about it.

If you're like Harriet with a basket full of problems, they would be more easily solved if you took them out of the basket and prioritized them. I'm not saying you can't solve all your problems with the Power Pause approach; I'm saying that you may want to deal with your problems one at a time. When you view problems all lumped together into one basket, they can seem overwhelming and unsolvable.

A visualization for all the Harriets:

See yourself taking your problems out of the hat, focusing on one at a time. See yourself rising above each problems, BEING its solution. You have now prioritized your problems, dealing with them in the order of their importance. You feel great about yourself because you're, finally, in charge of your life. You feel more alive and powerful now, more than you have ever before.

I solved a similar problem of having too much on my plate by asking myself, "Who I would be being if I had time for writing my book?"

My problem with finding time:

Before I got serious about getting this book written, I had that problem of not having enough time. My book had been on the top of my list for several months, but nothing was happening. I was kept busy publishing two newsletters, answering email from subscribers. I also attended numerous meetings each week. No time was left for the most important item on my list. The book was important but not urgent, and therefore, was not getting done.

In preparation for a Power Pause visualization, I asked myself,
Who I would be BEING if
I were writing on my book at least four hours daily
with full intention of meeting a scheduled deadline?

As soon as I formulated the question, the answer became obvious, and the visualization I needed became clear. To focus on

SOLVING SELF-IMAGE PROBLEMS

getting the book written, I had to give up being who I was being for a lot of people in my life.

Notice that the problem of having insufficient time for what we really want, almost always seems to be about having too much to do. But, in truth, the size of your to-do list is never where the real problem lies. The problem lies in not being clear about **who** you want to be so that you can choose the best path for getting you there. Who I was being was publisher of two different newsletters and a guru to my many subscribers. Who I needed to BE—how I needed to see myself—in order to get the book written was as the author of a best-selling book.

Without that focus, my number one priority, each morning, was to respond to my subscribers' questions before I did anything else. To make the not-enough-time problem go away, I had to make answering emails non-urgent and move the writing of my book to being the most important item on my to-do list.

Notice that changing my focus only seems to be about changing what I would DO. To get real value out of this example, you must see that changing what I would be doing required a major BEING change.

In my case, the visualization process was not necessary. Visualization is the blueprint for transforming yourself into BEING the one who has the problem handled. My problem was solved the minute I chose to BE the one who had put the writing of my book above all other priorities. But for the purposes of this discussion, this is what my visualization might have looked like had it been necessary.

My Power Pause visualization:

I see my daughter, Sherry, reading all incoming email, responding where necessary, printing out those messages which I must answer personally. I have reduced my counseling commitments to one or two a week. I now publish only one weekly newsletter, RICHBITS. I no longer attend numerous meetings. Now that I'm free of most everything that would keep me from my writing, I'm writing at least four hours every day. I see my book being finished within six months.

Once I created that vision, I became the one who would be finishing the book in six months. With that BEING choice, I could no longer be a health guru for a thousand subscribers to my Health, Wealth and Wisdom Newsletter. I could no longer be a personal prosperity-consciousness coach, urgently answering dozens of RICHBIT requests for advice each day. As a result of my BEING change, the reasons why my book wasn't being written no longer stood in my way. This book was written within that deadline.

Had I tried to change what I was doing without changing who I was BEING, the problem would not have been solved, because the urgency to answer all email daily would have still been there at the top of my to-do list, bugging me. I hope this helps you see the potential life-changing value in using the Power Pause to solve almost any problem; it works by changing your vision of reality, allowing you to make a new BEING choice.

When you know where you're going,
deciding which path to take will be easy
--Darel Rutherford

A Power Pause Success Story:

J. K. (we'll call her Jane) wrote,

I had a situation at work where someone else was being assigned clients that I thought should be mine. I was really upset and hurt. Mostly hurt and feeling unworthy. I declared a Power Pause, relaxed, focused on all the good that surrounded me, knowing that as one door closes, another opens. I knew that I had a gift to share, period. God would use my talents, and I gave thanks for the peacefulness that I felt, knowing the truth with a capital T.

Well, suddenly the floodgates opened and I have been getting new referral clients, great and interesting clients that are closer to home. I do not have to travel as much AND I was offered a second job (somewhere else) that is completely different from my first and allows me to soar. I just feel really blessed.

I have also taught the Power Pause to some of my clients and they say it makes them feel better and they can function better. I serve special clients with special health needs.

Jane's success story is just another example of what always happens with a change of consciousness. When you can see beyond the apparent condition of lack to the vision of who you would be BEING if

SOLVING SELF-IMAGE PROBLEMS

there were no lack, your impoverished condition will have no reality in which to exist. The pipeline of plenty is now open, and the lack is gone.

On feeling rejected

T. O. (we'll call him Tom) wrote:

> *When I thought about becoming rich, I had a feeling of rejection (a why-would-you-want-that attitude) from those close to me. Doing this exercise brought up a lot of old memories for me when I would be excited to tell my family or friends about something I wanted to pursue—something that was really important to me, and my goal or vision would not be accepted. This led to a feeling of being held back by those close to me.*

Tom's Power Pause logic:

If you're like Tom, your problem stems from allowing yourself to feel that you need someone else's approval for your decisions. By needing their approval, you give away your power. There's a hidden advantage in making them responsible for your decisions in life; by giving them the power to "hold you back", you can blame them, instead of yourself, when you end up not having what you wanted.

This is your way of setting yourself up to fail. You will need to replace your didn't-get-their-approval reason for failure with a vision of yourself succeeding in spite of their non-support. Ask yourself, "What would my life be like if I were as rich as I could ever want to be and didn't care one whit what THEY thought, one way or the other."

The question for all the Toms,

*Who would I be BEING if
I no longer needed anyone else's approval for what I do?*

Your Power Pause visualization:

See yourself celebrating the opening of your new store. Imagine looking at a sales report for the weekend with a sales figure that far exceeds your expectations. You have a grand sense of satisfaction about this new venture, knowing that you made the decision to open this store completely on your own without asking family, friends or anyone else for their approval. It feels great that you no longer need their approval in order to feel good about yourself!

BEING THE SOLUTION

Your vision of a new reality must be in present time consciousness. Declare a Power Pause to reinforce that vision every time you have self-doubts.

How do I stay elated?

D. R. (we'll call her **Dianne**) wrote,
I am reading the Eric Butterworth book, <u>Spiritual Economics</u>. He talks over and over about the importance of becoming centered in God-substance, of realizing that God will provide whatever we need (and want), but we must have the consciousness which corresponds. So how do I become centered in this idea of God-substance? I sometimes get this feeling of elation and pure joy when I think about the marvelous plan God has created for us all, and in those moments, I feel perfectly safe and happy knowing that I am part of God's glorious plan. The problem, of course, is in maintaining this feeling. Any help you can give me is greatly appreciated.

Dianne's Power Pause logic:

I agree with Eric Butterworth that God will provide whatever we have the corresponding consciousness to accept, but I disagree with the idea that concentrating on being centered in God-substance is the answer to having what you want from life. Without trying, you are already centered in God-substance, and you already have what belongs with you by right of consciousness—by right of your current BEING choice.

Wanting more from life is a waste of time until you acquire the consciousness to accept it by making a new BEING choice. The real truth is that you can't have IT until IT belongs to you by right of consciousness. Acquiring the consciousness (changing your self-concept) is the first step in the process of having the life you want. The feeling of elation and pure joy that comes with your changed consciousness is the presence of God expressing in and through you as you.

I suspect that a great many people on this planet believe that God has some sort of divine plan for their lives, but I have news for them. If they sit rocking on their back porch, expecting God to plow the field and plant the corn, they're in for a big disappointment. God will do for you, only that which He does in and through you as you. God's plan for you is that you reap the harvest only if YOU plant the seed.

The seeds you and I have to plant are seeds of thought. God has said, "You shall become what you think about." You've already done that; you thought your thoughts and are now reaping the harvest of those thoughts. If you don't like the fruits your thoughts have produced, you have the power to change your mind. I've given you the tool for that mind change. It's called a Power Pause.

When we know what God is,
we shall be Gods ourselves.
--George Bernard Shaw

God's plan for you

God's plan for you is that you grow in consciousness, finding with each new choice made that you've taken another step down the path toward self-discovery. You have the power of God behind your "I am" statement, and you've been left on your own to discover that you have this power. The game plan is that you be rewarded every time you create a new reality for yourself through the rediscovery and exercise of your power of choice.

It's also part of the plan that you live with the consequences of having chosen poorly. So, your BEING poor was part of the plan. The plan was that you experience being poor, so that when you grow tired of being poor, you would be ready to change your mind, and to be able to finally appreciate BEING rich. God's plan is not that you be rich or poor, but that you discover your power of choice. Other than that, sorry, there is no plan.

God's plan is that you and I will finally come to realize that we are Gods individualized. He gave you and I the power to choose who we would BE and the guarantee that we would reap the fruits of our choice. What more could He do for us? He gave us the magic wand (the power of thought) and left us alone, each to discover his/her own inner power. To do more would interfere with our power of choice, and we have His guarantee that He won't do that.

Before you can have that better life, you must realize that you already have everything that belongs to you by right of consciousness—by right of your previous choice of who to BE. Wanting more won't get it for you. Having what you want will require a change in consciousness. When you're ready for that quality-of-life change, you can use the Power Pause to change the blueprint that controls your life.

If you think God has a plan for you, here's your question:
*Who would I be BEING
if I knew that I, not God, chose the reality I now experience?*

A visualization for all Diannes:

In your Power Pause vision, you are elated and filled with pure joy in the awareness that you have created a new reality filled with all that you've ever wanted from life. You are empowered by the realization that you have the power to create your own reality by simply choosing who you will BE in it. You now see that you are always centered in God-substance and you are choosing a new and bountiful reality in full awareness of your God-given power. You feel better about yourself than ever before because you now know that you are BEING the source of your own good.

Just don't forget to say thanks to the spirit of God in you for giving you the power of choice and for allowing you to BE who you are!

The need-to-please disease

Note: The following is not a letter from a subscriber. It is a quote from the July-Aug 2000 issue of O, the Oprah magazine.

Oprah Winfrey says,
I was 40 years old before I learned to say no. Like Jane Fonda and Shay Youngbloood, I was consumed with the disease to please. The word yes would be out of my mouth before I even knew it.

...I spent my life giving everything I could to almost anyone who asked. I was running myself ragged trying to fulfill other people's expectations of what I should do and who I should be.

...I had to first get clear about who I was before I could beat the disease to please. When I accepted that I was a decent, kind and giving person—whether I said yes or no—I no longer had anything to prove. I was once afraid of people saying 'Who

does she think she is?' Now I have the courage to stand and say, 'This is who I am.'

Oprah's Power Pause logic:

Notice that Oprah cured her need-to-please disease by changing who she was BEING. This need to please is a self-image problem. If you can't say no, it's because you need other peoples' approval to survive. Oprah says this need for approval comes from having your "personal boundaries violated as a child." Whatever the root cause of this disease, you'll never be able to stand tall and be yourself in this world until you learn to BE the one who can say "no."

To remind herself, Oprah keeps these words at her desk:

Never again will I do anything for anyone that I do not feel directly from the heart. I will not attend a meeting, make a phone call, write a letter, sponsor or participate in any activity in which every fiber of my being does not resound yes. I will act with the intent of being true to myself.

Saying *yes* is easy, because it goes with the flow and allows you to be the nice guy; saying *"no"* is not so easy, because it goes against the grain. It takes guts to say *no*. Saying *no* requires standing tall, knowing whom you are. Finding the personal power to say "no" is a big part of the self-discovery process.

To create your Power Pause visualization for overcoming the need-to-please disease, ask yourself who you would be BEING if you liked yourself so much that you no longer needed their approval?

Oprah's question for you might be,

*"Who would you be BEING if
you had the courage to stand tall and say, No,
sorry, that request doesn't fit in with who I'm Being?"*

The Power Pause Visualization:

If the "need-to-please" disease is your problem, create an image of yourself having the power to say no. Then, every time someone asks you to do something that doesn't feel right, declare a Power Pause and revisit that image of being powerful, saying no. Before long, you will find that you have finally overcome the "need-to-please disease." You will love yourself

BEING THE SOLUTION

when you can stand tall and say, as Oprah says, "This is who I am, and I say NO."

Do yourself a favor and read Oprah's complete article, *What I Know for Sure*, in each issue of O, the OPRAH MAGAZINE. This magazine is filled with many inspiring, life-changing articles such as this.

To subscribe to O, call toll free, 888-446-4438.

The Power Pause habit

The greatest thing you could do for yourself, in terms of changing the quality of your life, would be to get the Power Pause habit. It's the magic tool that sidesteps your ego's resistance to change.

In each of the above examples, a self-image stood in the way of solving the problem, and a BEING change solved the problem. That's because our problem, as we have perceived it, is never the real problem. The real problem is with our perspective and the solution to that problem will always be in changing our perspective.

Knowing that to be a fact, I never cease to be amazed at the number of people who send me their problems in exchange for the Power Pause formula, and then tell me weeks later that they haven't found time to use the process. That's as silly an excuse as the woodsman I heard about who was about to lose his job. He was explaining that he couldn't chop as much wood as his boss expected because he didn't have time to stop cutting wood and sharpen his axe.

The woodsman in that story has two choices:
- He can stop cutting wood and sharpen his axe.
- He can blame losing his job on not having time to sharpen his axe.

And as I see it, you have two choices:
- You use the Power Pause regularly and create the life you want.
- You can not use it and complain about not having time.

The key to having life BE the way you've always wanted it is to change your self-image by making a new BEING choice. The tool for that job is the Power Pause. The choice is yours; sharpen your axe or you won't be cutting much wood.

If you don't have the Power Pause habit yet, read the following instructions again, and then, <u>set this book down and do the exercise</u>.

SOLVING SELF-IMAGE PROBLEMS
The Power Pause Exercise:

Here's how I want you to try it out. First, I want you to think about your worst problem. But don't just think about it, notice how you feel when you think about it; experience your fears and self-doubts, full-blown. Allow your fears to really take over for a moment.

- Then declare a Power Pause and go to that peaceful place in your mind. Really go there and experience being totally at peace for a full minute.
- Once you are at peace, allow yourself to visualize yourself BEING whoever you would be BEING if the reason for your problem were eliminated entirely. Feel as elated and joyful as you would feel if your problem were no longer a problem and your fear had been conquered.
- Say, "Thank you, God". It's important here that you be truly grateful that you problem is solved.

Time out. Stop reading now and do the exercise!

And now that you've done the exercise, how does it feel to be back in charge of your life? So, what's between you and acquiring the Power Pause habit?

After you've done the Power Pause a few times, you'll find your moment of peace coming automatically and immediately with each Power Pause declared. This allows you to go directly into your visualization.

As fear dulls your axe; from time to time, use your Power Pause vision to sharpen your axe. Once you've acquired the Power Pause habit, it should take you less than three minutes to cancel out fear and self-doubt each time it pops up. If sharpening your axe takes less than three minutes, wouldn't it make sense to sharpen it every time it gets dull—each time you experience self-doubt or fear? Get the Power Pause habit and take charge of your life!

Your self-esteem is determined by how you think and feel about yourself. You can increase your self-esteem if you will remember all the good things you've done in your life. The secret to building self-esteem is to just keep doing good things and keep remembering them!

Congratulations! You now have the power to transform the quality of your life forever!

In the next chapter, you will learn how the Power Pause can be used to solve relationship problems.

The Power Pause
Your way past the resistance

"Simple Solution to all Problems"
The Power Pause is the perfect formula for the simple solution to all problems. How do I know this? In all my 35 years of teaching the new thought philosophy, I've never seen anything work so quickly to change the quality of lives—Darel Rutherford.

- Hattie Pembrook used it to convert her unhappy marriage into a loving relationship.
- Sherry Jaramillo used it to permanently rid herself of migraine headaches
- Marie Mays, after five years of struggling, increased her massage business by 33% in only one month
- Dolores Jackson, after two years living in poverty, used it to land a song-writing contract in the music industry and a new job in just one week
- Jim G. used it to change his attitude from "ready to quit," to "my boss retired and left me the business" in six months
- Rev. Toni LaMotta's transformation in consciousness landed her the minister's job in a church ten times larger than the one she left. Three months after taking that position, she had increased attendance there by 55%, teaching these principles!

15
SOLVING RELATIONSHIP PROBLEMS
...with the Power Pause

Loving Relationship Vision

To solve your relationship problem
you must make a new BEING choice
--Darel Rutherford

A plea for help

When Hattie Pembrook first learned about the Power Pause, she wrote that she was tired of having her feelings hurt by a husband who constantly said unkind things. She wondered if the Power Pause would help to create a relationship with a man who adored her. Judging from her plea for help, I assumed the relationship to be all over but the shouting. But I was wrong!

A Power Pause Success Story

After using the Power Pause, Hattie Pembrook wrote,

My first attempt at the Power Pause was to think about what it would be like to be in a relationship with a man who adores me. Then I wondered if I could feel what it would be like having that relationship with the man I already have, my husband. So, I decided to feel good about being with him and seeing and feeling him loving me so very dearly.

One day we were in the car and he was feeling angry with me about something, which is not unusual. Instead of trying to respond with reason or logic, or get defensive, I turned my head, looked out the passenger window, and did the Power Pause. In a matter of seconds, he turned around and told me how sorry he was and how much he loved me. I was shocked, not so much about what he said, but that he had dropped the berating and was expressing his love for me. I was mesmerized and delighted.

Hattie's happy ending is a real living example of the seemingly miraculous and sometimes instantaneous changes that can happen in a relationship as a result of using the Power Pause for changing your own attitude and perspective. But it's really not a miracle; it's the law—a spiritual law—The Law of Correspondence.

Once you change who you are BEING, everyone in your reality will adjust to the new you.
--Darel Rutherford

Please don't misunderstand what happened here between Hattie and her husband. The Power Pause is not the means by which you can cast a spell on the other person and get them to change. The problem is not with them; it's with you. The Power Pause works its magic by changing who you are BEING relative to what you have perceived the problem to be. The other person's change will be in response to the BEING change in you and your problem will seem to have solved itself.

You have the power to change your reality. You've always had that power, but now, you have the tool for implementing the change. It's called the Power Pause. So use it!

What needs fixing

Before you choose to abandon a relationship that's not serving you, you might want to look at the real problem. Otherwise, when you leave to escape the problem, you may be taking the problem with you. As with all problems, a relationship problem is almost never what it appears to be. A closer look will reveal that the real problem is in whom you've chosen to BE relative to what has seemed to be the problem with the relationship.

SOLVING RELATIONSHIP PROBLEMS

I'd be willing to bet, that when you finally come to use the Power Pause to change how you relate to your perceived problem with the relationship, that problem, will dissolve and disappear.

Other men are lenses
through which we read our own minds.
--Ralph Waldo Emerson

In each instance of sharing problems, it will seem that a change in the other party's attitude would solve the problem. Instead, the solution lies in changing who you are being as you relate to the problem. If you have a relationship problem, perhaps you'll find your own problem and its solution in the following examples.

When choosing out of a relationship problem
make sure you're not taking the problem with you.
--Darel Rutherford

Relationship Problem Types

I've classified relationship problems into categories so that you can pick the one that would best apply to your situation. For each problem, I've offered:
- A logical way of thinking about the problem,
- A question that might help you see yourself BEING the solution
- A Power Pause visualization that will assist you in picturing a reality without the problem.

Notice that coming up with the answer for a problem is always easy. Because no matter what the problem seems to be, the solution will always be the same. To solve any relationship problem, you need only change your way of relating to the problem, and the problem will, most probably, be solved.

The following are relationship problem types we'll discuss:
- When they try to get you back in the box
- Giving your power away
- Handling criticism with the Power Pause
- Emotional abuse

BEING THE SOLUTION

- It's all their fault
- Getting even won't make you wealthy
- Worried about being sued

When they try to get you back in the box

Camelia wrote:
> *I feel I am still connected to my father...like an umbilical cord connecting me to his low thoughts and aspirations for his children—his need to keep us small so he can feel in control and superior, the "owner."*

Power Pause logic for all you Camelias:

My father also had a reputation for controlling others with a sharp tongue; he was good at putting people down. If my father's intention was to make me feel inferior, his faultfinding worked. I suffered from a severe case of inferiority complex. It took me years to outgrow my tendency to diminish myself as I continued to replay the tape he helped me make.

Feeling inferior in his presence, I saw my father as someone with the right to judge me. To gain back my self-respect, I had to eventually take him off that pedestal. When I finally rescinded his judging rights, I came to see his faultfinding as simply overcompensation for his own inferiority complex. His put-downs were his way of cutting others down to his size. It was when I stopped needing my father's approval that I began the slow process of regaining my personal power.

Camelia's real problem was not with her father, but in whom she had chosen to BE in that relationship. She'd given away her power and lost it for herself in the process. He will have that power over her for as long as she chooses to BE in his power.

Any time we allow ourselves to believe that we need someone else's approval, that person has great power over us. We may convince ourselves that we didn't give them the power—that they took it—but we're only kidding ourselves. The fact remains that we gave away our power and only we can take it back. Camelia alone can take her father off the pedestal of power on which she's placed him. So Camelia, and anyone else with the same problem, here's the question that would point you to your way out of that box:

SOLVING RELATIONSHIP PROBLEMS

If you have Camelia's problem, Ask yourself:
*Who would I be BEING
if I took away my father's right to control me?*

I would suggest for your visualization that you picture yourself changing places with your father.

Your Power Pause visualization:
Your father is looking up to you, because you are ten feet tall and he's only two feet tall. He has lost his power to control you. You feel amused at his put-downs. You laugh at his efforts to keep you in your box. You no longer need his approval. You've given yourself back all the power you will ever need to make your own independent decisions. You are back in charge of your life!

Once you've actualized the benefit of this visualization and regained your personal power, you will look back at your father's need for control and laugh about it. You won't hate him for who he has been or hasn't been for you; you'll feel a little sorry for him and a little silly for having given him power to control you. You'll thank him for giving you the problem that you've just outgrown.

Another example of power given away
L. J. (we'll call her Leona) was obviously having a bad day. When I asked why, she explained that she had been criticized and put-down by three different people in the past week. She had taken their criticism to heart and was still reacting to it when I saw her. Then I, in turn, added to her upset by telling her that something she was doing for me hadn't been done as requested. This just wasn't her week for feeling good about herself. I decided it was time to introduce Leona to the Power Pause.

But first I suggested that she had probably earned the criticism she received from them (yet another blow to her wounded ego). To explain, I said, "You are no longer the same person you were a year ago when you first married; you've obviously grown in consciousness." Her face brightened, and she said, "You're right, I have grown!" Then I continued, "You've come out of your box, but your husband and your sister keep trying to put you back into the old box. They need you in

BEING THE SOLUTION

there, being who you were before. This is so they can feel comfortable being with you."

I continued, "These two assume the right to criticize you, for not living up to the unwritten agreement you had with them, back when you were the old you. You broke that agreement the moment you changed your mind about who you would be. Those relationships are not working at the moment because you haven't made new agreements with them about who you're willing to be for them and they for you. Your choices: either you make the new agreement or live with their criticism."

"It boils down to this: you can no longer be who they want you to be; it's too late for that. They must accept you as you are <u>or not</u>. When they come to accept the new you, the new agreement will have been made."

Again she nodded in agreement and asked, "Yeah, but what do I do about the criticism?"

The strength of criticism
lies in the weakness of the thing criticized.
Henry Wadsworth Longfellow

Power Pause logic for Leona:

In the first place, their criticism is not the real problem; the problem is in how Leona has chosen to deal with that criticism. She can use the Power Pause to change her way of BEING with the faultfinding. So that it no longer has significance for her. Let's begin with the question.

If you're a Leona, the question for you is:
So, who would you be BEING
if their criticism was no longer a problem for you?

A Power Pause visualization for all Leonas

I see myself hearing their criticism and having no need to react to their attempts to get me back into my old way of being. In my vision I see myself being powerful and above their censure. I see myself understanding their problem and sympathizing with their need for the old comfortable me, but I'm not going back there just to please them. I feel great, BEING myself, liking myself as I am. I'm standing tall,

SOLVING RELATIONSHIP PROBLEMS

savoring this over-all sense of feeling good about myself. I feel empowered from having risen above their criticism.

A Power Pause solution:

If you have trouble reaching that self-assured state of mind, you might want to imagine the criticizers naked. Seeing them without clothes will bring a smile to your face, take the sting out of the criticism, and allow you to take the position of being unshaken by their words.

Using the Power Pause to solve a personal problem with a new BEING choice is your way of rising above that problem. It's you choosing a different way to BE as you view what you once thought was a problem. When you use The Power Pause to solve a problem, you change the problem into an opportunity for growing in consciousness.

Emotionally abusive

D. H. (we'll call her Della) wrote,

My husband is very negative and says things that at best annoy me and at worst hurt and enrage me. I think of them as being emotionally abusive. (This is similar to Hattie's story, but with a different ending.)

Later Della wrote,

There's a large amount of hurt, grief, anger and disappointment over the end of my marriage that I have yet to find a peace about.

Power Pause logic for Della;

When a marriage is on the rocks, the partners in that relationship often say things to hurt one another. When you're into the Destroy process in a relationship, the parties tend to berate each other, unconsciously hoping the other will make the first move to abandon the relationship. The Destroy process for a relationship is the means by which we detach ourselves from an alliance that no longer nourishes us. The hidden intent in the Destroy process is to make the other person wrong, so that you'll feel right about choosing out (detaching).

Again, the problem is never what it seems; the problem is in who you are BEING relative to the breaking up of the relationship. The key to solving that problem is in changing who you are being relative to the break up. So, all the Dellas out there, ask yourself this question:

BEING THE SOLUTION

Della's question:
Who would I be BEING if I were happy about being free of an hurtful relationship?

The key to dealing with the anger, grief, and hurt is to replace it with a happy thought. Visualize what your life would be like without the grief. How would it feel to be alive and free again (free to be yourself), loving yourself for who you are, happy and enjoying life?

A Power Pause visualization for Dellas:
I see myself free of upset and happy again! I'm going places, doing the things I like to do, and I am enjoying life. I see the rage and the annoyances are now gone and I am tranquil. I have many friends to keep me company and we do many fun things together. Now that the relationship is over, I can even see that my ex-husband's unkind words were just part of the process for ending a relationship that no longer served either of us. Now that the hurt and anger are gone, I am at peace with the world and myself.

When you can feel the joy of being free, your visualization is complete. Say, "Thank you, God."

Each time you feel anger, grief or fear, declare a Power Pause. When you've created the peaceful buffer between you and the grief, do your visualization. Each time you feel the joy and happiness of being a free soul, you'll be closer to being one. Before you know it, you will have become the free and happy soul in your vision.

It's all their fault
H. S. (we'll call her Helen) wrote:
No matter how positively I hold my consciousness on prosperity and even manifest it for myself and family, it is constantly impacted by the negativity of my partner's inability to see the glass half full, rather than half empty.

Power Pause logic for Helen:
If she used her prosperity consciousness to fill the glass, it would be neither half full nor half empty—but maybe running over? Maybe that's her solution to the problem?

SOLVING RELATIONSHIP PROBLEMS

We each are an individualization of God, with the power of the Universe behind every thought we think. With each and every thought, we unconsciously unleash that great power. That power "works by seeming not to work," producing poverty whenever we focus our thoughts on what we don't want.

Every negative thought we think produces a result; only our positive thoughts produce positive results. The last time I checked, each of us was in charge of our attitude and our thinking process. A negative attitude produces negative thinking, no matter who's doing the thinking (you or your spouse). If we will re-read Helen's words as she wrote them, we'll see that they are far south of being positive.

At the moment, it appears to Helen that her husband is the problem. The truth is that he's being whom he needs to be to correspond to her chosen way of relating to him; her BEING choice creates her expectations of him. Her praying in hopes of changing him won't solve her problem, because prayers designed to change the other person seldom work. Real power in life lies in being able change our reality, by transforming ourselves.

We do that by changing the pattern of our thinking with a new BEING choice. We can use the Power Pause to solve our problem by changing our relationship to the problem. Our lack of prosperity is a reflection of our own consciousness. Our transformation starts with the question.

The question:
*Who would I be BEING
if I suddenly realized that
my significant other was not the problem?*

Helen's Power Pause visualization:
Several of my authors' published books have become best sellers, resulting in a substantial increase in my income as their agent. My positive cash flow so far exceeds our expenses that even my husband feels positive about it. I love what I'm doing; business is great. The great new house we live in has a fantastic view of the mountains. Life couldn't be any better. My cup is full!

Helen, this is my imagination at work, not yours. But this is an example of what your visualization must look like if you are to change the vision that runs your life. Make no mistake about it. You do have a vision and your current condition of lack is kept alive by that vision. Your husband is your partner in it. You can take charge of and change the thought patterns that maintain that old vision by getting the Power Pause habit.

Getting even won't make you rich

G. P. (we'll call him **Pete**) wrote

I was divorced a year ago and am struggling to move forward! I want to be wealthy...I want to be able to help my children through college...and I think I want to show my wife I can do fine without her...if becoming rich can make her feel that she made a mistake, I want to do it!

Here's Power Pause logic if you're like Pete:

Your desire to get even with your spouse is not the type of motivation that can ever make you wealthy. Only positive emotions like enthusiasm and joyful anticipation can empower a person and move one toward becoming rich. Resentment is a power-draining emotion that takes you in the opposite direction. No matter how justified one feels in planning revenge, the one that gets burned is the one who builds the fire in their heart.

If you were sincere in your desire to be wealthy, your first step in that direction would be to forgive your ex-spouse, and the second step would be choosing to BE wealthy. Once one has chosen, you can begin to imagine what BEING wealthy would look like for you.

A Power Pause visualization for all the Petes:

I see myself going places, doing the things I've always wanted to do, but never before had time or the money for. Now I do! My new wife and I have just returned from our third ocean cruise this year.

As I sit here watching the sunset from the veranda of my beautiful new ocean-view home, I reflect that all my income is residual and flowing directly into my bank account. I don't even deposit the checks. I'm thankful that my wealth has allowed me to put each of my children through the college of their choice and even though we're no longer married, I now have a great relationship with their mother.

SOLVING RELATIONSHIP PROBLEMS

If you can create your vision of being wealthy and get excited about it, recalling that picture every time you have doubts, your dream must become your reality.

My suggestion is that you declare a Power Pause every time you think about getting even with your ex-spouse. By replacing the negative thought with a positive loving and forgiving one, you automatically change who you are being relative to what was once a problem, and the problem of wanting to get even will cease to exist.

This may not seem to fit

The next example may seem out of place in a chapter on relationships. But I think you'll eventually see that all problems can be solved by a change in the way we choose to relate to the perceived problem, and you'll agree that the following two problems belong in this chapter

Power Pause Success Story

M. D. (we'll call him Matthew) wrote:

> I had a very upsetting experience. I was attacked in a restaurant. I successfully defended myself, but in the mayhem, an innocent bystander got injured!
>
> *Bottom line ...I'm being sued. If proven guilty, I could go to jail! Or fined and cautioned, and still end up with a criminal record. Me, a professional businessperson.*
>
> *When all this started to happen, I felt like my world was dropping apart. I could see my long-established private practice going down the tubes. Bad newspaper headlines, effects on family, you name it, I was thinking about it. I spoke to my mentor, Darel Rutherford, about it, and he reminded me of the Power Pause.*
>
> *Using the Power Pause turned my head and belief system around. I still have to go through the hoops, but it's how I'm approaching them that has made the difference. The difference is, my life is no longer on hold. I no longer have the sword of Damocles over my head. Thanks to the Power Pause.*

Matthew said the worst part about the thought of going to court was the constant worry over the outcome. The Power Pause allowed him to take charge of the worrying. He told me that each time fear thoughts entered his mind, he declared a Power Pause. Setting aside the fear with a buffer of peace allowed him to visualize a positive outcome from the lawsuit. His life was no longer on hold.

If you have worry problems like Matthew, remember, you have the power to change who you will be and how you will relate to any problem. Once you've accomplished that change in consciousness, you'll feel the sense of power that always comes from taking charge of your life once more. You will feel in your heart the sense of elation that always comes from knowing who you are. In that moment of being reborn into a newly empowered sense of being, you will be a step closer to knowing and understanding the real source of your personal power.

As we move through life, we grow in consciousness, changing our minds from time to time about who we will be and how we will relate to life. Each change made in our relationship to life moves us a little further down the path of self-discovery. A relationship serves this growth process when it allows you to experience being yourself in it.

So, how powerful would you be if you no longer had anything to worry about and were supported in BEING yourself in every one of your relationships? And how powerful would your partners in that relationship be if, in the spirit of true love, they were being supported for being who they are? Love is a two-way street.

In my opinion, a relationship based on true love could not fail. That, of course, depends on one's definition of the word "love." Here's my definition:

Love is space that we create for each other to be who we are.
--Darel Rutherford

If a relationship were totally focused on providing this sort of freedom-to-be for each other, could it fail? I think not!

Think about that for a moment. My definition of love may very well be the most important thing you've read in this book, so far.

Your true purpose in life is to discover who you really are. If a relationship does not provide the sort of loving space in which you can BE yourself and grow, that relationship is not serving you!

Notice that once you set aside your romantic notion about what love is, my definition fits all relationships, including family, friends and your associates at work. If any relationship does not provide you with the opportunity to be yourself and to grow, it serves no real purpose in your life.

SOLVING RELATIONSHIP PROBLEMS

Your true purpose in life is to grow in consciousness, to become more and more aware of who you really are. The problems you face in life are the stepping stones that move you to the higher ground on the other side of the problem.

*The solution to almost any problem
is in changing how you relate to it.*
--Darel Rutherford

Your relationships allow you to experience BEING who you are at the moment. And when you change your mind about who you will BE, they should provide the space for that change of heart—a BEING change. Your Power Pause vision is the tool by which you will rewrite the script that runs your life.

In the next chapter you will learn you can actually use the Power Pause to improve your health.

BEING THE SOLUTION

RESIDUAL INCOME

This vision

can take you here

16
IMPROVING YOUR HEALTH

...with the Power Pause

Visualizing Good Health

*When my husband asked what I was doing
I told him, 'I'm killing cancer cells.'*

"...killing cancer cells"

When I visited my dentist, I was surprised to find Cindy, my favorite dental hygienist, back at work. The last time I'd had my teeth cleaned, I had been told she was terminally ill. When I asked her about that, she told me this incredible story:

Cindy said:

"For over a year, I was flat on my back in bed, paralyzed from the neck down, with brain cancer. I couldn't move a muscle, even to feed myself. I know my doctors had given up on me, but one day, I just made up my mind not to accept their verdict. I decided not to die!"

"Before long, my husband noticed something different about me. When he saw this new determined look of concentration on my face, he asked what I was doing. I answered, 'I'm killing cancer cells.' From that day forward, every day, I got better. Now, I'm completely cured of cancer

BEING THE SOLUTION
and happy to be back working again. My doctor just shakes his head in disbelief."

Think about that! If Cindy could cure herself of cancer, what could you do for your illness if you made up your mind to get well?

It is a part of the cure to wish to be cured.
Senca

My intention with this chapter is to convince you that there is a way out of your health problem. Once you believe that, you'll begin to look for a way to solve it. When you can believe in the possibility of good health for yourself, you will begin to visualize good health and to make your move in that direction.

The Power Pause as a healing tool

Often, when I suggest the Power Pause as a tool for solving health problems, I get that "are you kidding?" look and the raised eyebrows. We tend to think that good health is something we either have or don't have, when in fact, good health is actually a matter of choice. What? You don't believe that? I don't blame you for doubting me. But if you have even the slightest hope that I might be right, I challenge you to read on.

In the balance of this chapter, I intend to prove, with real-people examples, that even with supposedly incurable diseases, one can choose better health and then experience it. How does the Power Pause come into play? Being healthier, for you, will begin with your vision of what being healthy might look like for you and then in your decision to choose that better health for yourself.

Better health for you will actually begin with your intention to BE healthy. If you have a health problem you want solved, you will need to choose a different way of BEING relative to your health. If Cindy's story doesn't give you reason to hope, perhaps the other examples in this chapter will convince you that your health problem is solvable—once you've made up your mind to no longer BE sick.

The power to heal itself

When looking for a solution to our health problems, we often forget that our body has the power to heal itself. Within the cells of our body lives a self-healing miracle of nature called the immune system.

IMPROVING YOUR HEALTH

Given what it needs to stay healthy, that immune system stands guard on our health, ready and willing at all times to attack and repair any threat to our health.

If you suffer from some form of debilitating illness, your immune system is obviously not as healthy as is necessary to maintain adequate damage controls. To regain your health, you will need to nurse your immune system back to perfect health. The most important thing you could get from reading this chapter is that your immune system really needs help!

Your immune system needs your faith in the possibility of better health for yourself, but what it needs most from you is your determination to regain your health and then to stay healthy. Your immune system fights a losing battle in trying to keep you healthy if you've lost your faith—if you've decided to give in to a disease.

To get back your health, you must send an altogether different kind of message to your immune system.

You own it, now disown it

Your greatest barrier to regaining your health, will be your belief that that your health problem doesn't have a solution. Hopelessness is not an attitude that could ever make you well again. You can't solve any problem—health, wealth, relationship, or otherwise—until you first believe that the problem is solvable. Once you believe that, you will begin your search for the problem's solution.

Your belief system is so powerful that
once you see your health problem as unsolvable, it is.
--Darel Rutherford

Once you've bought into a health problem, you've given it power. By choosing to identify with that problem, you've made it a part of your BEING statement. Once your health problem becomes your reality, you no longer have a problem; that problem has you. You could also say that problem IS you. In each of the following examples of health problems being solved, the cure began as soon as that ailing person chose to disown their health problem.

Where did the cancer go?

Bobbie Nasci had been one of my bookkeepers for about six months when she announced that she would be taking two weeks off

BEING THE SOLUTION

work to have her semi-annual bone marrow transplant. This news came as a complete surprise to me. I had no idea that she had a serious illness.

I did, however, know enough about her personal life to ask this question: "Bobbie, why do you need bone cancer?" She was obviously shocked by my question, but said nothing. So I continued, saying, "I can understand why you needed bone cancer to escape a very unhappy relationship with an abusive husband, but that's over. You've been divorced for over six months. There's no longer a need for escape. You're already free. As I see it, you have no further need for bone cancer."

Bobbie made no attempt to respond, but I could tell my question had struck a nerve. She kept the appointment with her doctor, who did the usual semi-annual tests to check her condition. She came back from the doctor's office grinning like a Cheshire cat, to report:

Guess what, my x-rays showed I no longer have bone cancer! My doctor couldn't believe his eyes! He'd never seen total remission happen like this before.

Where did the cancer go? My guess is that it went away when Bobbie decided she no longer needed bone cancer.

Good health is not something to possess, it's a state of BEING—a choice.
--Darel Rutherford

About the immune system

Dr. Virginia Livingston-Wheeler has treated hundreds of cancer patients in her San Diego Clinic with remarkable results. She says:

We all have cancer in our bodies; its just that our immune system is keeping it in check... it's the breakdown of our immune system that allows cancer to grow... if you maintain a healthy immune system your chances of getting cancer are nil.
--Dr. Virginia Livingston-Wheeler
<u>The Conquest of Cancer</u>

When your immune system is healthy, your body has the power to heal itself. Bobbie and Cindy, who cured themselves of cancer, started the healing process in motion by first choosing not to be sick.

Once the image of BEING healthy became their chosen reality, the body's immune system got the message and did the necessary healing.
    Is that incredible? No, not really. You are an individualization of God with powers you haven't learned how to use. You have the power to choose to BE healthy. When you do, your immune system will get the message.

*The answer to cancer
will be found in the ways to prevent it.*
--Darel Rutherford

Good health is a choice

    If you are to regain your health, the first thing you may need to change is your attitude about it. You have the power to create your own reality; in fact, you've already done that concerning your health. If you've made up your mind that you have an incurable disease, your immune system can't override that decision. On the other hand...

*When you've made it your intention is to stay healthy,
your immune system will get the message.*
--Darel Rutherford

    When we can give our immune system everything it needs to stay healthy, including a healthy attitude, our chances of getting any debilitating disease will be nil. But once you have the disease, a healthy immune system could send that disease into remission.

Regaining control

    People with health problems tend to see themselves as victims of their illness. From a victim's point of view, their problems will seem unsolvable. The truth is that a simple change of attitude could make all the difference in your health. In the balance of this chapter, you'll find more examples of those who rebelled against their discomfort (dis-ease) and found their way back to health.
    If you've given in to it, your health problem is running your life. Isn't it time you put **you** back in charge? When you regain control of your life, spiritually and emotionally, your health problems will be improve-able. As with any other type of change you decide to make in your life, you must first rebel against the discomfort. Reject the pain;

choose good health and then create your picture of what improved health would look like for you.

You have more power to control your health than you have yet imagined. When you change your mind-set about who is in charge (you or your body), you can even control the pain.

Make the pain go away

I taught myself how to ride a bicycle the hard way on a bike much too large for the small boy riding it. My beginner's lesson: don't try your first ride barefoot! I learned that painful lesson when I wobbled that bike down the street and into the curb, scraping the flesh from my little toe clear down to the bone.

As I lay in bed screaming, the excruciating pain seemed unbearable. Even with my toe bandaged, I couldn't stand the weight of the sheet on my foot. My mother, a practicing Christian Scientist, sat on the edge of my bed to offer her words of comfort. What she said did more than comfort me. She actually showed me how I could make the pain go away!

She promised,

"Darel, if you want the pain to stop, just make up your mind that it doesn't hurt, and it won't."

With the faith of a small boy believing his mother, I said,

"Okay, it doesn't hurt."

I stopped crying, and like I had flipped a switch, the pain was miraculously gone, and I ran off to play.

Showing off

I couldn't wait to show off my new power. To impress my friends, I stuck pins in my arm—not just a pinprick, but all the way in, nothing showing but the head. I walked to school without a coat and didn't feel the cold. Don't misunderstand what I'm saying here. I didn't bravely endure the pain or the cold. The pain was no longer there. These were dumb things to do, but like a kid with a new toy, I reveled in my newly-found power.

After my first unhappy experience with numbed-lips dribble, I've never allowed my dentist to use his painkillers on me, even for a root canal. In fact, I've been known to doze off in the dentist's chair. Is that incredible? No, not really. It's not even extraordinary when you stop to think that hypnotists, have been demonstrating for years that the mind has power over the body—power to make pain go away, even the power to heal.

I often use mind-over-body power to get rid of the hiccups. I just snap my fingers and say, "Go away hiccups." and the hiccups are gone. You might want to try this the next time you get the hiccups. But I must warn you, that when you snap your fingers, you will prove to yourself whatever you expect to prove. If the hiccups don't go away, your mind power will have worked by seeming not to work.

Pain has a purpose

Pain sends a message that should never be ignored. But pain's real purpose is to alert you to a possible problem, not to keep you suffering. The pain message is sent from your nerve endings to your brain, telling you, "Move your hand, stupid; that stove is hot." You'd be wise to heed that early warning signal!

But once you've retreated to safety, the pain has already served its purpose. You no longer need it as a warning device, so why continue to suffer? It makes no sense to continue enduring the pain when you know how to make it go away. I'm not telling you that I don't feel pain. I do, but I have the power to make my pain go away whenever I choose. You also have that power!

I consider myself lucky to have had a mother who understood the power of the mind to control the body. Lucky for me that I learned that trick at a very early age. Actually, it's not a trick; it's a choice anyone can make. The only thing missing for you is your belief that it's possible. You have the exact same power to control pain, if and when you choose to believe in it and use it. It really is a choice you can make, so I challenge you with this question,

Who would you be BEING
if you made your pain go away?

Pain and fear are second cousins

Both your physical and your emotional pain can be controlled if you so choose. Both types of pain are messages, telling you to remove yourself from the source of your hurt as quickly as possible. With emotional pain, we often fail to heed the warning because we've become so attached to the other half of the problem—the other person involved.

Fear and pain are second cousins because both are early warnings of impending danger. Again, once you have been alerted and have taken appropriate action, neither fear nor pain serves a further purpose.

Fear warns you that you are about to lose something you hold dear. Once you accept that loss as a real possibility and make your move to avoid it, you have no further need for the fear. You solve fear problems when you rise to the challenge by facing the fear. Character is built through facing your fears and dealing with the pain.

*So, who would you be BEING
if you had faced your fear and moved past it?*

Stress is a form of fear. In the following success story, Sherry Jaramillo used the Power Pause to remove stress and eliminate her migraine headaches.

A Power Pause success story

Migraine headaches are often stress-related. When faced with deciding which of two obligations to meet, any indecision can cause stress. The stress-based headache is the result of a battle between "I want to" but "I can't" or between "I should" and "I shouldn't." In the end, stress is almost always, a conflict between choosing and not choosing.

Sherry Jaramillo said,

For years and years, for as long as I can remember, I've had frequent migraine headaches. All that time, I saw myself as the victim of those headaches. Why me, I asked? I had been told that these headaches were probably stress-related, but I hadn't a clue that there was anything I could do about it.

Then, I took my first step out of that box. I chose out, and looking back, it seems so simple. All that time and all that pain, and all I had to do was choose! I had finally made up my mind that it was time to get rid of the headaches, one way or the other!

Then I asked for counseling. That's when I was told that my headaches were not the real problem and neither was the stress that caused the headaches. The actual problem was in who I was BEING relative to the two conflicting ideas that were causing me to feel stressed.

Then I was told to use the Power Pause to visualize myself being who I would be being if there were no longer any stress. From that point on, every time I felt a headache coming on, I declared a Power Pause and visualized my life with no more headaches, feeling as I would if the headaches were gone. Every time I did a PP, I was able to get in touch with the two conflicting desires and/or obligations.

For instance: If my job-related duties interfered with making my husband's lunch, I felt stressed. But until I started doing the Power Pause, I didn't know what caused the stress. After doing a Power Pause on the problem, I was able to talk to my husband about my conflicting responsibilities. His response: "I'm a big boy. I can make my own lunch."

I was able to see through the stress and choose one of the two options. In another instance, if my housekeeping duties conflicted with my desire to do arts and crafts, I felt stressed. But each time I did the Power Pause, visualizing myself without stress, without feeling guilty about not doing the other. Living with the headaches was a terrible box, but now I'm free! Getting rid of the headaches was fantastic, but the greatest benefit to come out of doing the Power Pause was the great sense of personal power that came from taking charge of my thinking and rediscovering my power of choice.

- Notice that Sherry's headaches were the result of an emotional problem that lodged itself in the body in the form of a migraine headache.
- Notice that her health problem became solvable as soon and she made up her mind (chose) to get rid it.
- Notice that Sherry's first step in solving her health problem was to use the Power Pause to visualize a life without migraines.
- Notice that the solution to her health problem was in choosing a new way of BEING relative to the perceived problem.

Now, Sherry celebrates her newfound freedom from a debilitating health problem. The sad part about her victory over poor health is that she lived so many years of her life with a problem that was so easily solved. To this paragraph, Sherry says, "AMEN!"

BEING THE SOLUTION

A major cause and its solution

Pioneering research in the past decade has shown that the seven most deadly diseases (heart disease, cancer, stroke, diabetes, arthritis, osteoporosis, and Alzheimer's) and about 53 other diseases may be linked to one common cause—oxidative stress caused by free radical damage in the body. A free-radical is an oxygen atom seeking a replacement for its missing electrons.

Under ideal circumstances, the food we eat would contain enough anti-oxidants, and your immune system would produce enough of them to gobble up any excess free radicals and control the damage. Unfortunately, fast foods, over processed foods, and nutrient deficient produce makes it next to impossible for us to eat a healthy diet. And since we live in a polluted world, free-radical damage is now out of control. That's the other reason why your immune system desperately needs your help!

In his book, Healthy at 100, Dr. Robert D. Willix, writes:

> *The most important medical discovery in the last half-century concerns two substances called 'free radicals' and 'anti-oxidants' Free radicals have been linked to (at last count) about 60 diseases. We now have evidence that anti-oxidants can protect against, stop, and (in some instances) reverse the damage done by free radicals... These discoveries make clear that the most important single thing you can do, if you want to live long enough to dance the polka at your great-great-grandson's wedding, is to start an immediate regimen to make sure you get all the anti-oxidants you need—both through diet and through the use of nutrients and dietary supplements... I urge you to start taking antioxidant supplements now... You will see almost immediate, visible, tangible evidence that these substances are working to protect you from free radical damage. Patients who take this, report increased energy, positive changes in skin texture, and even loss of wrinkles—within a few weeks.*

The answer to cancer?

We've spent billions in a treasure hunt for a cancer cure. What if we are looking in the wrong place for the solution? What if the

IMPROVING YOUR HEALTH

answer to cancer was not in expensive drugs, but in the simple maintenance of a healthy immune system with anti-oxidant supplements? What if the answer to our health problems was a simple life-style change starting with a healthy attitude, and then in feeding our cells all the nourishment they need to maintain a healthy immune system?

Double blind clinical tests have proven that 1000-mg of vitamin C, given daily to heart patients reduces the incidence of heart attack by over 50%. Similar results were obtained when heart patients were given 450 IU of vitamin E daily. Bear in mind that only one of these two high-potency vitamins was given in each of these clinical studies. Doesn't that make you wonder, what if ...?

If only one optimal-potency vitamin, given daily, could make that much difference in the health of someone already diagnosed with heart disease, what would the effect be if we fed our bodies all the quality high-potency vitamins and minerals necessary to stay healthy on a daily basis? Would we even get sick? I don't think so!

The probable cause

In today's environment, your immune system can't keep up with free radical damage without your help. What it needs is your determined effort to stay healthy and your willingness to do whatever it takes, including a possible change in lifestyle.

If you are suffering from one of the 60 debilitating diseases mentioned in Dr. Willix's book, its probable cause is free-radical damage and its probable solution is an increased intake of anti-oxidants. Now that you know the cause and a possible solution, you can do something about your ill health. By taking Dr. Willix's advice to change your life style, eat a healthy diet, exercise, and take supplements, you could live to be 100 and "dance at your great-great-grandson's wedding".

Everything you find in this chapter has one purpose: to convince you that it's time for you to take charge of your health. The following examples of health problems solved should help to further convince you that there's hope even for you.

Fibromyalgia

Dr. Ray Strand's wife had Fibromyalgia for over 18 years. Early morning stiffness, mental fog, muscle spasm, fatigue and pain were daily occurrences with which she had learned to live. She had

BEING THE SOLUTION

thought being married to a doctor would help, but it hadn't. Because modern medicine has no cure for Fibromyalgia, Dr. Strand was frustrated in not being able to help his wife.

Then, one day, one of Mrs. Strand's friends gave her some nutritional supplements to try. She asked for her husband's approval to try them. Although he had spent 23 years advising his patients that they didn't need vitamins, he gave his okay.

Within a week, she was better, and within three weeks, she was back to her normal self and off medication. Dr. Strand said, "Obviously that got my attention! That's when I decided to read <u>The Anti-oxidant Revolution</u> by Kenneth Cooper." Ever since then, Dr. Strand has been treating patients with those diseases believing that the underlying cause of their degenerative disease was oxidative stress. The results he obtained from prescribing these high-potency vitamins have been nothing less than remarkable.

Diabetes

Even with Diabetes Type II, Dr. Strand has had several cases of complete remission when the patient followed his diet, took the recommended supplements and exercised on a regular basis. On Dr. Strand's web site, http://www.raystrand.com, you will find a description of the degenerative diseases and read about his successful treatment of them, all with nutritional supplementation. To learn his recommended dosage for a specific disease, you'll pay a modest fee for a pass-word, but his advice is well worth it. Again, I offer this information so that you'll have yet another reason for believing that there is a solution to your health problem. Once you see the light at the end of the tunnel of bad health, you will begin your move toward it. Until then you won't. This information is intended to turn on that light at the tunnel's end.

Candidas

My experience with the brand of vitamins Dr. Strand recommends is this: I had Candidas, a yeast condition probably caused by taking antibiotics, which tend to kill off friendly bacteria in the body. My Candidas symptoms: I got a headache if I ate bread, cheese, tomatoes, nuts, or sweets, and I couldn't drink coffee or beer. A medical Doctor prescribed *Nystatin* for my Candidas.

That prescription drug seemed to help, but one time when I was out of it, my friend, Dr. Norman Dawson, suggested that these supplements could be a better choice than my prescription drug. Three days after I started taking those vitamins, my Candidas symptoms were gone. I've been eating anything I wanted ever since, with no headaches.

The point of all this is to give you hope that there is a way out of your health problem. Vitamins don't cure anything, but a healthy immune system CAN cure you of what ails you. Now that you know this, YOU can give your immune system what it needs to keep you healthy.

But when you go looking for supplements, don't make the mistake of assuming that all vitamins are the same. They're not! To make a real difference in your health, you'll need a high-potency, quality-guaranteed vitamin manufactured in a FDA-registered facility that follows good manufacturing practices. Not many vitamins on the market today can guarantee pharmaceutical-grade quality.

Vitamin brands that brag about meeting RDA requirements are a joke because our government's **R**ecommended **D**aily **A**llowance is a joke. Those standards were not created to deal with today's environmental pollution and our nutrient depleted soils. RDA potency levels fall way short of that necessary for keeping you healthy. Again, not many brands on the market can offer the optimal potency guarantee.

It begins with an attitude change

Good health for you will be more than the absence of illness; it will be the rising up of your spirit. When you take charge of your health you'll find a new sense of aliveness, energy and joy flowing through you. Your good health begins with an attitude change.

The first step in the process of regaining your health will be to make up your mind to no longer accept your illness as the standard for your life. Set a new standard! Choose to be healthy, and then create your vision of what better health would look like for you. Once you've created your BEING-healthy vision, use the Power Pause daily to recharge that vision several times daily. When your belief system accepts good health as your new reality, you'll begin the process of nursing your immune system beck to perfect health with a healthy diet, exercise, and supplementation..

In Bobbie Nasci's case, she could latch on to a vision of perfect health the minute she realized that she no longer needed the bone cancer as an escape. We don't know what she thought, but we can

BEING THE SOLUTION

imagine that she saw herself being without the bone cancer and healthy. And as Christ might have said to Bobbie,

Not I, but thy faith has made thee whole.

Your Power Pause visualization of BEING healthy is the beginning step toward better health for you, no matter what your health problem.

Good Health Vision

In the following chapter you will learn how to attract wealth with the prosperity consciousness you will create with the Power Pause.

17
HOW YOU ATTRACT MONEY

...with a Prosperity Consciousness

ATTRACTING WEALTH

Yes! Ready money is Aladdin's lamp.
--Lord Byron (1788-1824)

A poverty consciousness

To get full value out of this chapter, I want you to imagine that you desperately needed a friend. So, in this imagined reality you go down the street asking everyone you meet, "Will you be my friend, will you be my friend?" How would most of them react to your approach? They'd be backing off, thinking, "Who is this nut?", and they would seek the nearest exit. You'd get the same sort of reaction if you were asking for money. This example provides a perfect picture of what life looks like when you have a poverty consciousness. The world keeps slamming the door in your face.

A prosperity consciousness

Now, let's reverse the picture. Go out into the world asking people, "Can I be your friend?," and you'll have all the friends you want if you sincerely mean to be their friend. If you'll ask them questions about themselves and really be there for their answer, you

BEING THE SOLUTION

will truly be BEING a friend. In terms of friends, you have a prosperity consciousness. With that consciousness, you will surely attract friends.

The same principle holds true for having money. When you go to the bank asking for a loan, *you can have all you want if you can prove you don't need it*; if you really need it, they'll tell you to get lost. A prosperity consciousness attracts money; a poverty consciousness repels it.

The genie in your Aladdin's lamp is
your prosperity consciousness.
--Darel Rutherford

You'll find this chapter filled with examples of the many ways you might create your own prosperity consciousness, replacing the poverty consciousness that keeps you in the state of mind that prevents your having what you want from life.

For whosoever hath, to him shall be given
and he shall have more abundance...
Mathew 3:12

What must one have?

Whosoever hath? Hath what? What does that bible quote mean? What must one have in order to have more abundance? Most of us would answer "more money," but that wouldn't be the right answer. Having money doesn't make you rich, but the right attitude about having it does. Like a magnet attracting metal filings, money flows toward those who have the consciousness to keep it and flows away from those who don't.

Wealthy people have a certain way of feeling about money that attracts more of it. If you're suffering from the effects of negative cash flow, you will NOT have the prosperous feeling necessary for attracting money. The prime ingredient to your becoming rich will be a "prosperity consciousness," best described as that prosperous feeling you would have if your income far exceeded your spending.

So, how can you feel prosperous when your credit cards are maxed out and you can't pay your bills? You can't! That's why I suggest that the shortest path to a prosperity consciousness is a positive cash flow.

HOW TO ATTRACT MONEY

It begins with your decision

Your condition of poverty is not caused by your lack of income; it's a direct result of who you've chosen to BE in your relationship to money. The sad part about your poverty consciousness is that there is no solution to your problem as long as you maintain your "poor-me" perspective. The other half of that bible passage above is:

...but whosoever hath not,
from him shall be taken away even that he hath.
Mathew 3:12

In other words, without a prosperity consciousness, you're doomed to life of wondering "Why a flat tire when I can't afford a new tire;" "Why is the roof leaking when I can't afford to have it fixed." The purpose of that spiritual law, *To him that hath...* is to push you so far into the have-not corner, you'll come out fighting.

The first step out of your "poor me" box would be your determined rebellion against your condition of lack. The moment you change your mind about how you will relate to money, you will begin feeling more prosperous. Once the cash flow is moving in the right direction, once your income exceeds your spending, you'll have that inner sense of well being—the beginnings of a prosperity consciousness. The greater the cash flow, the richer you'll feel, and the richer you feel, the larger the flow will become. The true meaning of the bible quote above is:

For whomsoever hath a prosperity consciousness,
to him or her shall be given more and more abundance.
Darel Rutherford

As you learn to use the Power Pause for maintaining the vision that will solve your problem, the one thing that should stand out for you is that all problems (including a shortage of money) are illusions created to maintain whatever reality you've chosen to experience. Your illusion will almost always point to some outside circumstance or condition as the cause, when the only real solution to any condition of lack will be a change in the way you choose to relate to the problem—a BEING change. So the question I would ask you is:

BEING THE SOLUTION
*Who would you be BEING
if money were no longer an issue?*

Take your time to really think about this question, because your answer truly is the solution to all your money problems! Perhaps the following shared examples will fit your situation in some way and point your way toward developing your own prosperity consciousness.

Can't see a way out

R. W. (We'll call her Rina) wrote:
I feel stuck in this temporary shack of a house (we rented it from a family member, intending to stay there for only three weeks—that was six years ago!) It would take away from paying our debt to move into something more suitable. The challenge is to see another way to solve our housing problem that would not keep us from becoming debt-free.

Power Pause Logic for Rina:

If you're stuck in a shack because you're afraid of being in debt, like Rina, you're asking for a doing solution to what's actually a BEING problem. What you need to solve your "stuck-in-a-shack" problem is a different way of BEING in regard to debt. To change your perspective on this, you will need to make a distinction between the spender's debt and the investor's debt. A spender's debt breeds a poverty consciousness by making you poorer, while an investor's debt does the exact opposite. Having your equity grow every month in that new home will help you create the prosperity consciousness that will make you wealthy. So, Rina, if you are ever to find your way out of that shack, you may want to rethink your obsession with being debt-free.

An investor's debt is when you purchase property with very little up-front money. This is called a leveraged investment. Your small down payment on that new home is the lever that allows you to purchase a much bigger home than you could otherwise afford. And by using that lever, you learn a secret of the wealthy. **Leverage** is the powerful tool all wealthy people use to create the multiple streams of residual income that make them wealthy. Now that you're on to their secret, you can do the same. Leverage is one of their secrets; residual income is the other.

If you are ever to BE the solution to your money problems, you will need to change your point of view about how money is earned. If you've spent your life trading hours for dollars, you would probably have a closed mind to the idea of residual income. Unless you're willing to open your mind to the possibility of YOU receiving some form of residual income, you can never ever be wealthy. Believe me, residual income will be a part of the picture in the BEING change that will make you wealthy.

Most of my residual income comes to me in the form of rent from commercial buildings, obtained through leveraged purchases financed by a bank. I made a down payment, borrowed the balance; my tenant paid the mortgage payments, and I now own the buildings. My wealth was created through leveraged purchases that would not have been possible, at the time, without the borrowed money.

Investing in a new home is a wise investment and a good reason for going into debt. On the other hand, credit-card debt created for the purpose of instant gratification is an unwise investment. At the moment, your obsession with being debt-free is a barrier to the possibility of making a wise investment in that new home.

"I can't see the way out" is your victim story, a reflection of who you've chosen to BE relative to your perceived problem. Maintaining that perspective won't solve your housing problem. From the victim's point of view, there can never be a way out. Your problem is not in what you are doing or failing to do; your problem is in who you are BEING relative to the problem of being stuck in that "shack" of a house.

A question for all Rinas:
*Who would you be BEING
if you decided to invest in that new home now?*

Your way out of that shack starts with your being able to visualize life being better. Once you allow yourself to create a mental picture of you and your family living in a more suitable home, the Universe will provide the means by which that can happen. Just make sure you don't slam the door on that opportunity because of you previous commitment to becoming "debt free".

What would your vision of a better life look like? What if your income doubled? Could you, then, afford a better house? What if you found a better house that you could buy for little or nothing down, with mortgage payments similar in size to the rent you now pay?

BEING THE SOLUTION

Impossible? Your dream of having a better house can be your reality as soon as you begin to think of it as attainable!

A Power Pause visualization for Rinas:
In your vision, you've already moved into that new home. Your family has just finished eating a great meal in your fancy new dining room, a meal you cooked with pride in your fancy new double oven. As you stand at the kitchen sink, putting dishes in the dishwasher, you can't help admiring your beautiful kitchen cabinets that have all the modern conveniences. You are enjoying the breathtaking sunset outside your kitchen window as you reflect on the fact that each affordable mortgage payment you make increases your equity in that new home. You're feeling prosperous!

Power Pause success story:
The following Power Pause success story is an example of how the visualization process worked for someone with almost the same problem as Rina.

A family of six, renting a small home, had five maxed-out credit cards and a credit rating that made approval for a mortgage loan seem impossible. Their way out began when the wife, **B. D.** (We'll call her Beth), created and maintained the vision of her new home. To make visualizing easier, she created a collage picturing all the features of the home she wanted.

Then Beth and her husband took an action step. They began looking at houses for sale. The looking went on for five months. During that period, they made several offers that were turned down for one reason or another but they kept looking. What I noticed during their period of looking and being in the market for a new home was a gradual change in who the husband and wife were being. One day, Beth's husband said, "I just got that we can have that new home! And I responded with, "That's it. That's the BEING change we've been looking for. Three weeks later they moved into their new home.

The Power Pause visualization works by changing who you are BEING into the one in your vision. Once your subconscious accepts your vision as your new reality, the Universe must fill in the rest of the picture—by putting you into that vision.

HOW TO ATTRACT MONEY

A side benefit:

Moving into their new home, just naturally, made them feel more prosperous, giving them the prosperity consciousness they needed. As a result of that prosperity consciousness, their income more than doubled in the year of moving into their new home.

Tired—physically, spiritually, and emotionally

N. O. (We'll call her Nell) wrote:

What can we, as a couple, do to expedite our journey to financial freedom? It seems we have struggled for so long and we are tired—physically, spiritually, and emotionally. Our persistence is paying off in that we are getting our credit back in shape. It's just that we don't want to struggle and fight and claw for everything we get from this point forward.

Power Pause logic for Nells:

If you're like Nell, getting to the top of a hill always seems more difficult when you focus your attention on the steepness of the hill rather than the prize at the top. Focusing on your problem (the struggle), rather than the solution, can make you weary of the battle and have you wondering if it's worth the effort. So change your focus!

The obvious answer to your problem is to move your attention from the darkness of the tunnel to the light at the end of it. When you go to bed at night, before you turn off the light, count your blessings. Pat yourself on the back for having the courage to budget your spending. Appreciate the fact that you owe less money every month. Like yourself for having the strength of character to stick by your guns. See if you can begin to feel more prosperous each day. Your real mission is to develop a prosperity consciousness.

*To him that hath a prosperity consciousness,
it shall be given even more abundance...*

The solution to your problem could be in the creation of some form of residual income. You don't need to know what form it would take before you create the vision as a possibility. In Chapter Twenty, you'll find some suggestions for ways you might go about creating your own source of residual income.

BEING THE SOLUTION

A question for all the Nells:
*Who would you be BEING
if your exciting vision of the future filled your heart with joy?*

A possible visualization:

In your vision for a prosperous reality, see yourselves receiving ever-increasing streams of residual income. Your income is increasing every month; your credit-card debt is paid off and you are feeling prosperous. You are looking forward to that day soon, when you no longer must work. You enjoy what you're doing and are happy that life is no longer a struggle.

Getting fired up (choosing to BE enthusiastic) about the possibility of financial freedom and a life without struggle is my recommended cure for your "life is a struggle" reality illusion. I've never seen anyone fired up with enthusiasm who was tired physically, spiritually and/or emotionally. Enthusiasm (God in us) seems to be a cure for all of those diseases. What? You didn't know tired was a disease (dis-ease)?

Envision life as it would be if you no longer had to struggle. Your life will change to match the vision. Don't forget the "Thank you, God." An attitude of gratitude is the most powerful prayer in the book.

Wanting too much

L. D. (We'll call him Lee) wrote:

My problem seems to be that I want too much. As we all know, God always says yes and my wanting has simply gotten me more of the same—wanting. I know this principle in my head, I believe it, but somehow the wanting creeps in to my every thought. I feel all my wanting has sabotaged me. How do I truly release and let go of the wanting and get around to the acceptance of all that is there for me?

Power Pause logic for Lee:

Yes, God always says "yes" to your "I am" statement! He doesn't care whether you say "I am poor," "I am rich," or "I want". He just says, "yes" to whatever you say! The problem is, "I want" very often turns out to be an "I am" statement, meaning "I don't have." The net result of this thinking is that you get to live your life wanting, always wanting, and never having! In Chapter Seven you learned how to convert your wants into the burning desire that would move you to the point of choosing to BE the one who would have what you want.

The Power Pause works as a powerful transformational tool because through visualization you change your "I am" statement from wanting to having. Your visualization changes your wanting to having and God says, "yes!" to your having it.

A question for the Lees:
Who would you be BEING if you already had everything you ever wanted from life?

A Power Pause visualization for Lee:
In your Power Pause vision, see yourself enjoying life as it would be if all your dreams had come true (you have what you want and are feeling prosperous). You are enjoying a luxurious life of not wanting for anything. You have an over-all feeling of wellbeing that comes with living your dream.

Resistance to goal setting
Rev. B. (We'll call him Baxter) wrote:
Currently, we are wanting to create a larger attendance to Sunday services. I am finding (within myself and others) that there is fear and resistance, confusion and sleepiness whenever we sit down to actually try and create a plan.

Power Pause Logic for that problem:
Your ego is fearful every time you think about changing the status quo. You can't change the content of your life without a change in the context; you can't have your life be different without a change in consciousness. Your ego doesn't want that change. Your sleepiness is just another one of ego's escape mechanisms, a trick designed to take you out of harms way.

I've been coaching Rev. Toni LaMotta for a year. She rose to the challenge and now gets a standing ovation every Sunday in her new church. In just three months, attendance at her church has grown from 500 to 800 each Sunday. The same is possible for you if you can rise to the challenge and commit to a new BEING choice.

If you're serious about wanting to grow your church, the Power Pause is your way of changing your consciousness. Your vision of a full

BEING THE SOLUTION

church every Sunday would gradually change who you were being, and the new you would attract the new members. Your problem would no longer exist. Your newfound enthusiasm would be so catching that your church would fill with people who wanted to share in that enthusiasm!

Who you are being now is a minister whose ego is comfortable with the size of church you currently have. If you are serious about wanting the congregation to grow, you may need to ask yourself:

The question for ministers might be:
*Who would I be BEING
if Sunday attendance in my church tripled?*

Frightening question isn't it? Notice that that question takes your right past the problem to its solution. The question challenges you to rise above your problem and BE its solution. If you can accept that challenge and feel as you would if you were living your dream, you will not only be thrilled by the spiritual awakening within yourself, but the new you will also inspire your congregation to similar spiritual growth.

A Power Pause visualization for ministers:
Imagine your attendance increasing every Sunday. See yourself getting a standing ovation every time you speak, not as a result of what you're saying, but because of who you're BEING. Visualize your new BEING message changing people's lives daily so much that they're bringing their friends to church. Because of the increased attendance, your board of directors just voted to give you a healthy salary increase and they've giving you a new car to drive. You now know what a prosperity consciousness feel like and it feels great!

Feels greedy and unspiritual: ...
L. H. (We'll call her Leah) wrote:
Wanting to be rich feels greedy and unspiritual, so it's hard for me to justify making a priority out of getting rich(er). Yet in my heart of hearts, I would love to be financially rich, because I have some wonderful ideas of what to do with a lot of money, for my children, for the environment, for my church, for social justice issues, etc.

HOW TO ATTRACT MONEY

Power Pause logic for all the Leahs:

"Rich" as a term describes who you are, your consciousness, and not the money you have in your pocket or purse. "Rich" is really more a measure of what you feel you have to give than it is about what you have. Once you accept "rich in consciousness" as your definition of rich, you should have no further need for guilty feelings when you think about becoming rich.

Your spiritual mission in life is to discover that you are an individualization of the spirit of God, being expressed in and through you, as the giver. Your choosing to BE rich is an expression of God being rich through you as you. Your fears of being greedy and unspiritual come from your ego, not from your indwelling spirit of God.

A question for Leahs:
*Who would you be BEING
if your wealth more than matched your desire to give?*

So, who would you be BEING in your heart if you were rich enough to share your wealth in all the ways you've always wanted to give? Who would you be BEING if you were wealthy and didn't feel guilty about it?

The Power Pause is your way of rewriting the script that's already been written on the blackboard of your mind. When you add feeling to your vision, you replace the fear with a positive emotion. This is like writing boldly over the old writing on that blackboard with a large piece of colored chalk. Your subconscious doesn't know the difference between your new vision and reality. When the picture you've painted becomes clear enough, your vision becomes your new reality.

A Power Pause visualization for Leahs:
For your visualization see yourself as rich as you could ever want to be and not feeling guilty about all that money. You realize that your becoming richer required a giant leap in consciousness. You've grown spiritually and are closer to God than ever before. You're doing for your children in ways you've always wanted and more. Your tithe is now healthy enough to satisfy your need to give to your church, and you spend much of your days working as a volunteer and donating your money to the organizations you've always wanted to support.

BEING THE SOLUTION

If I'm not struggling.

Michael Gonzales wrote,
I have realized that if I am not struggling to find that next paycheck, not juggling to make payments and being clever trying to outwit my bills, then I am doing nothing. I don't know what to do if I am not struggling. Please Advise.

Power Pause logic for Michael:
When who you are BEING gets value out of struggling to survive, the struggling becomes necessary to your experience of being who you've chosen to be. Michael, you are the struggle. Without the struggling, you would lose your sense of being. In other words, where would you be without your struggles?

So, if you're like Michael, the question you might ask yourself:
*Who would I be BEING
if I gave up my need for life to be a struggle?*

A Power Pause visualization for all you Michaels:
You'll need to give up your ownership of the struggling, using the Power Pause to repaint the picture.

In your visualization, see yourself living in total comfort with sufficient residual income so that you no longer need to work. It feels great that you no longer struggle to pay your bills. You are enjoying life, laughing at your history of struggle.

The Power Pause is not really magic. It always works, because the problem, as perceived, is never the real problem. The Power Pause works to change that reality. The solution to your problem will always be a change in who you are BEING relative to the problem.

How do you find your barriers?
R. W. (We'll call him Richard) wrote:
Do you have any suggestions as to how I might identify those thoughts (beliefs) that need changing, and having identified them, how do I change them to help me create my highest and best?

HOW TO ATTRACT MONEY

Power Pause logic for all like Richard:

For years, I thought it necessary to find and remove the hidden barriers before you could find your way past them. But I've changed my mind about that. All you really need is a new BEING choice. Once you commit to changing the quality of your life, you won't really need to find your barriers; they'll find you. When your barrier shows up, declare a Power Pause. You won't be removing the negative thought; you'll be replacing it with a positive one.

Your problem is nothing
but a way of thinking that needs changing.
—Darel Rutherford

But for now, be aware that those beliefs, whatever they are, belong with you. They are a part of your self-concept. You might as well leave them be there until you're ready to change your mind about who you are. And the best motivation for changing who you are is to want something so bad you can taste it, and then to choose to BE the one who can have it. (If you're not sure how to create that level of desire, go back and reread Chapter Seven.)

A question for all Richards:
Who would you be BEING
if you were ready now to choose your highest and best good?

A Power Pause visualization for the Richards:
Changing who you are is a simple matter of changing the pattern of your thinking. Visualization is your tool for accomplishing that purpose. Imagine yourself enjoying the benefits of having what you wanted and feeling good about it. When you think about your vision, your barrier to that reality will pop up and slap you in the face. Each time that happens, declare a Power Pause: go to that peaceful place in your mind, experience your vision as your reality, and say,. "Thank you God." Each time you do the Power Pause, you've replaced your barrier with the vision of that better life. Before long, that barrier will no longer be in your way.

I'm too old, and it's too late for me
B. H. (We'll call him Ben) wrote:

BEING THE SOLUTION

I am 65 years old and living on slightly more than fixed Social Security income. Is it possible—maybe practical is a better word—to become a millionaire at my age and financial state?

Power Pause logic if you think it's too late:
If becoming a millionaire seems too high a hurdle, lower the bar a notch or two; just choose to be rich. But if you need an excuse for not choosing to be rich, "I'm too old" is as good an excuse as any. But don't kid yourself, that's all it is, just an excuse.

I know several retired people that, starting from scratch, created six-figure incomes in home-based businesses. Opportunities to build your own businesses abound if you can rise to the challenge and BE who you would need to be in order to succeed at that sort of thing. And you don't need a great deal of money to get started.

How did they do that? I'll share that secret with you in Chapter Twenty. Actually, it's not a secret; you've been presented with the opportunity to be rich many times before, and have turned it down each time. You haven't heard the possibility in the offer, because the doing required didn't fit who you were being (poor). That's why knowing how is not the first step in the becoming-rich process.

The first step in the process of becoming rich is in choosing to be rich. I know this sounds too simple and too good to be true, but it is a fact. The Universe is set up so that you need only choose who you will be, and whatever belongs to you by right of that choice becomes available. Only then will the new you choose to do whatever is necessary to make it happen.

A question to ask yourself, if you're like Ben:
Who would I be BEING
if age were no longer my barrier to my becoming wealthy?

A Power Pause visualization for Bens:
Create a vision of what your life would look like if you had all the residual income you could possibly need for living comfortably for the rest of your life. Residual income is income that comes to you on a regular basis from a previous investment of time and/or money. This is income that doesn't stop when you do. Can you let yourself picture what your life

would be like having a great income without having to report to work?

Imagine having one million dollars invested at 5.2%, you'd have a residual income of $1,000 a week. When you think seriously about earning that level of income, your fears and doubts will pop up. That's when you would declare a Power Pause.

A Power Pause Success Story

Dr. C. F. wrote,

I tripled my income this year. I am thrilled. I have been so focused on using what I know, I forgot to get back to you. Thanks for the reminder.

She didn't tell me how she accomplished the tripling of her income. What you must know to be inspired by her example is that she used the Power Pause visualization process to convert a dream of tripled income into reality. She's so busy living her dream, she doesn't have time to talk about it.

Still trying to be successful

G. E. (We'll call him George) wrote,

I have had my own business for 16 years. I have never been terribly successful, but as you see, I'm not a quitter. I'm still trying to be successful. I have worked my fool head off with less than startling results. I am amazed at the number of compliments I receive at how good I am at such and such, but I have never been able to translate it into money.

And now this brings me to your question: "What's your reason for not being a millionaire?" First, I argued that this was not the right question. But the more I thought about it, the more I realized that I had never made the 'choice' to be a millionaire.

And then, I remembered the time many years ago, when I was trying to decide what to do with my life. People that mattered to me urged me to do something that would make a lot of money and provide security. I remember so clearly the conscious decision I made. I said emphatically, "I don't care about money. I want to do something that I enjoy and makes a difference."

I had seen my father go off to work for many years and hate every minute of it. I couldn't bear the thought of living that way. No, in hindsight, I see that he hated his work, but he gained a

BEING THE SOLUTION

freedom that came with a degree of financial security. On the other hand, I have loved what I have done (or I did something else), but I do not have the freedom that comes with security. Could it be that I have so programmed my mind to 'not care about money' that now when I really want to make money, my subconscious mind is reminding me of my vow. How frightening! How revealing! How freeing!

I hate where I am financially, but for some perverse reason, my ego doesn't want me to change. This has got to be one of the strangest things about human nature. We are constantly being sucked down to the lowest common denominator rather than being drawn to the greater good.

Power Pause logic for all Georges:

You're not alone in being a small businessman, working for peanuts. I also worked my fool head off for years, and for the first three of those years, I conned myself into believing I had made a profit when I had just barely made wages..

I worked 14 hours a day during those early years in business, earning less per hour that I could have made working for someone else, and that other job would have been without a business owner's headaches. The problems that come with owning your own business make it an unwise choice, unless you intend to make it pay a great deal more than just wages. Years later, while acting as a management consultant, I discovered that very few small businessmen are wise enough to ask for a profit over and above their wages.

During those early years, I blamed everyone but myself for my lack of profit in business. I thought the market was setting the price for me. Then one day, I woke up to the fact that what I called the market was actually following my lead. I was the one setting the prices. When I finally wised up and began making a profit, I realized that my own consciousness in those lean years had set prices too low to allow me a decent profit.

What you must realize is that you are not trying to be successful; you **are** successful! Your problem is that your success is measured in terms of how you defined success many years ago. You said, "I don't care about money. I want to do something I enjoy and makes a difference." In terms of your stated intention, you've been a success.

HOW TO ATTRACT MONEY

You are not financially secure because you've chosen not to be. You don't have the time freedom or the financial security that comes with having money in abundance because you said you didn't care about that. Now, you're thinking seriously about changing your mind, and your previous BEING choice is getting in your way.

Part of your problem in making a new choice is your idea that being financially secure means doing something you don't like. Notice that this idea precludes the possibility that doing what you like could pay well.

These are false ideas you picked up from watching your father going to work each day, hating his job. He was your model for creating financial security, but you, understandably, didn't like that picture. He gave you the worst possible example for the cost of security. A more accurate appraisal of the wealthy would reveal that they have something most people want and never have—the time freedom to enjoy their money.

Wealthy people don't work for money; their money works for them! Your vision of financial security needs to change from the picture of drudgery your father painted for you, to one that has you receiving multiple streams of RESIDUAL income.

So, my question for all the Georges,
*Who would you be BEING
if your business were remarkably successful?*

The Power Pause visualization:

So, for your Power Pause visualization, imagine what your life would be like if you were enjoying life, making a difference, and receiving more income from your business than you could spend? Can you create that vision, or does it go too much against the grain?

My challenge to you, is that you experiment with the Power Pause to transform yourself into one who can have what you want from life—financial security while doing what you love to do. Here's the experiment.

Choose to be rich—if you don't actually choose, this experiment won't work. Once you've chosen to be rich, you will hear your ego's reaction in the form of self-talk (mind chatter). When you're into self-doubting, declare a Power Pause. Be at peace for a minute and then visualize your life as it would be if

BEING THE SOLUTION

you were living your dream. Empower your vision with enthusiasm and all the good feeling you can muster. Say your thanks to God. h Habit. When you think of your goal and have doubts, declare a Power Pause break. Do this exercise several times a day, every day, for a month. I guarantee that at the end of 30 days or less, you will have transformed yourself into one who will be living your dream and feeling prosperous.

How can I make that guarantee? Christ made that same guarantee 2000 years ago when he said, Whatsoever you ask in prayer, believing, you shall receive. The Power Pause visualization is the process by which you see yourself enjoying the life you've wanted. Is this not the "asking in prayer, believing" that Christ was talking about?

Making riches your entire life
Darlene R. Hess wrote:
I would like to know how you address the issue of being rich vs. making it your entire life.

Power Pause logic for Darlene

Darlene's question tells me that she has a mistaken idea about what it takes to become rich. Becoming rich is not about being obsessed with the idea of having money. It's not about chasing riches. Most poor people spend the majority of their time chasing the dollar just to survive. Becoming rich is about having riches come to you as a result of who you are BEING.

Becoming rich is about having a consciousness that attracts riches instead of repelling them; becoming rich requires a transformation in consciousness, a self-worth change. You can not change a poverty consciousness into a prosperity consciousness without a giant leap in consciousness or spiritual growth. If who you're being now, does not allow you to have the good life you've always wanted, a change of consciousness is in order. That change of heart is not obsession; it's a BEING choice that just naturally attracts riches.

So, the question you might ask yourself:
Who would I be BEING if I were rich, but not obsessed with riches?

HOW TO ATTRACT MONEY

A Power Pause visualization for all Darlenes:

See yourself having more than enough residual income to live comfortably without having to work for a living. You are doing all the things you love to do, being with the people you love. Even though you no longer need the income, you're still working, because you love your work and you're making a difference. But now you're rich enough to have the time freedom to enjoy the good life.

"But I don't feel prosperous"

C. B. (We'll call her Catherine) wrote:

My income level already ranges from $70,000 to $100,000 annually. It was a huge surprise to me that I was having trouble visualizing being and feeling prosperous.

Power Pause logic for Catherine:

I appreciate Catherine's sharing this because it fits so many who have good incomes, but do not feel prosperous. No matter how much you make, you can't really feel prosperous if you spend everything you make. As I said earlier, your prosperity consciousness begins with a positive cash flow.

Wanting stuff you can't have because you can't afford it can make you feel poor no matter how much you make, and that's the exact opposite of a prosperity consciousness.

Your Power Pause visualization:

To solve this problem, set your vision on a positive cash flow and multiple streams of residual income. See yourself investing in your future instead of spending it all. In your vision, you are feeling prosperous. Your new prosperity consciousness attracts more and more of the residual income that's making you wealthy.

In the following chapter you'll learn about a repeating cycle of life that has those who are unaware of this cycle on an emotional roller coaster.

BEING THE SOLUTION

The Genie in your aladdin's lamp is your prosperity consciousness

18
FIND THE UNWRITTEN AGREEMENT
...and the solution to your problem

*A relationship is an agreement
about who you will be for them and they for you.*
--Darel Rutherford

Life works by agreement

If your dog jerks you around from pillar to post when you're taking it for a walk, you have an agreement with your dog that it, not you, is in charge of the walk.

If your boss jerks you around at work, you must realize that he/she couldn't do this without your permission. Your response to mistreatment, when it happened the first time, set the stage for it to happen again and again. If you see yourself as the victim in a relationship, you may be surprised to learn that you have an agreement with that person that it's okay for you to be pushed around.

For the purpose of this discussion, we're not concerned with who's doing what to whom; what matters is that you come to realize that your relationships are based on unwritten agreements about how you will relate to each other.

BEING THE SOLUTION
You will be the victim in any relationship for only as long as you agree to play the victim role.
--Darel Rutherford

Smile and then change the agreement

One of life's greatest revelations is the realization that you have, unconsciously made an agreement with each and every person in your reality—an agreement about who you will be for them and they for you. Once you begin to see your relationships as unwritten agreements, you will have found the power to transform the quality of your life forever. From that moment on, when a relationship rubs you the wrong way, you'll simply smile and propose a change in the agreement!

When you're tired of being jerked around by your dog, a gentle pull on the leash, from time to time, will let your dog know that you are taking control. When it gets the message, you will have made a new agreement with your dog. The solution to your relationship with your boss or a friend might be handled just as easily. You may want to begin by asking yourself who you would be BEING if he or she no longer felt free to treat you in that manner. Then, having made your new BEING decision, you would be empowered to make a new agreement with that person about how you will be treated in the future.

He or she may not agree, but so what? Without the new agreement, the relationship doesn't work for you anyway. You have made a new BEING choice, and the new you no longer fits the old mold.

You chose the role

Don't resent your boss for being the jerk (if he is). Your boss is doing you the favor of allowing you to experience life from the role of being the victim in that relationship. The value gained from such an experience comes when you finally realize that you chose the victim role because you needed the experience. Accepting this truth gives you the power to make a new BEING choice, and your newfound power makes your victory even sweeter.

A relationship fulfills its purpose by allowing you to experience BEING whoever you've chosen to be.
--Darel Rutherford

FIND THE UNWRITTEN AGREEMENT

This relationship definition may seem nonsensical until you begin to think about the meaning of the word "being." As a stand-alone, "BEING" means "existence" or "presence." But the word takes on whole new meaning for you when you ask yourself, "Being, relative to what or to whom?"

Your BEING is defined as your way of relating to everything and everyone in your chosen reality. All those people and things in your life are defined by your attitude about them. When you say, "I love apple pie, a la mode", you're telling us whom you've chosen to BE relative to apple pie with ice cream. The important thing to get from this example is that the apple pie didn't choose the relationship, you did.

They send a message

If you want to know who you are, take a good hard look at what you have in your life, and an even harder look at what your friends are telling you about yourself by how they treat you.

When I asked Jeannie if she had any problem relationships, she told me about a friend who had called from the airport on her way out of town to ask that Jeannie clean her house. The friend said she wouldn't be back from her trip in time to clean her house and she was scared to death about what her husband would say if he came home to a dirty house.

Jeannie resented her friend's request, but she didn't say *no*. She cleaned the house. When I ask her why she gave in to this outrageous request, she didn't know. I offered to coach Jeannie on finding the power to say *no* in situations like this. I also suggested that a new agreement with this friend might be in order.

If you're allowing someone you know to take advantage of your good nature in that relationship, you've chosen to relate to that person as their servant. They're using you. To regain your power, change your mind about who you will BE in that relationship. Then, see how you feel about yourself once you've chosen out of the victim role with the power to make a new agreement.

When seen as an agreement

Notice how much more powerful you feel about yourself in that relationship once you see it as an agreement about whom you will be for that person and he/she for you. Notice that you represent half or more of that agreement, and it's your half over which you have control.

BEING THE SOLUTION

Armed with this new perspective on relationships, you will have the power to solve your relationship problems by changing who you are BEING in them. From your new position of power, you can easily make a new agreement. Notice that both the BEING solution and the new agreement take you outside the victim role, putting you back in charge of your life.

Every written contract, to be validated, must be signed by both parties. Your unwritten agreements should be seen in the same light. Just remember, "it takes two to tango." If you don't like that dance, change the music!

Oh, no, I didn't agree to that!

As a complaining victim of a non-working relationship, your first reaction to this idea of being party to an unwritten agreement would be to claim, "Oh no, I didn't agree that they could treat me like that!" Oh, but you did!

In each relationship, an unwritten agreement about who or what we each will be for the other becomes firmly entrenched as we adjust to each other's way of being. The problem with such unwritten agreements is that we were not aware that an agreement had been reached simply because we failed to protest at the time. Acquiescence is not the best way to create agreements.

When I reflect on the subject of unwritten agreements, I'm reminded of Rose's reaction when I suggested that she had an unwritten agreement with her alcoholic husband about his "lost weekends." She violently disagreed when I explained, that years ago, she had made it okay for him to spend whole paychecks on drunken three-day binges.

That's the agreement!

To help her understand, I asked, "Rose, what happened the first time he did that?" She replied, "I stayed mad at him for several days, but forgave him when he promised never to do it again." And I continued, "Rose, that's the agreement—that he can go on a toot; you will be mad at him for a while; he'll make promises, and then you will forgive him. You now live your life, in bondage to that agreement!"

Rose saw the light and decided, in that moment, to make a new agreement. She had played the victim in that relationship until she realized that she shared equal responsibility for creating the unwritten agreement that had made her life miserable for years.

FIND THE UNWRITTEN AGREEMENT

So, if you think you didn't agree to the way you're being treated in that relationship, think again. Your response, or lack of response, to whatever he or she did or didn't do, created an agreement about who you would be for them under those and/or similar circumstances. So, you DO have an agreement. The question is, what do you intend to do about it?

If you want out of the old agreement, acknowledge its existence with the other party; voice your dissatisfaction with that agreement, and then announce your intention for a new agreement.

He who is firm in will molds the world to himself.
--Johann Wolfgang von Goethe

It takes courage

Finally, Rose found the courage to lay down the law to her alcoholic husband, in no uncertain terms. It takes courage to take a tall stand for a new agreement, because from that position, you're seeing yourself outside the relationship offering to re-start the relationship under a more workable arrangement.

Most people are so attached to a relationship that they can't imagine being out of it. Fear of losing the relationship stops them cold when they think about confronting their partner with some sort of ultimatum. Instead, they gripe and complain, playing right-wrong for months, or even years; they argue and fight, saying hurtful things, making each other miserable. In the end they destroy any possibility of the new agreement that could have made the relationship work for both of them.

Relationship problem solutions

The three possible solutions for any relationship problem are:
1. Change your way of BEING with him, her or it (a job, for instance)
2. Make a new agreement with him or her
3. Choose out of the relationship

The first of the three solutions begins with asking yourself:

Who would I be BEING if his or her behavior was no longer allowed to be a problem?

BEING THE SOLUTION

- By choosing a new way of BEING in that relationship you would, more than likely, cause an automatic BEING change in the other person.
- If they don't change, your new BEING choice should empower you to negotiate a new agreement about who you will be, each for the other, in that relationship.
- The other option, of course, will be to choose out of the relationship because no agreement could be reached.

No matter which new way of BEING you choose as your solution, it's important that you no longer be at the effect in that relationship.

*A man without decision
can never be said to belong to himself*
--John Watson Foster

The power to negotiate

You won't find the power to resolve your relationship problems as long as you continue to see yourself as the victim. Please get that you chose whom you would BE in that relationship. Until you accept full responsibility for having chosen that role, you will be powerless to make a new choice.

The place of power from which you must negotiate your new agreement is a stance that has you outside the relationship, intending to choose back into it with a new understanding. If a new agreement cannot be reached, there's no basis for a continuing relationship. This attitude may seem cold and hard until you stop to consider that the real purpose of a relationship is to provide you with the experience of being who you are.

All your relationships serve that purpose—even those that seem to upset you. What I'm saying here is that the job you don't like serves you by allowing you to be the victim of a boss you don't like, doing work you don't like so you can be the lightweight you've chosen to be in that relationship. Your way back to power is to give up your role as the victim.

Out of choice, not attachment

When I suggest choosing out of a relationship with the intention of choosing back into it under a new agreement, I'm never surprised by the fearful reactions and the looks of disbelief that I would

FIND THE UNWRITTEN AGREEMENT

even suggest such a thing. Let me assure you that the greatest possible relationship you could ever have would be one where you were clearly there in that relationship by choice, not because you were afraid not to be.

When you're in a relationship only because you're afraid of what life might be like out of it, you don't really have a relationship; you have an attachment. If you can't see yourself outside the relationship choosing back in under new rules, you are hooked. The basis for your relationship is fear, not love. If you remain in a relationship because you are afraid not to be in it, you are firmly attached. Don't tell me that's love, because it isn't!

Finding the courage
Let us never negotiate out of fear.
But let us never fear to negotiate.
--John Fitzgerald Kennedy

Finding the courage to make a new agreement begins with changing your focus from the problem to its solution. Notice that any solution to the relationship problem will require some change in who you are being relative to that problem. To find your courage, visualize what your life would be like if the problem were no longer a problem. When stated in this way, you will see that a change in your attitude about the problem must be a major part of the solution.

Another significant part of the solution to your relationship problem is in being able to detach yourself from it.

It does not take much strength to do things,
but it takes great strength to decide what to do.
--Elbert Hubbard

In this step, you must accept the possibility of an end to the relationship. This is the hard part, but if you are to negotiate from strength, you must be able to see yourself outside the relationship, choosing back into it under a new and mutually beneficial arrangement.

Speak softly
I'm not suggesting that you threaten your partner with divorce. In fact, I would suggest that you don't allow that threat to enter the

picture. If you've found your power to negotiate, it should come through as love in your negotiating, not as a threat.

> *He that complies against his will*
> *is of his own opinion still.*
> --Samuel Butler

President Theodore Roosevelt once said, "speak softly and carry a big stick." Being able to handle the emotional upset of seeing yourself out of a relationship gives you all the power (the big stick) you will need to negotiate.

Having power, in and of itself, is enough. Your relationship partner will get the message that you mean business without the need for you to wave your big stick. Anyway, using bully tactics during negotiations is a little like *throwing out the baby with the bath water*.

It's your willingness to stand your ground that gives you the power to negotiate fearlessly. With love in your heart, you will win your new deal if you take more than your share of the responsibility for causing the problem, and if you'll come to the negotiating table with something positive to offer (your new way of BEING in that relationship).

> *Resolve, and thou art free.*
> --Henry Wadsworth Longfellow

The new agreement

Your negotiations will begin with your acknowledgment of the existence of an unwritten agreement and your explanation for why that way of being no longer works for you. Make it clear that you're offering a deal that will make life easier and happier for both of you.

At this point in your negotiations, you can't play right/wrong and expect to win a better deal. His or her cooperation in putting together a new deal will begin with you taking a major portion of the responsibility. Example: somehow the old agreement seemed appropriate to who you were being back then, but that's not who you are now.

As you negotiate, it must be clear (in your mind and in your heart) that you are dealing from outside the relationship with every intention of choosing back into it.

FIND THE UNWRITTEN AGREEMENT

Courage is almost a contradiction in terms:
It means a strong desire to live
taking the form of readiness to die.
   --Gilbert K. Chesterton

You are offering to come back into that relationship as a different person if he/she will agree to the change in attitude and/or behavior that would make the relationship work for you. What you have to offer in the new deal is YOUR new way of BEING. The other side of the bargain is what you expect from him or her in this new arrangement.

Agreement defined

Agreement is defined in the dictionary as:
   a harmony of opinion.
According to the law, an agreement is:
   a properly executed and legally binding contract

A practice session

To test out this way of solving relationship problems for yourself, I suggest you do a practice session. Don't start with your worst relationship problem. Think of a recent misunderstanding with a friend. You'll be more objective with a relationship where you are the least attached and have less to lose if negotiations fail. Do you have a problem relationship in mind?

At first, your problem's source will appear to be with the other party, not with you. But to solve the problem, the first place you must look for a solution is within yourself. To get you started with the solution, here are some of the questions you might want to ask yourself:

- *What makes this relationship a problem for me?*
- *What would happen if I suddenly decided that I would no longer be concerned about it? Would the problem go away?*
- *So, who would I be BEING if his/her actions had no effect on me one way or the other?*
- *Who would I be BEING if I were standing tall, no longer the victim in this relationship?*

BEING THE SOLUTION

- *Who would I be BEING if I were totally detached from the relationship, outside of it, looking objectively at how I would like the relationship to be for me?*

How does it feel?

Now, which of those BEING choices works best for you? Remember, you're solving this relationship problem for practice. Begin by seeing yourself out of the relationship, ready to choose back into it under a new agreement. How does it feel to have chosen out?

If you're taking this practice session seriously, you should be experiencing some heart pangs from seeing yourself out of the relationship. If so, good! This is good practice for the main event. Now, think seriously about the benefits you would enjoy from being in this relationship and choose back into it with a sense of personal power you didn't feel before.

Your newly-found power comes from knowing that you are in the relationship out of choice.

Now that you're feeling powerful, decide what new, mutually beneficial agreement you will propose to replace the one that's not working for you. When you have your new deal in mind, you're ready to negotiate. I suggest you stop reading, pick up the phone and make that appointment with your friend.

Negotiating in the main event

We'll assume that you've done the practice negotiations and made your new agreement with your friend. If you haven't, you should really do so before you read on.

Now, you may be ready to tackle the relationship that gives you the most grief—the one that would cause you the most emotional upset from choosing out. But here's a word of warning: Your power to negotiate comes from being willing to choose out of the old non-working relationship in favor of a new and better alliance. If you can't deal with the idea of possibly ending the relationship don't do this—don't attempt to bluff your way in your negotiations!

Threats without power
are like the powder without the ball.
--Nathan Bailey, 1776

FIND THE UNWRITTEN AGREEMENT

If you are bluffing, negotiating out of fear, your partner in negotiation may sense your fear, call your bluff, and then you'd be worse off than before—even more in bondage, or maybe clear out of the relationship and feeling sorry for yourself. A good rule to follow:

*If you can't handle the heat in the kitchen,
don't present yourself as a cook.*
--Darel Rutherford

Find the unwritten agreement

When the attitude or actions of the other party in a relationship continue to upset you, look for an unwritten agreement. When you find it, you will understand why you're having the problem and you'll know how to fix it.

For example:
- If your son or daughter plays the role of an independent dependent, living at home but refusing to play by the rules, you obviously have an unwritten agreement here that will be the source of your problem with that relationship.
- If your neighbor borrows your tools but never returns them, you've made that okay by your lack of confrontation. You and he have an agreement.
- When you put up with constant nagging without comment, you've created an unwritten agreement that the nagging is okay.

Some unwritten agreement examples
- I know I'm over 21, but you still owe me a living.
- I know I'm loved because you give me what I need.
- I know you love me because you need me.
- I'm over twenty-one, but my father still gives me orders like I was seven.
- I'll soon have made you over into the person I want you to be.
- He never picks up after himself.
- He never pays back money he borrows.

Why relationships don't survive

From time to time in life, we grow up. When that happens, we sometimes forget to tell others in our reality that we are no longer who

BEING THE SOLUTION

we originally agreed to be in the original relationship. And sometimes we don't tell them because we're afraid of that truth destroying the relationship. An example of this might be your relationship with a parent who still tries to run your life.

The problem with pretending to be who you're not, is that it defies the real purpose of a relationship—that you get to experience being who you are. Living this lie also denies the other person any chance of getting to know the real you. A relationship based on a lie is always in danger of self-destructing. The solution to this problem, in all cases, is a new agreement.

So, there are two times when a new agreement should be negotiated:

1. When either party changes his or her mind about who they will be.
2. When one of you is assuming a privilege not offered or is working under a misunderstanding about what is acceptable behavior.

Making a new agreement

When you've figured out the unwritten agreement, acknowledge its existence; explain your displeasure with that agreement; and announce your intention to arrange for a new agreement.

Being the solution

The first and best solution to any problem will be your determined change of mind about who you will be BEING relative to that problem. The second best solution will be when you come to a new agreement with the other party about it.

In the last five chapters you have looked at examples of BEING the solution to every type of problem imaginable. Each time we can BE the solution, we've risen above the problem.

Finding the power to BE the solution
is the self-discovery process of consciousness evolving.
--Darel Rutherford

As an individualization of God in the process of evolving, you can speed up the evolutionary process by seeking BEING solutions to your problems.

FIND THE UNWRITTEN AGREEMENT

The true purpose of a relationship

It will help you understand relationships if you can think of them as the places where you will get to experience being who you are. You are a diamond in the rough. With each and every relationship in your life, you experience a different facet of your being. Your job in life is to polish those facets and become the polished diamond. All relationships serve that purpose, even though some may not seem to.

So, when you're having problems with a relationship, here are some questions you may want to ask yourself:

- *Who am I BEING that invites this problem into my life?*
- *Who am I BEING that allows this person to take advantage of me?*
- *How did I invite the unwritten agreement I have with this person?*

For instance: BEING the giver presents an open invitation for all takers, and the taker searches for and finds someone with a need to give. When the giver and taker find each other, we have a match and a codependent relationship. When you're willing to look at answers to the question of how you invited that unwritten agreement, you will know how to answer the greatest problem-solving question of all:

Who would I be BEING
If that problem were no longer a problem?

The importance of group support

When you're ready to make a major change in who you are BEING, you'd be wise to set up your Powerpact support group. Your BEING change will be met with automatic ego resistance. You'll need a support group that will get you past that resistance and keep you on purpose during the transition period.

All relationships reflect who you're being back at you. Your Powerpact support group will do the same. The difference is that they know your intention for a BEING change. They will remind and encourage you when you are not living up to your intention, and they will reinforce and commend you when you are on purpose.

In a Powerpact support group, you will be given the support you need to enhance, multiply, and increase your personal power. Your purpose in life is to grow in consciousness and find your true self. A

BEING THE SOLUTION

Powerpact provides you with opportunity to find yourself in a bigger way.

The power of keeping your agreements

It may never have occurred to you that the most important relationship you have in life is the one you have with yourself about who you will BE. Your life experience is ultimately nothing more than a reflection of how you feel about yourself. Your self-worth sets a limit to what you can have in your life, and your self-image is the channel through which your abundance must flow.

The most important agreement you have is the one you have with yourself. The most important discovery you could ever make is that you have the power to change the quality of your life by making a new agreement with yourself about who you will be. Any agreement you make with anyone else in your life starts out as an agreement with yourself about who you will BE in that relationship.

And now we come to the funny part. It never ceases to amaze me at how many people out there make promises they don't keep. They don't have a clue that they destroy themselves by breaking their word. The resulting loss of integrity destroys the self-respect upon which any success in life must be built. They shoot themselves in the foot and wonder why they never win a race.

When you speak your word, you're saying *This is who I am*. When you break your word, you are saying, *Well, I guess I'm not*. You destroy yourself a little more every time you show up late for an appointment, every time you don't do what you said you would. You are your word, and that's all you are. What does that make you when your word is no good?

Life is a game

Life is a game. Whether you like it or not, you are in life's game. It's a simple game. You get to choose who you will be, and then you get to experience life from that BEING choice. If you don't like what you are experiencing, you have the option to bitch about it, accept it the way it is, or make a new BEING choice.

In the meantime (between choices), life will reflect your BEING choices back at you from every direction. If you care to look for the evidence, each experience in your life, every relationship, will show you who you are being at any particular moment. The lesson to be

FIND THE UNWRITTEN AGREEMENT

learned from these experiences is that you can, at any moment, make a new BEING choice and make the problems go away.

In fact, the problem actually exists in your life for the purpose of inspiring you to rise above it. You literally chose the problem to be in your life so you could make the BEING choice that would take you beyond the problem. Overcoming problems is your path to the growth in consciousness that will allow you to discover who you really are.

Summary of this chapter

- When you understand BEING as your way of relating to everyone and everything in your life, you know that you can change the quality of your life by changing your way of being in it.
- Understanding life as an agreement gives you the power to change agreements and make your life work.
- When you understand that the purpose of a relationship is self-discovery, you will see the importance of always being yourself in it.
- When you find the unwritten agreement in a difficult relationship, you will know how to solve the problem.
- By changing your mind about who you are, you've broken the unwritten agreement. Isn't it time you made a new agreement?

Understanding your life

You will better understand your journey through life if you can think of it as an agreement with yourself, the universe, and anyone who shares some part of your reality. You've chosen who to BE; now you need to find those who will agree with and support your BEING choice.

Your life on this planet will go much more easily once you realize that there is actually an unwritten agreement between you and all those other people in your life about who you will be for them and they for you. Your whole life is an agreement. The first and most important agreement is the one you have with yourself about who you will be. If you're still confused about this, it may be that you don't really know who you are. In that case, there is no agreement—yet.

If you have a relationship that no longer serves you or nourishes you in a way that pleases you, find the unwritten agreement and cancel it.

~~The Unwritten Agreement~~

Then make a new agreement.

The New Agreement

Create, Persist, Destroy
In the next chapter, you'll learn why we tend to destroy relationships rather than make the new agreement that would put the relationship back on solid ground.

19
FIND YOURSELF ON THE CYCLE

...a roadmap for the rest of your life

*Life is too short to spend it in relationships
that can never support or nourish.*
--Darel Rutherford

Into the Destroy Phase

In tears, Jane said, "My husband constantly says things to hurt me and put me down". I have no idea how Jane responds to these put-downs, by way of getting even, but when she asked for my advice, I said, "First, see yourself outside that relationship, with the option of choosing back into it under a new agreement. If either of you is unwilling to make or keep a new agreement, there's no solid foundation for the relationship".

Of course, this simple logic is easy advice to give when you are a casual observer, not personally involved in the relationship. But my premise for this advice was based on two truths:

1. All relationships are unwritten agreements, and
2. Our lives revolve around a cycle which I call CREATE PERSIST DESTROY.

BEING THE SOLUTION

From what I knew about their relationship, Jane and her husband were quite obviously too far along in the Destroy Phase of the cycle to turn it around. If they could have seen their relationship as being in the final stages of the Destroy Process, they might have avoided a great deal of unnecessary emotional pain that often goes with ending a relationship.

"I'm not quitting!"

When my daughter, Sherry, began complaining about her boss, I asked, "When are you quitting?" She reacted to my question by saying, "I'm not quitting! I love my job." And I replied, "That's not what it sounds like to me."

When Sherry realized, a few days later, that she was actually into the Destroy Process with her job, my advice to her was the same as with Jane. "First find the courage to choose out of the job; decide what the job would be like if you could really enjoy going to work each day; then make a new agreement with your boss based on that new job description."

Sherry's dissatisfaction at work stemmed from the fact that, she had outgrown the job she had originally hired on to do. As an objective observer, I could see that Sherry was obviously in the process of destroying her attachment to that job so she could quit and not feel guilty about it. But until I pointed this out to her, Sherry had been totally unaware of the fact that she had begun the detaching process with her job.

Discontent is something that follows ambition like a shadow.
Henry W. Haskins

If you've outgrown a relationship, the hard way out of it would be to play ego's right/wrong game with the other party for long enough to make him or her so in the wrong that you'd feel justified in choosing out. But that's not really the best way to solve your relationship problem. The sensible solution for a relationship problem would be to create a new relationship based on a new agreement—and before it's too late.

Not really serving them

When I suggested a Power Pause solution for one of his counseling clients, a relationship counselor told me just enough about the case history for me to know that the relationship was no longer

FIND YOURSELF ON THE CYCLE

salvageable. His attempts to help the couple in creating a new agreement and a better attitude toward each other had failed. The Destroy Process had been allowed to continue for far too long, so that the resulting damage to the relationship by both parties made a new agreement next to impossible.

My advice to my friend, the counselor: "They're obviously not into making a new agreement. Why are you wasting your time and theirs? You can't really serve them by helping them prolong the agony. Just show them where they are on the CREATE-PERSIST-DESTROY cycle and help them move on with their lives."

Life's too short to spend it in any relationship that has reached the point of no return. Prolonging it is not serving either of you. If you've tried negotiating a new agreement with no success, choose out. You will find an unexpected surge of personal power in being able to say "no" to a relationship that gives you no reason for liking yourself while in it.

Wasting half your life

The most interesting thing about being in the Destroy Phase of the cycle is that from the inside of the relationship looking out you won't realize that you're into destroying your attachment to it. You could waste a year, or a lifetime, making the other party out to be the bad guy just so you can choose out without guilt and never realize that that's what you were doing. I'm here to tell you that relationships do not need to end that way.

Once you understand the cycle as an on-going process in your life and pay attention, you can catch yourself playing right/wrong and reverse the damage. When you realize that you are on the Destroy side of the cycle, you can back off and make a new choice about who you will BE in that relationship. If it is not too late, you can make a new agreement with the other party in time to save the relationship in a way that works for both of you.

Whether or not the relationship survives is not really the point here. What's important is that you not waste half your lives destroying each other's happiness just so you'll feel justified in choosing out.

If you're into despair

If you've reached the point of bitching about conditions at work, you can bet that you're in the Destroy Process. If you're unhappy in a relationship with a friend, a member of your family, or with your job, you're probably in the process of detaching yourself from the

BEING THE SOLUTION

relationship. You won't necessarily be ready to admit to yourself that you are on the Destroy side of the cycle, but you probably are. And if you are, you'll need to complete the process and get on with your life.

Detaching yourself sensibly simply means seeing yourself outside the relationship with the option of choosing back into it under a new agreement. For as long as you're attached to a relationship, you'll be powerless to negotiate the new agreement necessary to the relationship's survival. But once detached, you'll move yourself past the emotional upset of the Destroy Phase and into a new reality in that relationship. Each of you will be choosing a new way of BEING in that relationship, growing in the process.

The detachment process

One would assume that the first step in the creating of a new reality would be to create. Not so! The first step toward that bright, shiny new reality for you is when you sever your attachment to the old reality. Once you accept the detachment process as a necessary part of the on-going creative process, you can move in, through and out of it quickly. Once you learn to read the signals, you can short-cut the sadness and the unhappiness in the detachment process and get on with your life.

When you're into the Destroy Phase, in any aspect of your life, you will usually have three options.
1. You can continue with the destructive process—with the fault finding.
2. You can create a better relationship based on a new agreement.
3. You can simply choose out, because it's too late for a new agreement.

A relationship test

Here's a simple test you can use for any relationship: Ask yourself, "Do I like myself when I'm with this person, in this job, etc?" If the answer is "no," you'll need to make a new agreement that allows you to be yourself and to like who you are in that relationship. Otherwise, you would be wise to choose out. Life is too short to spend it in situations that can never reinforce or nourish us.

First, find your inner power
...seek ye first the kingdom of God
and all these things will be added unto you.

FIND YOURSELF ON THE CYCLE
--Luke 12:31

What does that mean—"*seek ye first the kingdom*"? It means to first find your inner power and then, "...all these things will be added unto you." This bible passage promises that you can have whatever you want from life if you can find your way out of your box. It means that you must first find the spirit, the power to choose a new way of BEING; it promises you that life will respond, by providing everything that belongs with your new BEING choice.

It further means you can choose a new way of BEING with your problem, and have that problem cease to exist as a problem. It means that when you seek for and find your inner power, the power of choice (the kingdom), you can choose a new reality and everything necessary to experiencing that reality will be made available to you. How could you ask for more? Life makes that promise if you're willing to come outside your box and play the game at a new level.

You say you'd rather play it safe in your box? Life is offering you this fantastic deal and you're turning it down? How could that be? Why would anyone elect to stay in their box when the good life is just outside it? Let's look again at what keeps you in your box and see if we can figure out why you're turning down life's generous offer for that better life.

The Game

In Chapter Three we established that life is a game designed to keep us traveling our own yellow brick road toward self-discovery. Our urge to grow comes from the spirit of God in us, seeking self-expression outside the box and around the next turn in the road. But our ego resists the changes that would be necessary for our growth. Seeing the game through the eyes of our ego, we have trouble understanding why we're on this road when we'd rather stay where we are.

In this chapter, you'll be given a roadmap that will help you understand where you've been so far, and allow you to see where you're going on your yellow brick road to self-discovery. By the end of this chapter, you'll have an overview of life that will help you to understand the game in a way that will let you win big and more often.

Your stake in the Game of Life is your old self-concept. Each trip around the game board, you must trade in the old you in favor of the new version. What you win each time you pass Go is a new self-image with more personal power and a better understanding of who you really are. At all times in this game, we're being urged to grow, and in growing, to finally discover that we are individualizations of God. That's God's game plan for you.

We are reading the first verse of the first chapter of a book whose pages are infinite.
--Author Unknown

It's only one inning

Our problem in playing the game is that we play each round as if it were the whole game when, in fact, it's only one inning in an endless game. We get upset when we're forced to face the fact that we don't really have it "made in the shade" now that we've reached our goal. We get stuck, because we lack an overview that would allow us to see the HAVING part of the BE DO HAVE process we talked about in Chapter Nine as the end of an inning, not the end of the game.

A new perspective will allow us to see that HAVING what we want has no real value compared to the growth in consciousness that results from each new trip around the game board. Wanting to be richer and happier is our motivation for moving to the next level of the game. Choosing to be rich is not something about which you need to feel guilty.

Most misinterpreted

One of the most interesting and misunderstood passages of the bible is the one that reads:

It is easier for a camel to go through the eye of a needle than for a rich man to enter the kingdom of God.
Matthew, 20:24

Since a camel could not possibly go through the eye of a needle, most of us interpret this bible passage to mean that you can't be rich and go to heaven. That's not what it means, at all!

Back when Christ said this, most cities had an inner and an outer wall. The inner wall allowed entry only through an opening shaped like the eye of a needle—an opening too small for a loaded camel to pass through. To take his favorite camel into the inner city for the night, the rich man was forced to unload it. Back then, a rich man could not easily take his riches with him into the inner city. Notice that unloading his riches outside the wall didn't make him poor.

The load on your camel

If you think rich people are the only ones with a loaded camel, you are mistaken. Metaphorically speaking, whatever you've attached yourself to—your job, a relationship, your way of life—is the load on your camel's back. Whatever you've made more important than being free and out of your box, is your wealth. What that bible quote should mean to you is:

To find that greater dimension of your own being,
you must first unload your camel—
--Darel Rutherford

If you've used the "rich men don't go to heaven," reason for choosing not to be rich, you'll have to look for another excuse. That bible passage is meant as a message for you and I. What! You didn't know you were rich?

Each time around the cycle in the Game of Life, we become attached to whatever way of life we've created in that level. That way of life is your riches and you're extremely attached! To reach the kingdom (to play at the next level of the game), you must first unload your camel.

He does not possess wealth
that allows it to possess him.
--Benjamin Franklin

We become attached to many things in our lives: our jobs, our relationships, our possessions, even our problems. Before we can create the reality of a better life for ourselves, we must first detach ourselves from whatever we've made more important than our SELF. The Destroy Side of the cycle is simply that part of the game where we unload the camel.

Without the big picture

Our biggest problem in winning the Game of Life is that
we can't have what we want
without giving up our attachment to not having it.

BEING THE SOLUTION

As a pawn in this game, we have next to nothing; as the king, we would have everything. But the king and the pawn cannot occupy the same space on the chessboard. To be a king, you must give up your attachment to being the pawn. Therein lies the problem.

Because we don't see the big picture, we don't really understand what's happening to us when we are being forced to give up our attachment to one way of life in favor of one that would serve us better. For lack of an overview, we haven't seen that the Destroy Process takes up about half of our lives and serves only one real purpose—that of detaching ourselves from a reality that no longer serves us. And because we don't understand the Destroy Process, we go through life destroying relationships when all we needed was to give up our attachment to it so we could make a new agreement.

One trip around the cycle

The creative process for mankind is BE DO HAVE.
- BE = *Making a new BEING choice*
- DO = Persisting in the being and becoming
- HAVE = The satisfaction of completion

The creative process is quite simple. In order to have what we want from life, we must first choose to BE the one in whose life it belongs. Once committed to BEING the one in our vision, we move into DOING whatever necessary to being and becoming who we need to BE and have what we want from life. Wow! We finally HAVE it.

But here is where we all go wrong. Unfortunately, HAVING is not the end of our growth; it's only one of the many new beginnings and endings necessary to our growing in consciousness, moving toward discovering that we are, indeed, individualizations of God.

Life is a repeating cycle

You've been around this cycle, down this road many times before. Take the time to think back on the times in your life when you've discarded unhappy circumstances in favor of new and better ones. Think of the trying circumstances in your life that caused you to rise above your problem and grow. Those triumphs over adversity were each only one trip around the cycle in the Game of Life.

Your personal power is reinforced when you remember how powerful you felt each time you rose to a challenge, each time you became the solution to your own problem. Each trip around the cycle was an instance of your seeking the kingdom, making a new BEING

FIND YOURSELF ON THE CYCLE
choice and having your problem be solved

Create Persist Destroy, the Cycle

Notice that BE and CREATE occupy the same lower left quadrant of the cycle. DO and PERSIST take up the upper left quadrant; HAVE and DESTROY take over the whole right half of the cycle. Most of us spend at least half our lives in some aspect of the Destroy Process. When you can see the creative process as a repeating cycle, the episodes of your life will make more sense. By paying attention, by monitoring the way you feel about relationships, noticing how you're dealing with or reacting to life, you'll know where you are on the cycle.

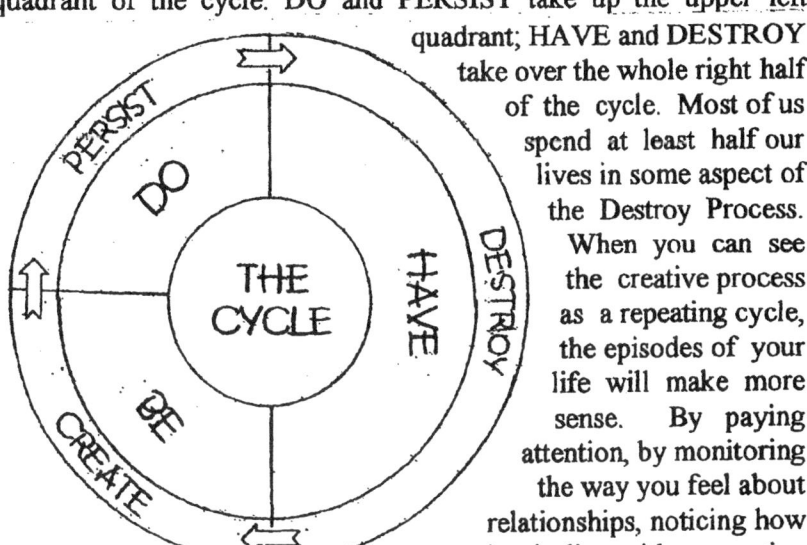

When understood, this cycle becomes a blueprint for the rest of your life. When you learn to read the road signs, you will put more hope, desire and excitement into the Create Phase. You will be a great deal more enthusiastic and joyful as you persist in the process of accomplishing your mission, and when you've achieved your goal, you'll see your success as a BEING triumph rather than a HAVING triumph. With your new outlook, you won't get stuck in the idea that having what you wanted was the big win, and you won't have nearly as much trouble detaching yourself from your winnings.

The best of times

The absolute best times in my life were experienced while I was inspired with some goal or purpose that captured my full and enthusiastic attention. The very worst times of my life happened when I found myself mired down in self-pity and without purpose. We tend to look at the "up times" as our good fortune and accept the "down times" as unfortunate twists of fate. But that's not what they are!

BEING THE SOLUTION

Both are BEING choices

Would you be surprised if I told you that the "up times" and the "down times" in your life were both BEING choices? Once you accept the premise that every reality you've ever experienced was the result of a BEING choice, you'll see how a different BEING choice during the detachment process could put you back into creating a great new reality on the up side of the cycle.

Your trips around the cycle in the Game of Life will be emotional roller coaster rides until you learn how to avoid the downside—the depression and emotional upset that almost always accompanies the Destroy Process.

We'll be taking an imaginary trip through some of the emotions you might experience in a trip around the cycle. If you will put yourself into this picture, you will have a better feel for the cycle. See if you can feel the feelings and relate this sample trip to your current reality or to a previous episode of your life.

You've been here before

Each trip around the cycle represents only one round in the never-ending Game of Life. You've been around the cycle many times in your life, never once noticing that you've been here and done that, each time at a different level in the game. It's time you realized that the pattern repeats itself. Once you learn to read the road map, you'll be able to choose a different way to go—a route with a more pleasant view.

The Destroy Phase is necessary

The most difficult part of the cycle is in destroying our attachment to what we've most recently created. Once you accept CREATE PERSIST DESTROY as a repeating process, you'll be able to find yourself on the cycle and clear up the mystery about why you feel so bad when you're into the Destroy Side of the cycle.

The benefit in finally understanding the cycle is that you'll be able to take the destruction out of the Destroy Phase. You'll simply detach yourself and move on.

FIND YOURSELF ON THE CYCLE

A Roadmap For The Rest Of Your Life

Find yourself on this cycle and then choose a better route.

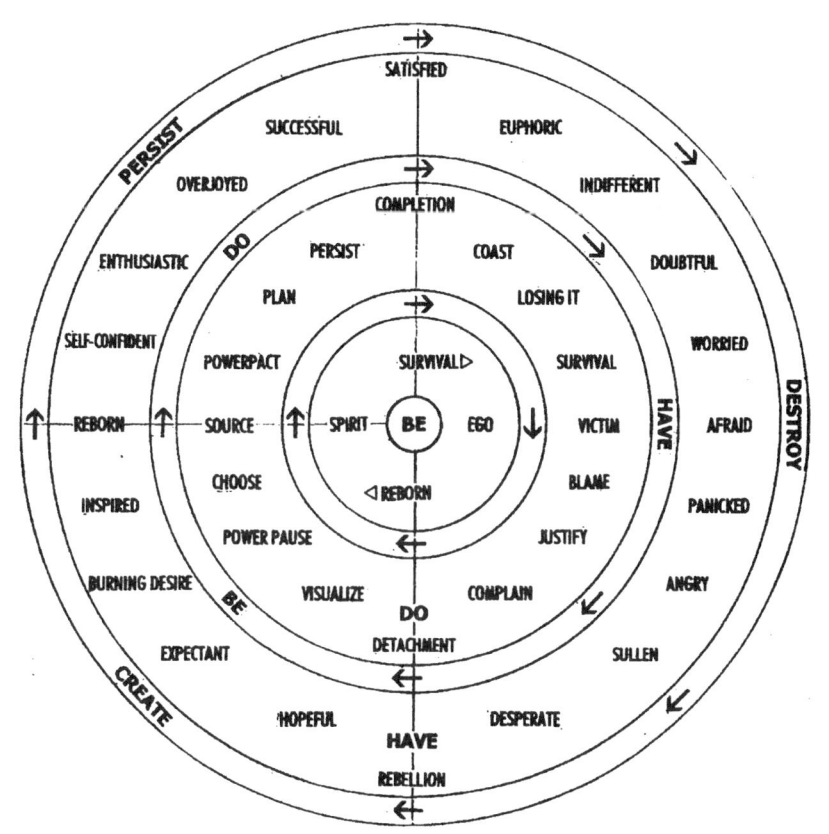

[Diagram: Concentric circular roadmap with BE at the center, surrounded by SPIRIT and EGO. Outer rings contain labels including SATISFIED, SUCCESSFUL, EUPHORIC, OVERJOYED, INDIFFERENT, COMPLETION, ENTHUSIASTIC, PERSIST, COAST, DOUBTFUL, PLAN, LOSING IT, SELF-CONFIDENT, WORRIED, POWERPACT, SURVIVAL, SURVIVAL, REBORN, SOURCE, SPIRIT, BE, EGO, VICTIM, AFRAID, CHOOSE, BLAME, INSPIRED, PANICKED, POWER PAUSE, JUSTIFY, BURNING DESIRE, VISUALIZE, COMPLAIN, ANGRY, EXPECTANT, DETACHMENT, SULLEN, HOPEFUL, DESPERATE, HAVE, REBELLION. Quadrant labels: PERSIST, DESTROY, CREATE, with DO, HAVE, BE axis labels.]

The (BE) cycle

Take a look at the above illustration. Notice that the word BE occupies the center circle. The words in the donut-shaped space just outside the central BE circle are "spirit" and "ego." These are both BEING choices. The message in this center donut is that you have, at all times, the option of being your ego and living life defensively and in the survival mode, or of being your spirit and choosing out of your box to be reborn into a new and exciting reality.

Follow the road signs

Follow the road signs and find yourself on this roadmap for the cycles of your life. Then, when the road gets rocky and rough, you can take charge of your life by making a new BEING choice with better scenery.

The (DO) aspect of CREATE

The next larger donut-shaped circle in this illustration shows some of the things you might be DOING on one trip around the cycle. Your new life begins with your detachment from whatever you've been clinging to in your current reality. Your new reality is born with your visualization of what life might be like outside the box. But whenever you think about that better life, fear shows up, attempting to scare you back into your box. You deal with the fear each time by declaring a Power Pause. With determination, your vision gains power. Finally, you choose to BE the one in that vision, and now that you are committed, you know for sure that you've been transformed into being the one who can have what you want from life. You now see yourself as the source of that which you seek in life.

The (DO) aspect of PERSIST

To empower your success, you create your Powerpact support group and you share your action plan with them. Empowered by your Powerpact, you DO whatever is necessary—persisting for as long as necessary for completion of your mission.

The (DO) aspect of DESTROY

Now your long climb up the hill to success is over; you finally HAVE what you've always wanted and it's time to settle back and enjoy the fruits of your labors. Notice that you are very much attached to your most recent success, but you no longer work at it. You begin to coast—downhill. Your success gradually slips away, because you are no longer aggressively seeking it. You fall into the survival mode; you're definitely losing it. As your success erodes, you begin to see yourself as a victim of circumstances over which you seem to have no control. You look for and find others to blame for your problems. You justify your failure with all sorts of plausible reasons and constantly complain about your bad luck. Does this sound familiar?

Notice that this whole Destroy process had only one real purpose: detaching you from your current reality so you could move into creating the new you who will play in the next level of the game. If you're like most people, you've wasted half your life in the Destroy

FIND YOURSELF ON THE CYCLE

Phase, when you could have side-stepped the destruction and started your enthusiastic pursuit of your next mission in life instead.

We've just reviewed some of the things you might be DOING on your journey around the cycle. Now let's look at the cycle as an emotional trip.

The (HAVE) aspect of CREATE

Let's see how you might feel about life in each segment of the cycle. Your first step out of the box will be taken with an attitude of rebellion against circumstances you consider unrewarding. You've begun to think about what life could be like outside the box, you've created that picture, and are now hopeful for that change. The more you think about it, the clearer your vision of that new reality. In fact, you have now reached the point where you are actually expecting life to get better. You've created 20 reasons why you want that new reality, and you have a burning desire for having it happen. You are now inspired with the possibility of a new reality—a new you.

The (HAVE) aspect of PERSIST

You've had a breakthrough in consciousness. You've been reborn into a new conscious awareness of who you really are. In your new empowered state of BEING, you now know that anything is possible for you. Your new level of self-confidence impresses everyone you meet on your way toward BEING a success, and your natural enthusiasm infects them all. You are overjoyed with the many ways your life has changed for the better, and you seem to be successful in everything you attempt.

The (HAVE) aspect of DESTROY

At this point, you are experiencing the satisfaction of having completed your mission—so pleased with life that your state of mind could be called euphoric. You are enjoying your success, but the fire of desire has burned out, and your ambition has gone with it. Now you begin to notice that your new feather bed no longer feels all that comfortable. Your attitude about success has slipped so far that you are now indifferent to the little problems that pop up. That's when you begin to notice signs that all is not well in paradise. Your doubts about the way things are going soon turn to worry and then to being afraid that you could actually loose it all. At this point, when everything seems to be going wrong, your fear turns to panic. You become angry

BEING THE SOLUTION

with those you blame for your failure. You pout often and grow sullen. Things are now so bad they couldn't get any worse, and you find yourself desperate for a way out of your depression. It is obviously time for the rebellion that will bring you to the point of starting your next trip around the cycle.

If you've put yourself into this picture, you will see how you've lost control of your life during the Destroy Process, probably many times in your life. You'll see how much of your life you've wasted, and perhaps you'll be able to see just how easy life would have been had you simply completed the detachment process and gone on to create a new game to play.

From a position of power

If you were to decide not to let yourself become attached to your most recent success, you could unload your camel, go into the inner city and plan your next round in the Game of Life. Your next trip will begin with your visualization of how great life will be outside the box you've just recently created for yourself. Your new reality will be more easily created from a position of power than from the powerlessness you will find on the lower end of the cycle.

I'm telling you that there's no need to ride the Destroy Process all the way down before you decide on your next hill to climb. When you play the game with self-discovery as your purpose, you won't become quite so attached to the material manifestation of your new consciousness.

Taking charge

At this point in reading this chapter, you should have an overview about life that would allow you to take charge, avoiding the bad times by simply creating more of the good times. The big rule of any game is that:

> *You can never win what you can't afford to lose.*
> --Darel Rutherford

If you can't even image life outside that relationship, you are not in a powerful enough position to negotiate a new agreement. You can't win in that relationship, because you can't deal with the possible loss.

FIND YOURSELF ON THE CYCLE

As long as you are afraid of losing your job, you probably won't risk negotiating a raise, no matter how much you think you deserve it. In any negotiation, the one with the least to lose will have the most power in making the better deal. In other words, the one with the most "no" power will almost always win.

What's at stake

What you bet in the Game of Life is your self-concept. If you can find the courage to wager your old concept of reality, you'll win a new self-concept with a greater understanding of who you really are. Your new level of self-awareness will give you a sense of personal power that far exceeds anything you've known up to now. That's your win!

The yellow brick road of your life is taking you home to the realization that you are, indeed, an individualization of God.

The gem cannot be polished without friction,
nor a man perfected without trials.
--Confucius

BEING THE SOLUTION

If you truly have a desire to be WEALTHY,
you must maintain this vision!

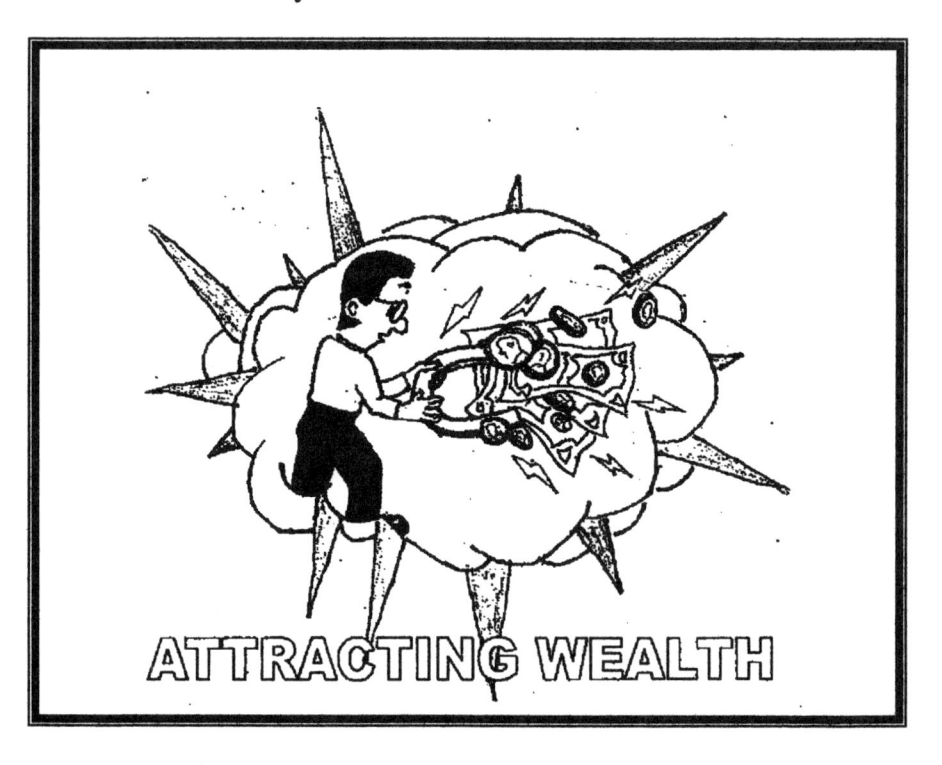

20
YOUR RELATIONSHIP TO MONEY
…will make you rich or keep you poor

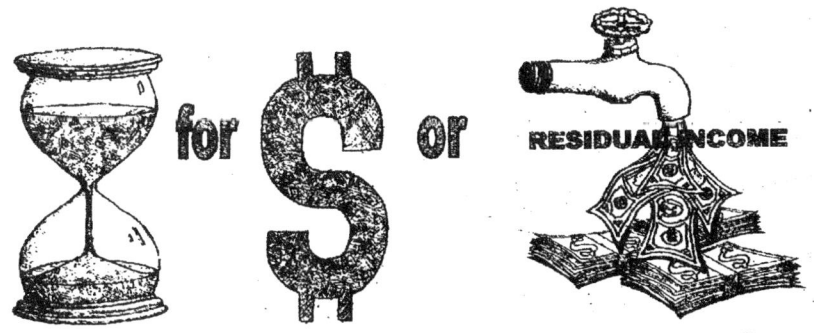

for $ or RESIDUAL INCOME

YOUR EARNING STRATEGY

*Money just naturally flows toward those
who have the consciousness to keep it
and away from those who don't.*
--Darel Rutherford

She Was Rich

BEING rich is in having everything you need to make your life whole and complete. Mother Theresa was rich, and yet, in terms of material wealth, she had nothing!

BEING poor is in wanting something from life that you don't have. That definition for "poor" makes most of us poor! A millionaire desperate for more wealth is poor; having five maxed out credit cards makes you poor. In either case, you will have chosen a relationship to money that keeps you poor. It is the purpose of this chapter to change your relationship to money. So, think about this:

You do have a relationship

If you think you don't have a relationship with money, you may want to rethink your opinion. If you see money only as an inanimate object—just the stuff you receive on paydays, earnings which never quite stretch to the end of the pay period—then you are at the effect of the real cause of your money problems. As long as you persist in that point of view, your income problems can't be solved.

If you never seem to have all the money you think you need to make your life whole and complete your money problems are the consequence, not the cause of your predicament. And to resolve your financial bind, you must be able to see that the real problem is in HOW you've chosen to BE in regard to money.

The three ways you relate to money
Your relationship to money is expressed in three ways:
1. As **your prosperity consciousness**—or lack of it
   A prosperity consciousness can be defined as: feeling prosperous when you think about your personal finances.
2. As **your spending strategy**
   An insatiable need for instant gratification, will create negative cash flow and the resulting poverty consciousness will keep you in debt and poor. On the other hand, spending less than you make creates positive cash flow and the resulting prosperity consciousness that will make you rich.
3. As **your earning strategy**
   Almost no one ever became wealthy trading hours for dollars. The creation of multiple streams of residual income is your true path to wealth.

In Chapter Seventeen, you learned how to use the Power Pause for developing your prosperity consciousness. To feel prosperous and attract money, you will create a positive cash flow by spending less than you make. If you are to manage your cash flow, you'll need to understand the laws of money that control your spending habits.

In this chapter, I'll show you how your current earning strategy could be keeping you poor and I'll be offering some suggestions for changing your earning strategy. Once you are fully in charge of all three of the ways you relate to money, you should be on your way to becoming wealthy.

YOUR RELATIONSHIP TO MONEY

The Laws of Money

In my first book, So, Why Aren't You Rich?, I relate the stories of three workshop participants who thought their money problems could be solved with additional income. Even though their incomes varied greatly, each had the same problem of spending more than they made. It's called negative cash flow.

After the three compared notes, each came to the obvious conclusion that the real problem was not lack of income; it was in his/her spending habits. They were each over-extended financially, being controlled by what I call:

The Spender's Law of Money

Your expenses will always rise to meet the level of your income until you rebel against your addiction to spending.

If your spending habits are such that you consistently, pay out everything you make and more, you will never, ever, have enough income to satisfy your wants. Your desperate need for instant gratification makes your want list grow faster than your income. Your need for immediate gratification comes from the mistaken idea that spending money is proof of worth. The truth is that you can never spend your way to prosperity. If you are ever to find the financial independence you seek, you'll need to revolt against your spending habits and be governed by a different law of money.

The Saver's Law of Money:

10% or more of all you earn, invested wisely, will create multiple streams of residual income and make you wealthy.

The simple way to create a positive cash flow is to budget your spending so that you spend less than you make. As soon as you give up your need for instant gratification, you've changed your relationship to money.

*Your decision to save
is your commitment to retire wealthy.*

The first benefit from that changed relationship will be the new prosperous way you will feel about yourself once the cash flow turns

BEING THE SOLUTION

positive. Notice that changing how you relate to money is a BEING change.

*Your new relationship to money
will be your ticket to prosperity.*

Wealthy people can have whatever they want from life, because early in life, they gave up the need for instant gratification in favor of future gratification and the more desirable lifestyle they would enjoy later.

Once you've conquered your spending habits and solved your cash flow problems, you'll want to take a hard look at your beliefs about how money is wisely earned. Your chances of increasing your income will be limited if you refuse to look beyond your current earning strategy for ways to earn residual income. The following is a good example of the wrong solution to money problems.

Looking for a job in LA

When I graduated from high school, I sold my Model "A" Ford for $25, hitch-hiked out to Los Angeles, and went looking for work. I found the lines at the state employment agency long and jobs scarce. But in 1940, one nickel would buy two donuts and a cup of coffee. I knew I could survive on that until I found a job.

When the options don't make sense

For my first full-time job in Los Angeles, I worked in a fig cannery from 7:00 am to 3:30 p.m. It was good to have a job. Now that I had a steady income, I felt secure and prosperous for a while. But before long, I noticed that I wanted stuff I couldn't afford.

My natural solution: find a second job working evenings. For my moonlighting job, I worked six hours each evening, setting pins in a bowling alley. I was now working 14 hours a day, trading hours for dollars.

Once again, before long, my wants were not totally satisfied and more often than not, I ran out of money before the end of the month. My solution this time: volunteer for overtime. Bowlers paid double and sometime triple for a pinsetter willing to work after 11 p.m. My point here: when we're locked into trading hours for dollars as the only way we earn money, the options will be limited to a second job or working more hours.

YOUR RELATIONSHIP TO MONEY

Notice that neither solution makes much sense, because more hours means giving up one of the greatest benefits of having more money—the time to enjoy it. I hope you're getting the point; that trading hours for dollars is not the best earning strategy for you. Are you ready to consider a better way?

Who said that was a good idea?

Before we talk about changing your earning strategy, let's talk about how you and I came to believe that trading hours for dollars was the best strategy.

My father, a carpenter and construction superintendent, advised me, "Learn a trade and you will never go hungry." That sounded like good advice to me, and no one ever told me any different. So, when I was ready to settle down, I took my father's advice, learn the carpenter trade, and began yet another way of trading hours for dollars.

Other parents wisely advised their kids to go to college, get high marks and get a job with one of the major corporations. "You'll have it made for life," they said. That was considered good advice back then, but times change. We hadn't heard about downsizing.

Even in college, you are taught everything you need to know so you can get a job and trade your hours for dollars. Obviously, college professors, even with all their education, haven't figured out that there's a much better way to earn a living than trading hours for dollars. Like you, they're trading hours.

What's wrong with trading hours for dollars?

No matter what profession you choose—whether you're a doctor, lawyer, teacher, or a computer technician—you get paid only when and if you work. When you stop working, for whatever reason, the pay stops. That's just the way it is when your earning strategy is hours for dollars. But residual income doesn't stop; the money just keeps rolling in!

Obviously, those who taught you your earning strategy just didn't understand money.

We don't understand money

Everyone thinks they understand money, and hardly anyone does; otherwise, we would not have been taught that the worst of all earning strategies was the best. The fact is that about 96% of the

- 269 -

BEING THE SOLUTION

population work for the 1% who really understand how money is best earned.

Almost everything you were ever taught about money is false. The money you earn has nothing to do with age, gender, education, intelligence, or where you live. I know brilliant people who are dead broke most of the time, and I know some millionaires who don't seem all that smart. The only thing the millionaire had over you, before they became rich, was the motivation that got them to the point of choosing to be a millionaire.

*Your commitment to be rich
creates a polarity for attracting money.*
--Darel Rutherford

The three income earning strategies:
1. **96% of us trade our time for money**—that's not the best earning strategy. This list includes doctors, lawyers and all other highly-paid professionals
2. **Only 3% of the population invest to earn money**—a better idea. With this motive in mind, investing in the market is a good idea if you invest for the long term in quality stocks that pay regular dividends.
3. **Just 1% of the population multiply their efforts through others' efforts**

If you find yourself reacting to the idea of being an employer, know this: the top 10% of all earners earn 314% more than the bottom 90%.

Master or slave

As an employee, trading our day for a paycheck, we tend to think of our employer as a slave to that business. In some cases we would be right in thinking that. But that attitude about employers or people with money is a prejudgment trap that can prevent you from ever allowing yourself to BE one of THEM.

We have this notion that wealthy people are so obsessed with the idea of making money that they can think of nothing else. Some of them may be, but don't use those few as a basis for making your judgment call on rich people. Contrary to popular opinion, the wealthy are not the ones who slave for their money.

YOUR RELATIONSHIP TO MONEY

Those who can least afford to pay rent, pay rent. and those who can most afford to pay rent, build equity.
--Darel Rutherford

When someone expresses that sort of "bad guy" opinion about the rich, you might want to ask yourself, "Who's talking and what does this person do for a living?" If he/she spends 40 to 50 hours a week "slaving" for a week's pay, that person has no room to talk. The more accurate picture is that the poor sweat for every dollar they make and wealthy watch them work. Who is the slave in this picture?

The poor think of money only in terms of what it will buy

Wealthy people don't become wealthy by trading hours for dollars, nor by being a slave to money, but by leveraging their time and finding as many ways as possible to have their money work for them. In my book, you're wealthy if your income is enough so that you no longer must work for a living. If you are wise, you will begin to think of residual income as the ideal way for money to be earned.

The rich see money as a servant that provides, comfort, freedom, and financial independence.

The way to go

When you choose residual income as your way to earn, you're not just choosing to be rich; you're choosing your path to wealth, and some day, because of that BEING choice, you'll come to the conclusion that you no longer need to work.

Your reality is run by a vision—a concept of reality that got you into the financial circumstances you now endure. Your new financially secure reality will begin when you can create a new vision, a new reality built around a better earning strategy. The next time you think about wanting more income, don't think about getting another job. Think about how you might begin to create your own streams of residual income.

BEING THE SOLUTION
Planned your retirement, yet?

When I asked Jo Ann, a massage therapist, if she had done anything in the way of planning for her retirement, she said, "No, not yet." Why didn't that surprise me? A large percentage of the population would give you the same answer. We all think about retirement, but most of us do nothing about it, hoping the problem will somehow take care of itself. Believe me, it almost never does!

Retiring with sufficient income to live the rest of your life in comfort will require your commitment to making it happen. Unfortunately most of us will retire poor, simply because we just never got around to doing anything about creating a retirement income. We always thought, that someday we would prepare for old age, but that someday never came, and now we're now facing retirement without sufficient income to live comfortably. Your latter years on this planet should not end in poverty.

When it doesn't fit

When I suggested to Jo Ann that she think about creating some form of residual income, she reacted negatively to my suggestion. When I asked why, she said, "I don't feel comfortable with the idea of receiving money I haven't worked for." Her natural reaction is based on a common misconception most of us have about residual income.

Of the many different **residual income** types, most of them could be described as,

income received on a regular basis
from a previous investment of either time or money.

In other words, residual income is pay you will receive today, tomorrow, and the next day for work you did yesterday.

The problem, for Jo Ann, is that income earned by means other than working for it is outside the box called, "trading hours for dollars". It just doesn't fit her concept of reality about how money should be earned. It just doesn't feel right! It doesn't fit in with who she is BEING.

If, like Jo Ann, you are uncomfortable with the idea of receiving money in some form other than a regular paycheck, you will need to create a different attitude about residual income. Otherwise you become a bondservant to your weekly paycheck. Trading hours for dollars is a form of slavery, not to your employer, but to your concept of reality about money. Without a BEING change, you are doomed to living your life as a slave to money. Your role as the slave will persist for as long as you maintain the attitude that residual income is somehow not right for you.

What does a residual income check look like?
It looks like:
- Royalty checks from the sale of books, tapes, and movies
- Rent income from owned real estate
- Stock dividends
- Interest income
- Network marketing commissions
- Toll gate income when you own the bridge others must cross
- Oil well royalties
- Inventor's patent royalties
- Insurance policy-renewal commissions

So how do YOU feel about residual income?

When I asked Jo Ann if she was working on a vision for creating residual income she said, "Yes, but it's difficult. I was thinking I'd like to buy houses, fix them up and rent them. But in that picture, I see myself painting, fixing and repairing, working a lot of extra hours for much less per hour than I make in my profession. My vision of residual income seems to have me working a lot more hours, and that's not an inviting picture."

Jo Ann finds this visualization difficult because she has a mental block against residual income. Every picture she comes up with has her working more hours, not less. She's still locked into a concept of reality called, "If it is to be, it's up to me." If she were really in the business of buying, fixing, and renting houses, she wouldn't be doing the work; she would be hiring it done, BEING the supervisor.

To create a visualization of yourself receiving multiple streams of residual income, you will first need to feel comfortable with the idea. The picture Jo Ann needs to create is one of herself in a lawn chair next to the pool, shortly after depositing the rent checks each month.

BEING THE SOLUTION
Changing how you feel about it.

The following are exercises in changing how you feel about residual income. First, imagine you've written a book. You've spent almost every waking hour for the past year writing that book. During that whole period, you've received no pay for your labors.

Now your book is published. Your royalty checks for last year amounted to $52,000. You get paid a royalty every time someone buys a book. And since book sales are increasing, your anticipated royalty income will be even greater next year. Can you imagine that kind of work-free income? How does that feel? Will you feel guilty because you're being paid now, over and over again, for that year of hard work? Of course not!

Really imagine yourself into this picture, and allow yourself to feel what it would be like receiving regular residual income. That feeling is what you're trying to capture with this exercise.

*Money is like a sixth sense without which
you cannot make a complete use of the other five.*
--W. Somerset Maugham

If you invested one million dollars

Now, let's try another example for the purpose of changing how you feel about residual income. Imagine I gave you one million dollars that you invested in a money market account earning interest income at the rate of 5.2%. How much income would you receive weekly? Take your time and come up with your own answer before you read on.

If you did the math correctly, your yearly income would be $52,000; your weekly income would be $1,000. How would you feel about having your savings account increase by $1,000 a week in residual income? Take time to allow yourself to feel what that would be like having an extra $1,000 a week. How would you FEEL about receiving $1,000 a week that you didn't have to trade your time for? How much richer would you feel? How would that change your life?

To get the real benefit from this exercise, you must really put yourself into the picture, receiving the residual income and feeling good about it. The purpose of this exercise of your imagination is to change your attitude about residual income. If you are ever to be wealthy, you must change the way you feel about residual income; you must create a new vision of a reality that includes residual income for yourself. When you accept that vision as your reality, you've accomplished a BEING change that could have you on your way toward becoming wealthy.

Another example:

Let's say you invested a million dollars as a down payment on an apartment house. Your apartment house is fully rented and you have a live-in manager. After mortgage payments and all expenses are paid, you receive a net income of $104,000 a year. How would you feel about earning $2,000 a week without having to work for it? Are you feeling prosperous? Now, let's try one more.

So how do you feel about others working for you?

Instead of investing your million in an apartment house, let's say you decided to start your own business. Your business is successful and you now have 10 employees making a total of 1000 widgets a week. Your net profit per widget is $2. Your well-managed business runs so smoothly that you no longer need go to work. Your net income per week is $2,000. Would receiving income resulting from someone else's labors have you feeling guilty?

Remember, 96% of us work for the other 1%, who feel no guilt about being our employer.

The above examples were intended to help you change the way you feel about residual income. If the idea of residual income begins to feel right for you, you'll be able to create the vision and make that your new BEING choice. If one of the above income sources feels better than the rest, create your vision around that one. The important thing is that you expand your concept of reality about earning money to include some form of residual income.

The power of leverage

Next, let's look at some of the pros and cons for the various residual income types so that you can really decide which one is for you. As you review them with the intention of choosing the best one for you, I want you to keep in mind that in some cases, the power of leverage increases your earnings exponentially.

In the above apartment-house example, notice that compared to interest income your return on investment doubled. That increase was made possible through the power of leverage. When you make a small down payment and borrow the rest from a lending institution, that deposit becomes a leveraged investment. When investing in real estate,

BEING THE SOLUTION

you have the double advantage of residual income plus appreciation of your investment.

You might, for instance, own a million-dollar complex with a down payment of only $100,000. If your rental income, after the mortgage payment and expenses, were sufficient to give you a healthy cash flow, the investment would not only provide you with residual income, your tenants would also be paying off the mortgage for you. That's the power of leverage supplying residual income while in the process of turning your $100,000 investment into a million-dollar asset. Stop and think about that, because that's how the wealthy got that way!

With this example, it shouldn't be too hard for you to see that, leveraging could possibly double your original investment every three years while investing in real estate for the purpose of creating residual income.

But a word of caution: unless the income from your real estate investment exceeds all expenses, including taxes and maintenance costs, you haven't really created residual income; you've created the exact opposite—a drain on your bank account.

If your intention with a real estate investment is to create residual income, your income from that property must exceed all expenses, including unexpected maintenance costs. Money left over after you've paid all the bills is called positive cash flow or residual income. The more money left over at the end of the month, the better the deal.

Before we move away from the subject of real estate, let's consider an example that might be more affordable for you.

Another real-estate rental income

One of my workshop participants decided to create residual income through buying houses and renting them. Two years later, he owned nine houses. He had a plan and he worked his plan. To get started, he began looking at houses for sale—not buying, just looking. Each house he visited taught him what to look for, and what a good value would be. When he finally decided to get his feet wet and buy his first house, he was already an expert on housing values.

He buys run-down houses in neighborhoods where the homes on each side have been better maintained than the one he's buying. His first rule for buying a house is to pay less than the appraised value of the other houses in the same neighborhood (including fix-up costs) so that whenever he decides to sell, he can get his money back and then some. Before he buys a house, he visits the neighbors on each side, telling them that he intends to buy the house in order to rent it. He makes friends of the neighbors, telling them he intends upgrade the rundown property and improve the neighborhood.

He gives the neighbors his business card and asks them to let him know if the new tenant appears to be abusing the property. Each of his nine houses return a healthy positive cash flow over and above the amount needed to make mortgage payments, pay taxes, insurance and maintenance costs.

Residual income from these rentals has allowed him and his wife to quit their jobs and travel the country in their new RV.

The down side: that all sounds pretty good, but there can be serious problems with this type of investment. Your first mistake could be in not taking the time to become an expert before you buy your first fix-up house. The second mistake you might make, would be to rent the house to a tenant who would destroys your property.

To be a successful landlord you must be tough on credit and diligently check a prospect's references including a talk with a previous landlord before accepting them as a tenant. If you haven't the patience to become the expert, if you're not a good judge of character, if you're a soft touch who can't say "no" this is not the business for you. Before you decide to do this type of investing, the question you might ask yourself is:

*Who would I be BEING
if I were a successful landlord?*

Royalty from book sales

To BE the author of a best-selling book is a great ambition for any writer, and because you would receive a percentage of each book sold, the residual income benefits are great—if you become a best selling author.

The downside: the sad fact is that maybe 2% of all books submitted to publishers even get read, and only a small percentage of books read by editors ever get published. The writers who make it big are a miniscule percentage of the multitude of writers out there, vying for the publisher's attention. Those are pretty big odds to buck!

BEING THE SOLUTION

The common fallacy for most first-time writers is to assume that they'll have it made once their book is published. Not true! Publishers don't sell books; they print books. Distributors don't sell books; they distribute books. Bookstores don't sell books; they stock books. Only authors sell books. If you're not willing to do the sales promotion as well as be the author for your book, don't expect your writing to make you wealthy.

Dividend checks are residual income

If you've saved your money and invested it in dividend-paying stocks, your quarterly dividend checks will be residual income. The advantage of owning stocks is in the possibility that the stock will also appreciate in value. The hidden value here is that you don't pay income taxes on the gain in value until you sell the stock. If you choose this type of residual income, make sure you pick stocks that have a history of never missing a dividend.

The downside: dividends are paid quarterly and the percentage of return on this type of investment is usually small. Unless you can afford the very best advice, investing in the market can be a big gamble. Just so you know, stock prices don't always go up. Sometimes they go down.

Owning your own business

The advantage of owning your own business is that you get to pretend that you are your own boss. You get paid full value for your own labors and, hopefully, you also make a profit on your employee's labors. The power of leverage (hiring others to do the work) can make the well-managed business very profitable.

The downside: the failure rate in starting a new business is high; only about 5% of new startups will still be in business after the first five years. Most of those who don't succeed will fail within the first two years. Buying a franchise gives you a much better chance of succeeding because their name is known and their business mo. is tried and tested, but the $100,000 to $1,000,000 you will invest in a franchise is a great deal of money. And in many cases, you will have just bought yourself a job. Many business owners I know work 12 to 15 hours a day making less per hour than their better-paid employees. Downside summary: owning your own business is a big investment with a high probability for failure.

Network marketing commissions

Before I give you the advantages and disadvantages of network marketing, let me explain what network marketing really is and why it is the marketing revolution of the future.

The traditional way for the manufacturer to market its products is to sell them—through a jobber who buys truckload quantities to be shipped direct—to a distributor who stocks the product and distributes it in smaller quantities—to the retailer who sells it—to the ultimate consumer. When you add overhead, shipping and advertising costs for each of the above middlemen, I think you can see how the cost to the ultimate consumer finally ends up being four times what the manufacturer is paid for that product.

Think about this! In this standard distribution process, the manufacturer gets only 25% of the dollar you spend in the store.

In contrast, in the network marketing distribution process, the product is shipped direct to the consumer. This cuts out all those middlemen. There are no advertising costs because the product is promoted directly to the consumer through the referral system. You try the product and like it—recommend it to a friend—that friend recommends it—and the referral process goes on and on. Word of mouth is the best kind of advertising, and it costs the direct marketing manufacturer nothing. Who do you think pays for that expensive advertising that got you to choose that product from among all the others offered? You do. Direct marketing passes that savings on to you!

Why does this way of marketing work so well? Obviously, in order to be highly recommended a product must be superior to the competing products on the market. And because ¾ of the distribution costs are eliminated, the consumer gets a superior product for much less. Why wouldn't they recommend it? And they get paid for recommending it.

In relationship marketing (the correct name for network marketing), when you recommend the product as an associate, the manufacturer pays you a commission.

The advantages of network marketing

You have the advantages of owning your own business without the risk.
- The initial investment is small, usually less than $1,000.
- The risk factor is low.
- Overhead costs are minimal.

- You work from your own home in your pajamas.
- Your time is leveraged through the efforts of others. The people in your down line work for you, but are not on your payroll.
- You don't punch a clock.
- You choose the hours you want to work.
- Your income doesn't stop when you do.
- The income potential is high when you're good at it.

The downside: succeeding at network marketing will require some skills you may not yet have and may not be willing to acquire unless you're ready for a BEING change. The failure rate in network-marketing newbees is high because, in most cases, they were led to believe it would be easy.

No one told them that success in relationship marketing would require a change who they were BEING. Your greatest barrier to your network marketing success will be your own self-concept standing in the way. In other words, your success in network marketing will require a transformation in consciousness. Of course, that transformation would be necessary no matter what avenue you choose for creating your new relationship to money.

Downside summary
- You'll be doing things that are outside your comfort zone.
- Network marketing is not as easy as you've been led to believe.
- You probably can't succeed at it and continue being who you are now.
- You'll be recommending a product to friends who may resent being sold.
- Your rejection rate will be high.

Income types rated
To help you analyze your choice of a residual income type, I've created the following spread sheet analysis showing some income type advantages.

YOUR RELATIONSHIP TO MONEY

INCOME TYPE ADVANTAGES

Income Type	Low Start Up $	Leveraged Income	Low Risk	Low Overhead $ Costs	High Income Potential	No Payroll	Minimal Hours Required	Income Is Residual	Score
Owning A Business		X			X			?	2
Stock Dividends				X		X	X	X	4
Oil Well Royalties				X	X	X	X	X	5
Interest Income			X	X		X	X	X	5
Rental Income		X		X	X	X	X	X	6
Book Royalties	X		X	X	X	X		X	6
Network Marketing	X	X	X	X	X	X	X	X	8

Notice that Network Marketing comes out with a score of 8, the highest rating of all, because it takes very little up-front money to get you started and has such high earnings potential. It gives you the advantage of leveraging your time through the efforts of others without the disadvantage of having them on your payroll. It allows you to be in business for yourself without the high overhead cost in a conventional business. It's an opportunity of a lifetime if you can rise to the challenge.

It is better to have permanent income
than to be fascinating.
--Oscar Wilder

Everyone trades his or her life for something
What are you trading your life for? If you are trading your hours for $ in a job you don't like, you're making a bad trade. If you're working too many hours just to earn a living, you're not being wise.

The most valuable commodity you have in life is TIME, and everyone on this planet has a equal amount of it to spend. Yet some people have wisely awakened to the fact that you can buy quality free time with residual income. Wealthy people have a relationship to money that allows them to enjoy the good life; their money works for them to buy that free time. Don't envy them; be one of them. I say you're wealthy if you have sufficient residual income so that you no longer must work for a living.

Residual income buys you your place among the wealthy.

BEING THE SOLUTION

The whole difference between those who trade hours for dollars and those who don't is in their concept of self as it relates to making money. The key difference is that the ones who don't work have residual income as their earning strategy. If you haven't chosen a residual income type for yourself yet, don't worry about that decision for now. Your first step down the yellow brick road to wealth is into the vision of having multiple streams of residual income.

I suggest, to start, that you visualize yourself enjoying a life of leisure, being wherever you like to be when you're not working. You don't need to know what source of residual income you will choose in order to create your vision of receiving it and no longer working for a living. Just know that your new relationship to money starts with a vision of residual income and ends up BEING your reality.

Your vision will gain power and momentum as soon as you get fired up about it. When the visualization begins to feel real to you, when you are really feeling good about your life as it will be from having multiple streams of residual income, the means that best suits you will become clear to you. Then you can choose the one for you. In the mean time, work on your vision of receiving residual income.

Just in case you've forgotten what this chapter is about; it's about changing your relationship to money, making the BEING change that will allow you to retire wealthy instead of poor. Your new relationship to money will include one or more of the above mentioned forms of residual income.

If you're seriously thinking about becoming rich, I suggest you move that goal up a notch and choose, instead, to be wealthy. Most wealthy people got wealthy through the use of the power of leverage to create multiple streams of residual income. I'm suggesting that you do the same.

We trifle when we set limits to our desires
since Nature hath set none
--Christian Nestell Bovee

Self-discovery is outside the box

The spirit of God in you seeks growth through new ways of expressing itself in and through you as you. You won't find the kingdom of God inside the box where you now hide from the truth of your being. Self-discovery for you is outside the box!
"Seek ye first the kingdom."

YOUR RELATIONSHIP TO MONEY

To fulfill life's purpose, you must find your way out of that box. To find your way out, you must rediscover your power of choice. You must find in yourself, the spirit of God who seeks expression outside the box.

Thank God that life is not fair. Without problems, we wouldn't have the opportunities nor the desire to grow. Without the growth, we would never get to know who we really are—individualizations of God.

We'll get where we're going by unloading the camel from time to time, finding new forms of riches at new levels of BEING.

*You'll find your way past that problem
once you've chosen to BE its solution.*
--Darel Rutherford

If you liked this book and can't wait to recommend it,
DON'T—at least not just yet—not until I tell you about a great opportunity for earning some of the residual income we just talked about in the last chapter.

Consider becoming an affiliate of mine in the selling of this book. I just learned about the affiliate plan recently and am really very excited about the idea. I'm excited for you because you could earn almost a 50% commission off of every BEING E-book sale that comes from your recommending this book.

If you'd like to learn more about that,

Check it out at ➔ http://beingsolution.com/

P. S. I publish a free weekly online newsletter called RICHBITS.
To subscribe yourself or a friend, click on:

Subscribe at darel@richbits.com